THE LEGAL CHALLENGES
of GLOBAL CYBERSPACE

Why National Regulations Often Fail to Protect Digital Assets on Cyberspace

SECOND EDITION

TILAHUN MISHAGO

Library of Congress Cataloging-in-Publication Data:

Mishago, Tilahun.
　　The Legal Challenges of Global Cyberspace: Why National Regulations Fail to Protect Digital Assets on Cyberspace, 2nd Edition /Tilahun Mishago.
　　　　p. cm.
　　Includes bibliographical references and index.
　　ISBN-10: 1478393416 (paperback); ISBN-13: 978-1478393412
　　　　1. Cyber Security - Law and Regulation – United States and Europe. 2. Cybercrime - International Law. 3. Information & Communication Technology – National Security - United States and Europe. 4. Foreign Direct Investment – FDI in Digital Economy - all Nations. 5. Privacy & Data protection. 6. Jurisdiction on Cyberspace. I. Mishago, Tilahun
　　　　II. Title.
　　HD30.2.L363 2012; 658.40 038–dc22

Printed in the United States of America
　　10 9 8 7 6 5 4 3 2 1

TABLE OF CONTENTS

CHAPTER 3 CYBER LAWS: ADEQUACY, CHALLENGES, AND EFFECTS ON OFFSHORING.181

Preface

Progress in information and communication technology (ICT) has brought about both challenges and opportunities. While ICT has enabled seamless communication on cyberspace, it has also made every phenomenon, positive or negative on cyberspace possible. The good side of ICT is the endless opportunities provided to harness multiple features and capabilities of associated technologies while its side effect being the enormous security challenge on cyberspace.

This book examines legal challenges caused by malicious activities on global cyberspace that tend to counteract regulatory efforts of national jurisdictions.

Illicit events on cyberspace become increasingly complex as cyber technology advances thereby undermining the ability of existing regulatory instruments aimed at cybersecurity and deterring cybercrime. As existing laws cannot cope with newly emerging cyber security incidents, these incidents pose security risks for digital assets including those associated with cross-border trade and investment.

Effective legal and policy frameworks are needed to help mitigate cyber security threats and safeguard digital assets against such threats while promoting the benefits of ICT. To this end nations attempt to regulate cyberspace within their territories, but may quickly find that issues on cyberspace are both global and national at the same time, and as such not fully controllable at national levels only. If nations cannot adequately regulate ICT and cyberspace, such a regulatory deficiency will have negative consequences particularly with respect to digital investment. That is, investor's digital assets may not be adequately safeguarded by means of national legal instruments, which will deter potential investors. There is a need to analyze the question as to whether it is entirely possible for nation-states to individually address the multifaceted challenges of cyberspace with appropriate national legal and policy frameworks alone to protect digital investments.

It can be argued that, on the one hand, nations are behind in providing proper regulatory coverage for cyberspace, while, on the other hand, existing regulations have largely been unsuccessful in containing cyber security threats primarily due to complications caused by the ubiquitous global presence of cyberspace. Consequently, investor's digital assets are more susceptible to unauthorized access and use, or destruction, none of which can be addressed by currently possible and available legal or technical means. Of course this is not to suggest that issues on cyberspace will go away anytime soon. In fact, there is no guarantee that future regulations will fully address cybersecurity issues. In any case, there is a strong indication that digital investor assets demand more protection efforts from both investors and nation-states alike due to the involvement of cyberspace compared to the level of effort needed to protect and promote traditional Foreign Direct Investment (FDI).

Concept and Significance

As evidenced in current literary sources and observed in cybersecurity practices, national law makers have generally failed to adequately secure cyberspace to provide sufficient protection for critical infrastructure in particular through legal instruments. There are policy and regulatory pitfalls in cybersecurity caused primarily by technological intricacies in cyberspace. It can be argued that advance in cyber technology may have led to such shortfalls due in part to lack of adequate normative coverage and legal interpretation of cybersecurity laws. The consequence for this shortfall is that criminal events on cyberspace continue to undermine efforts aimed at securing digital assets belonging to FDI engagements.

While the main focus of this research has been FDI in IT-enabled service business, we look into cyber security problems of cross-border data transactions, those involving FDI in particular, more comprehensively. Since FDI projects are not just service oriented, there is a need to explain the main occurrences of FDI, i.e. this book first lays out major differences between FDI in goods and services, albeit at a high-level.

A significant volume of literature has dealt with legal means to protect investor assets (usually tangible assets) within host state territories compared to intangible assets from an offshore IT investor's perspective. Even if issues related to misuse of Intellectual Property Rights (IPR) have been discussed in various scholarly works, the focus has been on copyrighted content; such as, music. Even then, much of the literature has been devoted to generic issues like software piracy and theft of digital media, instead of discussions emphasizing regulatory and cybersecurity safeguards for all digital assets in an offshore business setting.

Specifically, there has been very little theoretical or empirical work conducted directly addressing peculiar issues faced by foreign investors in protecting investor's digital assets through legal and policy measures. The focus in this research inquiry was on intangible assets; such as, investor's sensitive information, though the scope of information protection must include IT-hardware that houses/hosts, processes, or stores information that also needs to be protected.

Literary sources in both legal and information systems security fields are investigated. Looking at issues from various angles with the help of interdisciplinary materials and expanding the discussion topics to international economics, as well as business are critical steps in providing a detail analysis of the problems identified in this research. The versatility of the materials and topics presented in detail, thus, allow this work to serve an audience that includes but is not limited to students, teachers, and practitioners in legal, economics, business, and information technology fields.

This book is as relevant for regulators, lawyers, judges, attorneys, and juries as it is for information security professionals like ISSOs, CISOs, CIOs, ethical hackers, engineers, administrators, and other power, as well as regular system users. This book was developed with the international community and global cyber users in mind as well. As such, it will benefit international lawyers, cybersecurity professionals from other countries, and government agencies, as well as leaders in international organizations. The fact that this contribution addresses many of the legal and security questions foreign direct investors, and multinational business entities face in doing business abroad, makes it very useful and handy for all these stakeholders.

This book provides an overview of various modes of service-oriented FDI engagements by analyzing relevant literature in both IT and legal fields. In particular, it defines and clarifies the distinct nature of FDI in IT-enabled/based services as opposed to FDI in services in general thereby shifting the focus to legal and policy frameworks to protect digital assets within offshoring or IT-enabled FDI.

While cross-border outsourcing or offshoring is not new, the concept of offshoring service FDI (captive center) with emphasis on IT based services and the need to secure information and information systems associated with such an FDI is a relatively new phenomenon. Therefore, the difference among traditional IT outsourcing and offshoring FDI on the one hand, and service offshoring and IT specific service offshoring FDI on the other hand is discussed in detail. This ensures that the emphasis of this research is on the protection of digital assets within the scope of only IT-enabled offshoring service FDI, which has not seen much scholarly contribution from legal communities. It is also important to look at how offshoring service FDI came to existence, how it is different from traditional FDI, or what the driving forces are behind the recent upward trends for offshoring service FDI in IT-enabled services.

This book further identifies the types of investor assets that are unique to the IT-enabled business process that maybe subject to information security threats and vulnerabilities, and as such deserve protection with appropriate technical measure and legal, as well as policy frameworks. The focus again is on digital or electronic data that can be processed, transferred, or stored in the offshoring service FDI business process.

Data at rest (backed up and stored), in transit (e.g. logistics of procured hardware and software, as well as other data being exchanged online for instance using e-commerce), and in process need to be equally protected. Empirical and theoretical sources of literature in the information systems security field were analyzed to assess capabilities of existing tools, techniques, and mechanisms utilized to secure information and systems at all phases of data and systems handling. Best practices and standards in security policy measures, as well as technical approaches are identified, analyzed, and in limited circumstances recommended for use.

E-commerce can be considered part of tradable services, but whether e-commerce by itself can take place in the form of an offshoring business model depends upon several considerations. This book looks at the possibility of e-commerce being at least part of an offshoring service FDI in IT-enabled services. We find that e-commerce can be utilized by a service FDI business model and thus the book outlines some practical approaches as to how e-commerce transactions of an offshoring service FDI can be protected from cyber attacks.

The enormous technical, security, and legal challenges of the Internet era on cyberspace, and how those challenges might directly affect the IT-enabled offshore investment are also covered. The fact that a foreign digital investor might now be facing a new paradigm of perceived threats to investment assets requires a closer look into regulatory problems and viable solutions. That is, unprecedented challenges posed by cyberspace against digital assets require new technical and legal solutions. Unlike the ways traditional investment assets can be protected by host nations, digital investment assets need new regulatory norms for protection. These new approaches are discussed in detail. Wherever necessary, this book also outlines technical tools/security measures that may be available to investors in order to protect investors' digital assets against internal and external threats, and what legal remedies an investor has in the case of loss or destruction of those assets.

More importantly, this book assesses the effectiveness of the current legal and policy environments provided by existing regulations and policies based on examples from a few countries. Specifically, the investigation covers the fact as to whether existing national legal norms, in particular cyber security laws, if any, of selected jurisdictions contain reliable, enforceable, appropriate, and sufficient provisions to address security issues originating from cyberspace. It answers the question as to whether the existence of policies and regulations benefits the FDI promotion efforts as regulators may anticipate.

Depending on certain circumstances, too much or too little regulation might harm these efforts. As evidence suggests, some jurisdictions have cyber security related laws and policies that are either too strict or too lax presenting a possibility that offshoring IT services might be discouraged after all. Home or host state regulations and policies, especially those aimed at national security in general can have adverse impact on offshoring service FDI. Studies suggest that cyberspace has complicated the determination of jurisdiction on transnational legal disputes including cybercrimes. Thus, possible effects of such jurisdictional complications on offshoring FDI are investigated in more detail.

Chapter Organization

The book, excluding appendices, is organized into three parts. Part I is an overview, while the remaining two parts present the contents and main deductions from the materials discussed in more detail. Part I defines various modes of FDI and provides an overview with the focus on legal and technical problems associated with IT offshoring. It states the significance as to what this research contributes to and lays out the methodology as to how these problems were analyzed in the research.

Chapters one through three in Part II present the bulk of the research materials and analyses focusing on technical details of information security threats, vulnerabilities, and counter-measures (security controls, legal, and policy measures to counteract those threats), among other things. Part II presents the central problem of cyberspace and the Internet, their being transnational or global in nature, which results in the fact that existing legal and policy frameworks may or may not adequately solve cyber security issues affecting IT offshoring. Illegal actions on cyberspace and their impacts on user community are dealt with. The impact of security threats on IT offshoring with respect to digital assets belonging to an investor is discussed.

Part II also compares existing regulations and policies from a few sample jurisdictions. The regulations and policies under consideration are from both host and home countries. In addition, this section investigates adverse effects, if any, of these regulations on investment promotion.

Part II finally addresses the legal complexities of cyber security and cybercrime, which arise out of the borderless characteristics of cyberspace, and discusses proposed approaches to dealing with the Internet governance and global cyberspace security. It discusses problems of jurisdiction and attribution that are peculiar to legal issues emanating from cyber security flaws.

Finally, Part III sums up all relevant findings of this research under 'conclusions'. It provides a summary of the overall content materials and relevant research outcomes, as well as the need for further investigation based on constraints of the current research.

Acknowledgements

Work on this research would not have been possible without the constant support and encouragement of a number of people. First and for most, I wish to thank my biggest supporters, my parents: Gago Bande and Mishago Butule for their many sacrifices over several years that helped me get to this point. I'm especially inspired by their selfless dedication to educate me despite the fact that they have never had an opportunity for themselves to access formal education. Limited but yet the only possible opportunities I have been exposed to by them have shaped my career and allowed me to experience many adventures in life.

My family has been patient and tolerant during my research and writing. My loving wife, Misty Matewos, has been very enthusiastic, supportive, and provided me invaluable encouragement in this journey. Her selfless devotion of time has allowed me to dedicate my time to this project. And because of that, I am very grateful to her and my entire family. Special thanks to my sons Joseph, Daniel, and David Mishago for their patience and love throughout.

Many thanks to those, whose insightful suggestions helped to improve the quality of the manuscript. I would like to extend appreciation and thanks to Professors: Christian Okeke, Nancy Yonge, and Michael Daw. I owe my deepest gratitude to Dr. Christian Okeke and Dr. Sompong Sucharitkul, Distinguished Professor Emeritus, who have shared with me over the years their vast experience in international jurisprudence. Working with these scholars eventually led me to conduct a research in cybersecurity issues associated with the contemporary international economic law.

Finally, my sincere gratitude goes to all staff, particularly John Pluebell, of the Golden Gate University School of Law, Graduate Program. Without them, the research and writing of this project would have taken years off my life.

Dr. Tilahun Mishago,
March 2012

Acronyms

ACM	Association for Computing Machinery
ACPA	Anticybersquatting Consumer Protection Act
ADR	Alternate Dispute Resolution
B2B	Business-to-Business
B2C	Business-to-Consumer
B2G	Business-to-Government
BIT	Bilateral Investment Treaty
C2B	Consumer-to-Business
C2C	Consumer-to-Consumer
C2G	Consumer-to-Government
CaaS	Computing as a Service
CEO	Chief Executive Officer
CFAA	Computer Fraud and Abuse Act
CFO	Chief Financial Officer
CIA	Confidentiality, Integrity, and Availability
CIO	Chief Information Officer
CISO	Chief Information Security Officer
CNSS	Committee on National Security Systems
COMESA	Common Market for Eastern and Southern Africa
COTS	Commercial off-the Shelf
CPC	Civil Procedure Code
CRS	Congressional Research Service
DDoS	Distributed Denial of Service
DNA	Deoxyribonucleic Acid
DNS	Domain Name Server
DOJ	U.S. Department of Justice
EC	Electronic Commerce
ECHR	European Convention on Human Rights
ECJ	European Court of Justice
ECLAC	Economic Commission for Latin America and the Caribbean

E-Commerce	Electronic Commerce
EDI	Electronic Data Interchange
EFF	Electronic Frontier Foundation
ERP	Enterprise Resource Planning
ESEC	Ethiopian Spice Extraction Company
EU	European Union
FDI	Foreign Direct Investment
FET	Fair and Equitable Treatment
FIPS 199	Federal Information Processing Standard 199
FISMA	Federal Information Systems Management Act
FPS	Full Protection and Security
GATT	General Agreement on Tariffs and Trade
GDP	Gross Domestic Product
GLBA	Gramm-Leach-Bliley Act
HIPAA	Health Insurance Portability and Accountability Act
IaaS	Infrastructure as a Service
ICANN	Internet Corporation for Assigned Names and Numbers
ICC	International Chamber of Commerce
ICD	Internal Control Disclosure
ICJ	International Court of Justice
	Industrial Control System
ICSID	International Center for Settlement of Investment Disputes
ICT	Information and Communication Technology
IDS	Intrusion Detection Systems
IIA	International Investment Agreement
ILC	International Law Commission
IP	Internet Protocol
IPR	Intellectual Property Right
ISACA	Information System Audit & Control Association
ISO	International Standards Organization
ISSO	Information Systems Security Officer
ISP	Internet Service Provider
ISS	Intelligence Support Systems
ISSA	Information Systems Security Association
IT	Information Technology
ITU	International Telecommunication Union

MNC	Multinational Corporation
MNE	Multinational Enterprise
NAFTA	North American Free Trade Agreement
NIST	National Institute of Standards and Technology
ODR	Online Dispute Resolution
OECD	Organization for Economic Co-operation and Development
OMS	Order Management System
P2P	Peer to Peer
PCI DSS	Payment Card Industry Data Security Standard
PII	Personally Identifiable Information
PIN	Personal Identification Number
PKI	Public Key Infrastructure
R&D	Research and development
RAM	Random Access Memory
SaaS	Software as a Service
SADC	Southern African Development Community
SAN	Storage Area Networks
	Supervisory Control and Data Acquisition (SCADA)
SEZ	Specialized Economic Zone
SOX	Sarbanes-Oxley
SSA	Sub-Saharan Africa
SSL	Secure Socket Layer
SWF	Sovereign Wealth Fund
SWIFT	Society for Worldwide Interbank Financial Transfers
TCP	Transmission Control Protocol
TCP/IP	Transmission Control Protocol/Internet Protocol
TNC	Transnational Company
UNCITRAL	United Nations Commission on International Trade Law
UNCTAD	United Nations Conference on Trade and Development
USSR	Union of Soviet Socialist Republics
VPN	Virtual Private Network
WiMAX	Worldwide Interoperability for Microwave Access

Part I

Overview

Issues with cybersecurity are not limited to doing business within national borders. While conducting business activities across national borders often requires firms' indirect involvement, e.g. in the form of international trade, many firms do business overseas through direct management control of operations in the form of Foreign Direct Investment (FDI)[1]. The question of cybersecurity becomes relevant regardless of the nature of cross-border business engagement if such an engagement involves the exchange of electronic data over cyberspace. Cybersecurity issues with regard to FDI in IT-enabled services is the focus of this book because FDI tends to be subjected to both foreign and home state legal provisions, the interaction of which sometimes defeats protection efforts for digital assets. The applicability of foreign and national laws on FDI both complicates cybersecurity efforts and weakens protection mechanisms in the case of weak or dysfunctional legal systems, which puts digital investment

---

[1] Defined as: "…[A]n investment involving a long-term relationship, and reflecting a lasting interest and control, of a firm or individual from one country in another", see Richard D. Smith, Foreign Direct Investment and Trade in Health Services: A review of the literature; in Social Science & Medicine 59, pages 2313–2323, at 2315 (2004). Usually distinguished from portfolio investment which, unlike FDI, does not entail management control over the investment activity; see Leon E. Trakman, Foreign Direct Investment: Hazard or Opportunity? The George Washington Int'l L. Rev. [Vol. 41], 5 (2009).

through FDI at more risks.

FDI can take place in both manufacturing (goods) and services; however, recent trends indicate that FDI is increasingly shifting towards services[2]. Changes in international business environments coupled with the emergence of physically and geographically unconstrained digital economy[3] have brought about rapid growth in doing service oriented international business[4]. FDI in services now accounts for more than sixty percent[5] of the overall worldwide FDI activities. FDI in services include FDI in IT-enabled[6] or core IT services, which generally

---

[2] FDI in services accelerated not only in terms of size but in terms of location due to competitive pressures caused by factors; such as, rise in cost of labor and improved conditions within FDI destinations, see the United Nations Conference on Trade and Development (UNCTAD) Information Economy Report, Science and technology for development: the new paradigm of ICT, 123 (2007-2008); see also the UNCTAD: World Investment Report - The Shift Towards Services, UN, NY, 97 (2004). Meanwhile, the trends in service FDI has a bit slowed down, FDI flows in financial industry being the hardest hit, due to the global financial meltdown since 2010; see UNCTAD, Non-Equity Modes of International Production and Development, at xii (2010).

[3] Digital economy is the new kind of economy that converges computing and communications technology on the internet, as well as other networks to enable the flow of information that stimulates e-commerce and vast organizational changes. For more on the concept , definition, and emergence of digital economy, see Georgios Zekos, Foreign Direct Investment in a Digital Economy, European Business Review, Vol. 17 No. 1, pp. 52-68, 62 (2005).

[4] See Lilach Nachum & Srilata Zaheer, MNEs in The Digital Economy? ESRC Centre for Business Research, University of Cambridge Working Paper No. 236 (June 2002).

[5] See Rashmi Banga, Foreign Direct Investment in Services: Implications for Developing Countries, Asia-Pacific Trade and Investment Review Vol. 1, No. 2, at 55 (November 2005).

[6] Meaning - a business process usually involving information technology and provided by usually IT TNCs (for digital IT services) or non-IT TNCs which

involve global business processes most recently referred to as offshoring.

Today there are various IT-enabled services being offshored in the form of either conventional outsourcing or Captive Center[7] where a foreign investor retains operational control. The Captive Center - also known as offshoring service FDI or simply offshoring FDI[8], often involves delivery of technology-intensive services or business processes taking advantage of ICT. Foreign investors either open overseas branches or in the case of multinational corporations, engage their directly controlled subsidiaries. Offshoring service FDI includes IT and IT-enabled services or IT-enabled business processes[9]; such as, reading X-ray images of patients (Tele-radiology)[10], processing financial data, Research

---

"use the Internet and networked information technology to deliver their commercial service products", see Catherine L. Mann, International Trade in the Digital Age: Data Analysis and Policy Issues; Testimony Subcommittee on International Trade, Customs, and Global Competitiveness of the Senate Committee on Finance, 1 (November 2010).

[7] Involves an 'FDI-type' offshore activity where the client retains control over the business process including management due to intellectual property concerns and the need to control end to end business process, inter alia, see Sudin Apte, Shattering the Offshore Captive Center Myth, Forrester Research, Inc., 5 (2007).

[8] As used in the 2004 UNCTAD report, see UNCTAD (2004), supra note 2, at 213; But literary sources do not always differentiate this as 'Offshoring FDI' and Offshoring service FDI' although there is an important difference, i.e. the former includes production oriented IT related investment, whereas the latter is limited to service FDI in IT or IT-related engagements.

[9] See Aspray et al., The Economics of Offshoring, in Globalization and Offshoring of Software, A Report of the Association for Computing Machinery (ACM) Job Migration Task Force, ACM 0001-0782/06/0200, at 20 (2006).

[10] See Kalyanpur et al., Inter-organizational E-Commerce in Healthcare Services - The Case of Global Teleradiology, 1 (2006).

and Development (R&D), and testing, building, and maintaining software for customers, as well as call centers supported by application systems maintaining customer data[11].

While advance in ICT has made offshoring much more feasible and cost effective, the Internet with its inherently insecure building block, the Transmission Control Protocol/Internet Protocol (TCP/IP) stack[12], has also introduced a new set of technical challenges in securing information. Thus, cyber security[13] and information protection have become the new frontiers of policy and regulations for regulators[14]. The Internet and e-commerce, both of which exhibit inherent global characteristics have resulted in new legal challenges[15] for

---

[11] For more categories of offshored services, see UNCTAD (2004), supra note 2, at 151.

[12] Unfortunately, any new technology tends to bring with it not only "blessings", but "curses" too (as Professor Okeke put it) and this is not limited to ICT, but all other products of science and technology; such as, biotechnology, atomic energy, etc, exhibit these dual characteristics, see Christian N. Okeke, "Science, Technology and the Law", Lectures & Speeches, Paper 2, at 42f (1992); Also available at: http://digitalcommons.law.ggu.edu/lectures/2, (last visited October 16, 2011). Also see Kelly A. Gabel, Cyber Apocalpyse Now: Securing the Internet Against Cyber Terrorism and Using Universal Jurisdiction as a Deterrent, 19 (August 14, 2009); Also available at: SSRN: http://ssrn.com/abstract=1452803, (last visited January 10, 2012).

[13] Defined by the ITU's Telecommunication Standardization Sector (ITU-T) Recommendation X.1205 as "the collection of tools, policies, guidelines, risk management approaches, actions, training, best practices, assurance and technologies that can be used to protect the cyber environment and organization and user's assets"; available on: http://www.itu.int/osg/csd/cybersecurity/gca/global_strategic_report/chapter_2.html, (last visited October 12, 2011).

[14] See Sushil K. Sharma, Socio-Economic Impacts and Influences of E-Commerce in a Digital Economy, in the Digital Economy: Impacts, Influences, and Challenges, at 2 (2005).

domestic lawmakers and international legal communities.

The Internet has become the nervous system for societies, where it is vital for digital communications among general public and businesses. Besides, critical infrastructures that are vital for public safety and national security gradually become dependent upon the Internet and cyberspace[16]. This reliance has made the largely unregulated Internet, in particular a good target for cyber terrorists and hackers. In fact, the Internet has not only attracted such illicit actors, but it has provided them with the tools necessary to initiate attacks[17] thereby making all kinds of Cyber-attacks including Cyber-terrorism the reality. Due to the nature of the Internet, cyber-terrorism has posed concerns becoming one of the most significant threats to national and international

---

[15] See GERALD FERRERA ET AL., CYBER LAW: TEXT AND CASES 301 (2000).

[16] For some it denotes the separate space created by the Internet (though sometimes synonymous with the Internet per se) – see Vishnu Konoorayar, Regulating Cyberspace: The Emerging Problems and Challenges; Cochin University Law Review, 413 (2003). For others (and this approach is more plausible); however, it is a "global domain within the information environment consisting of the interdependent network of information systems infrastructures including the Internet, telecommunications networks, computer systems, and embedded processors and controllers", see Committee on National Security Systems (CNSS), National Information Assurance (IA) Glossary, CNSS Instruction No. 4009, at 22 (April 26, 2010). The Internet itself is a network of networks utilized by cyberspace as it resides partially on the Internet as well, unlike somewhat confusing definition provided by Folsom, who limits the Internet to be just a gateway to cyberspace, see Thomas C. Folsom, Defining Cyberspace (Finding Real Virtue in the Place of Virtual Reality), Tulane Journal of Technology & Intellectual Property, Vol. 9, at 77 (2007), also available at SSRN: http://ssrn.com/abstract=1350999, (last visited December10, 2011).

[17] See Kelly A. Gable, Cyber Apocalpyse Now: Securing the Internet Against Cyber Terrorism and Using Universal Jurisdiction as a Deterrent, at 24 (August 14, 2009), also available at: SSRN: http://ssrn.com/abstract=1452803, (last visited Dec. 25, 2011).

security[18]. As a result, the security of the Internet and cyberspace is a high priority for governments, businesses, and the public alike.

Not only do the majority of cross-border transactions for offshoring service FDI take place over the Internet thereby exposing such transactions to possible cyber attacks, but also the same FDI business process provides opportunities for host country or foreign personnel to access and mishandle critical investor information. Such information may include sensitive customer data (e.g. personal and credit card information), intellectual property, and financial data. Such information and technology being used to process or handle this information (information system) can easily be exposed to unauthorized parties and misused while in transit over a network (e.g. logistics of procured hard- and software[19]). This information can also be compromised during online data transfer to a server location or otherwise exchanging data by means of e-commerce, or while being processed overseas, and/or at rest in an investor's overseas facility.

Investor's sensitive information, especially when it is made available on the public network (the Internet), is vulnerable to unauthorized use or other forms of attacks. The security of this data heavily depends on the safety and integrity of data networks[20] being utilized to connect to the Internet both at host and home

---

[18] Id. at 2.

[19] Erwin van Zwan, Security of Industrial Control Systems, in ISACA Journal Volume 4, at 4 (2010).

[20] The World Bank Group, Cyber Security: A New Model for Protecting the Network in International Policy Framework for Protecting Critical Information Infrastructure: A Discussion Paper Outlining Key Policy Issue, 2 (July 2006).

country locations.

The Internet has not only made a faster information transfer possible anywhere in the world, but it has also been effective in masking the Internet user community thereby providing "unprecedented opportunities for anonymous perpetration"[21] of illegal acts. This anonymity coupled with the global nature of the Internet has been a challenge for legal community and so the investor has to deal with attribution and jurisdiction issues.

Jurisdictional issues in FDI disputes are nothing new; however, the problem with lack of consistency and consensus on what suffices to assert jurisdiction, for instance, whether or not a mere existence of a website justifies a jurisdiction[22] is unique to IT offshoring service FDI. Jurisdictional issues along with the problem of the anonymity that makes identification of the source (attribution[23]) of damage in cyberspace nearly impossible[24] are relatively new and peculiar to FDI in IT-enabled services. It can be argued that individual jurisdictions have not been successful in coping with legal issues emanating from the global cyberspace or the Internet that has no national boundaries[25]. Yet clearly any

---

[21] GERALD FERRERA ET AL., CYBER LAW: TEXT AND CASES 302 (2000).

[22] Richard Johnston and Ken Slade, Jurisdiction, Choice of Law, and Dispute Resolution in International E-Commerce, Boston Bar Association: International Arbitration Committee, 15 (January 2000).

[23] See Kendra Simmons et al., Cyberspace Security and Attribution, in National Security Cyberspace Institute (NSCI), 2 (July, 2010).

[24] See GERALD FERRERA ET AL., CYBER LAW: TEXT AND CASES 321 (2000).

[25] Joanna Kulesza, Internet Governance and the Jurisdiction of States: Justification of the Need for an International Regulation of Cyberspace, 1 (December 2008).

single source of regulation whether it is national, regional, or international alone cannot solve the problem partly because of conflicts in legal systems[26]. It can be anticipated that no plausible, adequate, and universally applicable rules can be achieved by any level of jurisdiction anytime soon.

Meanwhile, attracting FDI in the form of offshoring is among the key components particularly in many developing countries' national initiatives in an effort to improve national economic development. However, relevant studies indicate that such initiatives have been impacted by factors; such as, level of economic development[27], nature of regulatory frameworks and level of sophistication in technology, especially ICT. The willingness of foreign investors (mostly transnational companies) to do business in developing countries still depends on some level of sophistication in terms of service industries and skilled labor, inter alia, on the host side unless the host has abundant natural resources that can easily be exploited and a large local market size for higher demand[28].

---

[26] See Mohamed S. Abdel, Identity Theft in Cyberspace: Issues and Solutions, 7 (2006).

[27] See Marc Proksch, Selected Issues on Promotion and Attraction of Foreign Direct Investment in Least Developed Countries and Economies in Transition, at 4.

[28] S. Ibi Ajayi et al., Foreign Direct Investment in Sub-Saharan Africa: Origins, Targets, Impact and Potential, African Economic Research Consortium, 12 (2006).

Part II

Global Nature of Cyber Security Issues: Challenges of Protecting Systems, Data, & Privacy via Regulation

Chapter 1 Introduction

Offshoring service FDI that deals with an IT-enabled[29] mode of business process involves digital assets, which can be processed, stored, or transferred over cyberspace using the Internet across national boundaries. These assets include digital data and information technology that processes, stores, and transfers the data. The data itself could be sensitive, disclosure of which can have privacy consequences or can result in financial loss. No matter in which state the investor's digital assets find themselves, there is no question that they need to be protected against illegal or unauthorized access, change, destruction, or use by known and unknown threat sources from cyberspace.

Not only has the advance in ICT and the Internet made offshoring possible for any service business far more than ever before, but this advance has brought about plenty of challenges for national regulators. The Internet is both global and national in nature as some aspects of it may be controlled through regulations within a national boundary, while some other aspects are international and as such not necessarily governed by national

---

[29] For its definition, see Catherine L. Mann, Offshore Outsourcing and the Globalization of U.S. Services: Why Now, How Important, and What Policy Implications? - In the United States and World Economy, at 281 (undated).

laws and policies. The characteristics that make the Internet global and services such as e-commerce that use the Internet and become global by very nature of using this infrastructure have complicated the ability of existing national regulations to cover every aspect of cyber-based transactions. The Internet poses security threats due to flaws in its building block, TCP/IP stack[30]. These flaws have introduced technical challenges of dealing with cyber security. The security threats posed by the Internet and all services that use the Internet have become, thus, an added challenge for domestic law and policy makers[31], who attempt to promulgate laws and provide policies for protecting information and systems on cyberspace.

National laws and policies have faced with an added problem of not being able to apply existing traditional regulations on cyberspace due to a multitude of factors. Meaning traditional laws cannot deal with new challenges created by cyberspace because of practical difficulties[32] including jurisdictional plurality, legal vacuum[33], technical difficulties, and exorbitant cost of persecution, as well as attribution.

Many jurisdictions have attempted to provide policies and

---

[30] Kelly A. Gable, Cyber Apocalpyse Now: Securing the Internet Against Cyber Terrorism and Using Universal Jurisdiction as a Deterrent, at 19 (August 14, 2009), also available at: SSRN: http://ssrn.com/abstract=1452803 (last visited Dec. 25, 2011).

[31] Sushil K. Sharma, Socio-Economic Impacts and Influences of E-Commerce in a Digital Economy, in the Digital Economy: Impacts, Influences, and Challenges 2 (2005).

[32] Vishnu Konoorayar, Regulating Cyberspace: The Emerging Problems and Challenges, Cochin University Law Review, 424 (2003).

[33] Id.

regulations which deal with cyberspace albeit in more general terms. However, while few regulations and policies aim e-commerce security and protection mechanisms for digital investment, any attempt to regulate the Internet also fails chiefly because a sovereign power cannot impose rules on other governments without expecting conflict, for the Internet is technically and economically global[34]. Besides, divergent national policy orientation and other factors; such as, tax differentials[35] make it harder to regulate the Internet and standardize policy requirements across Nation-states.

Part II investigates existing laws and policies of a few jurisdictions (both from host and home states' stand point) to see what aspects of cyberspace have been regulated or not. In particular, we look at whether or not current regulatory norms targeting cyberspace are sufficient to address possible data protection issues emanating from cyber security flaws for an offshore investor. Too much or too little regulation may negatively affect offshoring, rather than help promote it. Thus, part II further analyzes cyber security related laws and policies of certain jurisdictions, which have either too strict[36], too lax legal

---

[34] Christoph Engel, The Role of Law in the Governance of the Internet, Preprints aus der Max-Planck-Projektgruppe: Recht der Gemeinschaftsgüter, 8 (Bonn 2002).

[35] Catherine L. Mann, International Trade in the Digital Age: Data Analysis and Policy Issues; Testimony for Subcommittee on International Trade, Customs, and Global Competitiveness of the Senate Committee on Finance, 5 (November 2010).

[36] EU's data protection directive with a stringent privacy standards is a good example, see Madhu T. Rao, Key Issues for Global IT Sourcing: Country and Individual Factors, in Information Systems Management Journal, 17 (Summer 2004).

norms, or contain too many loopholes.

Depending on the nature of the data communication tools used to handle the data of an offshore investor, in a case of data breach, the investor deals with various parties causing the damage or acting in an illegal manner to gain access. These parties may not be limited to the host state or citizens of the host but could be anyone from any other jurisdiction. If the investor cannot rely on forum and home state regulations to take legal actions against these perpetrators or sources of illegal actions emanating from neither a forum state nor a home country, there is the possibility of dealing with laws of various other jurisdictions. Thus, in cases of unauthorized access, change, use, or destruction of investor data, the investor faces not only an anonymous actor,[37] but also may end up pursuing legal remedies with different national regulations and international legal norms, if any, in addition to those provided by host and home states.

The global nature of cyberspace, thus, proves to be an enormous challenge involving multiple legal systems for the legal community and the offshore investor alike. The investor now has to deal with issues of attribution[38] and jurisdiction absent agreed upon forum by means of a valid choice of law clause[39]. Jurisdictional issues in FDI disputes are nothing new; however, the problem with lack of consistency and consensus on what suffices

---

[37] FERRERA ET AL., CYBER LAW: TEXT AND CASES, 302 (2000).

[38] See Kelly A. Gable, Cyber Apocalpyse Now: Securing the Internet Against Cyber Terrorism and Using Universal Jurisdiction as a Deterrent, at 6 (August 14, 2009), also available at: SSRN: http://ssrn.com/abstract=1452803, (last visited Dec. 25, 2011).

[39] Richard Johnston & Ken Slade, Jurisdiction, Choice of Law, and Dispute Resolution in International E-Commerce Boston Bar Association: International Arbitration Committee, 15 (January 2000).

to assert jurisdiction, for instance, whether or not a mere existence of a website justifies a jurisdiction[40] makes the problem of jurisdiction on cyberspace more peculiar to FDI in IT-enabled services.

The fact that national regulations have proven to be ineffective in addressing all aspects of cybersecurity issues has resulted in debates among scholars and lawmakers around the world. A few solutions have been proposed by some. But many see viable alternatives from the international legal arena to compensate the inability of national laws to fully address cyber security issues as well as provide governance mechanisms for the Internet. Among those proposed possible alternatives are, for instance, calls for international legal frameworks, as well as global data privacy standards[41] to deal with data protection on cyberspace. There are several other proposals that range from using universal jurisdiction[42], treaties[43] to more efficient and interoperable technical tools[44] to augment national regulations.

---

[40] Id. at 5.

[41] Christopher Kuner, An International Legal Framework for Data Protection: Issues and Prospects, 2 (2009).

[42] See Gable, supra note 38, at 7.

[43] Ron Keys & Jim Ed Crouch, International Cyberspace Considerations, in CyberPro May, 10 (2010).

[44] The White House, Draft National Strategy for Trusted Identities in Cyberspace: Creating Options for Enhanced Online Security and Privacy, 12 (June 25, 2010).

Chapter 2 FDI in Services: IT Enabled Services & the Need for Securing Investor's Digital Assets

A. *FDI in IT and IT-Enabled Offshore Services*

1. FDI in Goods vs. FDI in Services

a) Comparative Look at Characteristics and Trends

Scholarly sources have dealt with both investment in goods and services for the most part, but the same sources have been inconclusive in terms of providing clear definitions for both modes of investment. Instead of attempting to define both, much of the literature tends to elaborate on conceptual differences and come up with what the distinguishing factors are in order to deduce definition there from for each. One approach sees storability of products of goods and services as a determinant factor for differentiating between FDI in goods and services[45]. Accordingly, unlike goods, services must be produced and consumed right away, thereby being non-storable in the form of stock or inventory. Since some, but not all, services can be separated in a manner that they are produced in one place and provided in a separate location, regardless of the use of ICT, this approach is no longer plausible.

To clarify the above situation, others would categorize service FDI into two: those that require physical proximity of

---

[45] See Rashmi Banga, Foreign Direct Investment in Services: Implications for Developing Countries, Asia-Pacific Trade and Investment Review Vol. 1, No. 2, at 58 (November 2005).

service provider and user, and those that do not, where the latter can be separated in terms of time and space for production and consumption. The ability to separate service in terms of time and space has come about primarily due to advance in technology[46]. Based on the above premise, one can conclude that service FDI differs from FDI in goods mainly due to its non-storability, non-transferability, and that services are more complex conceptually, as well as flexible in production. But such a conceptual distinction is not as straightforward as it sounds because both goods and services have certain elements of each other. For example, some services are visible, tangible, and storable, whereas some goods are intended to provide service[47]. For this reason, an approach based on sectoral differences, i.e. variation with respect to economic activities in various sectors has been proposed and often adhered to. Accordingly, all activities not included in primary and secondary sectors are considered services[48].

With regard to growth trends in both FDI in goods and services, the same forces, i.e. improvements in ICT that have enhanced tradability of services seem to have helped accelerate inward FDI in services in the last decade[49]. Compared to increase in FDI in goods, cross-border spending in "digital IT products (software and IT services)"[50] and in all other IT-related services

---

[46] Id.

[47] UNCTAD, World Investment Report - The Shift Towards Services; United Nations New York and Geneva, 145 (2004).

[48] Id.

[49] See Catherine L. Mann, Offshore Outsourcing and the Globalization of U.S. Services: Why Now, How Important, and What Policy Implications? - In the United States and World Economy, at 286.

[50] This is one of the three ways a service oriented FDI can be setup, also known as efficiency seeking FDI, to provide low-cost export oriented service

has risen to date. The share of globalization in service oriented business and service FDI is expected to continue to grow at a faster pace. That is attributable to the increased use of advanced technology that enables broad range of knowledge to be digitized and codified, which in turn makes the separation of time and place, and transfer of services based on this knowledge possible.

b) Types of FDI in IT Intensive and IT-Enabled Services

Regardless of the definition blur observed in previous section, services in general and offshore service FDI in particular can be subdivided into two broad categories: producer and consumer, both of which can be technology intensive and IT-enabled for the purpose of ease in understanding based on the scope of this discourse. For both IT and IT-enabled service FDI, companies involved are both of those engaged in purely IT functions and those that perform non-IT business functions and do not pursue IT-business as their core business function. The latter is comprised of a far larger set of transnational companies, which often use the Internet and networked information technology to deliver their service products[51].

Thus, in terms of investment sector or type of engagement, services within offshoring FDI may include IT intensive activities (e.g. software engineering, development and testing, and IT R&D) undertaken usually by IT companies and IT-enabled service activities (e.g. sophisticated financial analyses, architectural

---

production in chosen destinations, see Nathan Associates Inc., Foreign Direct Investment, Putting it to Work in Developing Countries, U.S. Agency for International Development (USAID), 35 (June 2005); see also Id. at 281.

[51] Id. at 282.

designs, R&D, X-rays, films, and advertising clips) of non-IT companies. In terms of investment strategy, a service FDI can be classified as market or efficiency seeking, among others. And a large portion of FDI in services has been classified as market seeking; however, this is changing as more and more services become tradable utilizing improved ICT. More comprehensive list of the various kinds of IT and IT-enabled services that are being offshored can be found in the 2004 World Investment Report[52].

2. Foreign Investment in IT and IT-Enabled Services – Offshoring

a) What is Offshoring Anyways?

Before attempting to define offshoring in general and offshoring service FDI in particular, it is important to describe outsourcing as this appears to cause some confusion. Outsourcing refers to sending work by one company or organization to be done by another organization[53]. Outsourcing involves legal arrangements; such as, (sub)contracting with external entities, regardless of location, for providing goods and services to supplement or replace internal efforts[54].

---

[52] UNCTAD, supra note 2, at 150 (2004); also see UNCTAD, World Investment Report: Non-Equity Modes of International Production and Development, 137 (2010).

[53] Aspray et al., Offshoring, The Big Picture, The Economics of Offshoring; in Globalization and Offshoring of Software, A Report of the Association for Computing Machinery (ACM) Job Migration Task Force, 2, ACM 0001-0782/06/0200 (2006).

Offshoring, on the other hand, is considered an outgrowth of outsourcing efforts[55] and, thus, a recent phenomenon. IT related offshoring is more likely an outcome of the expansion in 1990s[56] of international ICT solutions as part of the overarching outsourcing arrangement. Offshoring refers to the location or place outside national boundaries where the outsourced work is done. With respect to location, of course, offshore conventionally means overseas, i.e. across the oceans for example from the U.S. point of view. Such locations include Europe but not Canada and Mexico though these lie across the U.S.-borders as well). The majority of outsourcing, in the case of the U.S., occurs within the United States, but since there is also outsourcing by U.S. companies taking place outside the U.S., especially in countries like India, the term offshoring may have come about. Some classify offshoring into two based on geographical distance between the client and vendor[57]: offshore outsourcing (for U.S. clients, this would include countries like China and India) and near-shore outsourcing (to include Canada and Mexico in the case of U.S. clients).

Yet, there is a shift in the most recent application and understanding of these terms as can be seen below under section (b). That means the difference between offshoring and

---

[54] See Hirschheim et al., Information Technology Outsourcing: The Move Towards Offshoring, 1 (2004).

[55] United States Government Accountability Office (GAO), Offshoring of Services: An Overview of the Issues, Report to Congressional Committees, 10 (November 2005).

[56] Economic Commission for Latin America and the Caribbean (ECLAC), Foreign Direct Investment in Latin America and the Caribbean, 65 (2008).

[57] See Hirschheim et al., Information Technology Outsourcing: The Move Towards Offshoring, 4 (2004).

outsourcing will no longer be significant and will not always be based on just geographical distance, location, or oceanic landscape. Rather, the focus, with respect to overseas outsourcing in general, is on whether the overseas outsourcing engagement involves a significant control shift in the management of the outsourced operations. The question, thus, becomes whether such an operation is a conventional offshore outsourcing for services provided by an external vendor or captive center/captive offshoring for in-house or internally controlled operations abroad. And depending on the analyses of key factors that determine the nature of outsourced operations, the concept of 'Offshoring service FDI' becomes a subset of offshoring in general and captive offshoring in particular.

b) Types of Offshoring and its Trends

i.   *The Difference between Conventional Outsourcing & Offshoring FDI*

There are technical differences among the sometimes interchangeably used terms: Outsourcing, offshore outsourcing, offshoring, and captive offshoring. Outsourcing means in general sense transferring organizational functions to a third party, where the party can perform the assigned functions within or across-borders. The latter is referred to as offshore outsourcing. As stated earlier, offshoring refers to a geographical location/distance beyond national borders where the work is done regardless of who manages or performs the actual work. Offshoring, thus, combines all out and in-sourced activities abroad, and comes in a variety of flavors, but the vendor controlled (conventional[58]) offshore outsourcing and captive offshoring described below are the two most common ones. Offshore outsourcing involves a scenario where the management responsibility for the delivery of outsourced service shifts to an external vendor based in a foreign country. E.g. a U.S. client in conventional offshore outsourcing concludes a contract with an offshore vendor, which could be an overseas based firm operating from an offshore destination or a Transnational Company (TNC) operating in the offshore location. The client can establish relationship with such vendors for certain fees either through a direct relationship with the offshore vendor/TNC or through a partner organization engaged in channeling work to offshore contractors[59].

Captive center also known as captive offshoring, on the other hand, can be qualified as offshoring service FDI involving an FDI scheme, where a foreign affiliate organization carries out offshoring investment while its operating decisions are dictated by the sourcing organization[60] (e.g. a parent corporation at the home country). It is believed that captive offshoring by definition involves FDI because the client company, often a TNC, is engaged in a self controlled offshore operation and that in a country other than its home country. So the key difference between conventional offshore outsourcing and offshoring service FDI is the management control over operational decision making process of the outsourced efforts in the globally sourced

---

[58] Id. at 5.

[59] Id. at 6.

[60] Aspray et al., Offshoring, The Big Picture, The Economics of Offshoring; in Globalization and Offshoring of Software, A Report of the Association for Computing Machinery (ACM) Job Migration Task Force, 2-2, ACM 0001-0782/06/0200 (2006).

operation. Captive centers strive to benefit from both cost-cutting and management control strategies based on an in-sourcing model[61], rather than outsourcing.

---

[61] Madhu T. Rao, Key Issues for Global IT Sourcing: Country and Individual Factors; in Information Systems Management Journal, 20 (Summer 2004).

Sourcing Organization		Geographical Location			Management Control over Overseas Operation			
		Domestic	*International*					
E.g. A U.S. Client	Organizational Functions	Within the Continental U.S.	Near-Shore (e.g. Canada, Mexico)	Off-Shore (e.g. Europe)	Parent/ Investor Control	Vendor Control	F D I	Type of FDI or Outsourcing Operation
	Out-sourcing	External Vendor within the U.S. (National or Foreign Contractor) - Conventional Outsourcing	External Vendor Abroad (National or Foreign Contractor) - Conventional Outsourcing	External Vendor Abroad (National or Foreign Contractor) - Conventional Outsourcing	No	Yes	N O	Conventional or Offshore Outsourcing
	In-sourcing	Branch Operation within the Parent company	Branch Operation/ Foreign Affiliate/ Another TNC	Branch Operation/ Foreign Affiliate/ Another TNC	Yes	No	Y E S	Captive Center, Offshoring FDI, or just *Offshoring*

Table 1: Summary of Offshoring and Outsourcing Activities

ii. *Trends in Foreign Outsourcing and Offshoring Service FDI*

The captive center version of outsourcing seemed to have won momentum over the past few years due to certain factors ranging from intellectual property concerns to more cost-cutting, to the need to control end-to-end process[62]. These benefits even galvanized some firms to back-source their outsourced operations

---

[62] See Sudin Apte, Shattering the Offshore Captive Center Myth, 5 (2007).

and streamline their foreign presence with the fully controlled offshore operation. However, recent trends indicate that such an enthusiasm in companies' decision to go solo in offshoring has somewhat faded. The reason appears to lie in the strength of intellectual property protection. With respect to technology oriented investment, the benefits associated with control over intellectual property rights seem to outweigh other factors in FDI decisions. However, these benefits exist only where there is a workable and functioning intellectual property protection. The strength of IPR, thus, has an impact on FDI decision, as well as inflow and technology transfer in general.

The impact of non-existent or dysfunctional IPR is particularly obvious with respect to offshoring service FDI in information technology and IT-enabled services. Weaker IPR regulation and treatment in a given FDI destination means that the investor cannot rely on IPR protection mechanisms for the investor's proprietary technology. This may hold true even when other influential determinants like location advantages (e.g. market size) are present[63]. Studies show that weak IPR protection has the highest negative correlation with the inflow of technology-intensive FDI[64]. The overall implication is that the weakness in IPR protection will deter FDI in IT and IT-enabled services as well, thereby making licensing a viable alternative. The licensing option may very well favor and encourage outsourcing in contrast to in-sourcing/offshoring service FDI. Thus, the licensing option through outsourcing instead of relying on weak IP

---

[63] See Michael W. Nicholson, Intellectual Property Rights, Internalization and Technology Transfer; Federal Trade Commission, 2 (2001).

[64] Beata K. Smarzynska, Composition of Foreign Direct Investment and Protection of Intellectual Property Rights in Transition Economies, World Bank - Development Research Group (DECRG); Centre for Economic Policy Research (CEPR), 11 (June 1999).

protection in in-sourcing might have as well contributed to a weaker trend in offshoring service FDI.

By the same token, there has been a slight reversal of the upbeat trends in offshoring service FDI as observed in popular destinations like India. These downward movements can additionally be attributed to factors; such as, high attrition rates and lack of management support from headquarters, as well as failed process integration between headquarters and affiliates[65].

All these factors imply that the offshoring service FDI in technology-intensive and IT-enabled services generally faces added challenges in the global market place. IT offshoring decisions, thus, can be affected by additional factors, especially associated with technology transfer and intellectual property protection that may continue to impact global expansion of IT offshoring negatively. It may seem that there will be a decline in offshoring service FDI due to these deterrents even when compared to conventional FDI.

Yet, while such downward trends may turn out to be true for IT intensive offshoring, service FDI in general has shown to grow more rapidly over the last decade compared to manufacturing FDI[66]. And there is enough evidence that this trend has been enabled by improvements in the global ICT. As stated elsewhere, rapid transformation in ICT resulted in the fact that more and more services continue to become tradable. Meaning, services can be digitized and easily transferred electronically from provider location to consumer location regardless of time and place thereby drastically minimizing required cost, time, and in

---

[65] Id., at 6.

[66] Catherine L. Mann, Technology, Trade in Services, and Economic Growth; OECD Trade Committee Conference: Trade, Innovation, and Growth "Global Forum on Trade" 15-16, at 3 (October 2007).

some cases quality of delivery, as well as product. Some have argued that growth in tradable services can lead to more trade in services than investment[67]. The problem with such an argument is that, although this may turn out to be true for some types of services, whether a service product should be provided for trade (sold on global market) or should be provided at the consumer location through an FDI engagement is dependent upon management decisions and other factors affecting investment returns. Arguably tradability of services will promote both service FDI and trade. Yet, it is up to a service provider to decide, based on benefits and drawbacks of either of the two modes of service delivery, whether to engage in providing overseas service through an FDI presence and management control (what is also termed as commercial presence[68]) or simply to deliver service products for sale abroad via international trade. Since host countries will benefit more from positive spillover effects of service FDI[69], e.g. technology transfer and employment, inter alia, hosts are often pressed to attract service FDI with all means than simply purchase service products. Service FDI, thus, most likely benefits from host-based incentives more than trade, which will in turn positively impact growth trends in service FDI.

c) Information Technology Offshoring

---

[67] See Rashmi Banga, Foreign Direct Investment in Services: Implications for Developing Countries, Asia-Pacific Trade and Investment Review Vol. 1, No. 2, at 55 (November 2005).

[68] Id. at 56.

[69] See UNCTAD, supra note 2, at 26.

i. *Progress in ICT and its Impact on IT Offshoring*

Unlike any other outsourcing or offshore business undertaking, international engagement in information technology operation requires reliable and functioning information and communication networks. Simply put, global IT outsourcing and offshoring heavily depend on the quality and reliability of ICT globally and within national boundaries. An unreliable telecommunication system only exacerbates the problems by compounding the challenges already exist due to the long-arm management relationship for an offshore investor[70]. Global ICT has come a long way, but its transformation at least in the last decade has been remarkable. The impact of such transformation, especially that of the progress in telecommunication networks on global IT trade and investment has been felt globally via an unprecedented surge in multi-national IT offshoring and outsourcing. Of course, there are other drivers in general affecting offshoring with push or pull effects from both home and host countries' perspectives; such as, changes in business process, pace of innovation, and quality of higher education just to name a few. However, software platform standardization and adoption of low-cost, high bandwidth communication media, among others, have been the major factors that not only revolutionized IT services offshoring, but tend to have push or pull effects on IT service FDI[71]. Countries in the developing world in particular now compete against each other to attract as many IT offshoring and outsourcing services as they can by building better, wired and wireless telecommunication infrastructure. A few even created designated enclaves ('technology parks'[72]) within their territories

---

[70] See Hirschheim et al., supra note 57, at 13.

[71] See Aspray et al., supra note 9, at 60.

equipped with a state-of-the-art technical infrastructure, in some cases rivaling those in the developed high-tech world[73]. These facilities are often capable of providing IT offshoring industry with the high technology support like high bandwidth fiber-optic networks needed to support massive data server farms and high speed connectivity. As multi-nationals continue moving at least low-end IT services from high-wage locations to low-wage countries (many of them in an FDI type operation), more and more developing countries continue to compete against each other in attracting these TNCs recognizing the benefits of accommodating these investors for all FDI associated advantages.

ii.   *Trends in IT and IT-Enabled Services Offshoring*

Traditionally, IT service offshoring activities are focused in software development (simple design, coding or programming, testing, and maintenance) using low-cost of labor. In fact, some argue that offshoring itself came about as part of the larger trend of software globalization, where software products and services were created in low-wage/low-cost environments and sold across the world[74]. These include IT research and development, software architecture and design, IT project management and consulting. More recent IT outsourcing and offshoring undertakings, for instance, involve high-end application development, specifically web-based applications and e-Business to enable firms to

---

[72] See Madhu T. Rao, Key Issues for Global IT Sourcing: Country and Individual Factors, in Information Systems Management Journal, 17 (Summer 2004).

[73] See Hirschheim et al., supra note 57, at 14.

[74] See Aspray et al., supra note 9, at 60.

embrace the e-Business era. However, offshoring and outsourcing are not limited to just IT resources. IT-enabled services - business processes not necessarily heavy on IT per se, but use IT resources to meet their business needs by enhancing their business processes with IT are very much active in offshoring. Very common IT-enabled offshoring services that are among the fastest growing offshoring service FDI include customer service or call centers, medical billing, accounting and financial processing, and x-ray reading, among others[75].

So far multi-nationals have pushed offshoring of mostly low-end IT and IT-enabled services to the scale seen today, especially in search for low cost to increase the bottom-line, meet global demand, and be on the edge with regard to fierce global competition. However, many believe and project that even high-end IT and IT-enabled services will continue to be of greater interest for these same TNCs for offshoring since they can now use the same cost benefit with highly educated labor force in developing countries, India and China being the best examples[76]. It is no surprise that offshoring services have moved up the value chain also to provide more sophisticated IT-enabled service sometimes called knowledge processing. So high-end or knowledge processes like x-ray reading and patent checking are increasingly being part of the services provided via offshoring today. Therefore, as far as what the offshoring future may hold, there is no doubt that more high-end software and IT service tasks will be, if not already, among the often offshored activities as more and more developing economies pave the way for such activities by providing, among other things, low cost – highly skilled labor force.

---

[75] See Aspray et al., supra note 9, at 55.

[76] Id. at 53.

3. Tradability of Services and the Need for Cross-Border E-Commerce

a) *Non-Tradable Services and Cross-Border Trade*

The need for cross-border services trade and investment has always existed. As trade in services entails international transaction costs in a big way, the cost factor has greatly hampered this type of trade. Technical infeasibility and host country policy frameworks had been additional factors until recently which had negatively affected growth in cross-border trade and services FDI. But, again advance in ICT, especially since 1990s has made a difference in alleviating some, if not most, of these problems. The ICT revolution has helped businesses overcome some of the technical obstacles associated with transferability and storability of services by providing means to digitize, codify, and fragment much of the service information for many types of services. Yet not all services can be technically divisible and digitized for ease of transport, thereby being non-tradable as tradability is not just a matter of technology[77]. Trade may not always be possible even when technical issues of tradability for services are resolved. That is because for some services there is a set of other equally determinant economic factors that should also be available or must be possible for the service trade to take place. These factors include proximity to

---

[77] Id. at 149.

markets, interaction with customers, and trust and confidence, which could outweigh the possible benefits[78]. It turns out most of these trade barriers can be addressed via physical presence of the service provider in the host forum through offshoring service FDI itself, instead of trade.

b) The Role of Electronic Commerce in Offshoring Service FDI

i. *What is Electronic Commerce?*

Most recent scholarly sources define electronic commerce (e-commerce) as the process of buying, selling, or exchanging products, services, and information through computer networks while others follow the broadest definition adopted by the WTO General Council in 1998[79]. Evidently the current definition takes into consideration the strong association of the term with commercial activities on the Internet[80]. Yet it can be argued that the term 'e-commerce' should be conceived as involving business activities to include not just buying and selling goods and services online, but other transactions as well. Such transactions include electronic funds transfer, information exchange, and business communications using all devices and networks that facilitate electronic data transfer as well as communication. In the case of an IT services FDI, this could include any and all online business

---

[78] Id.

[79] Andrew D. Mitchell, Electronic Commerce, Legal Studies Research Paper No. 353, at 1 (2006).

[80] Id. at 1

activities/transactions involved in all phases of the offshoring supply chain. Devices and network tools that facilitate e-commerce include not just the Internet and its technology as it appears to be today. There was e-commerce before the advent of the Internet and associated technology that utilized other technologies to include EDI, computer systems, and predecessor communication devices (facsimile, analog telephone, and internal data networks). The Internet has just improved the e-commerce platform by making the communication digital, much easier and faster, and the scope of e-commerce presence much broader, as well as ubiquitous.

ii.   *Types and Platforms of Cross-Border E-Commerce*

Basic e-commerce infrastructure has evolved to include core functionality for navigation, shopping cart, and checkout that includes a payment mechanism, shipping and handling, and taxes. Most advanced e-commerce solutions nowadays also include features that range from some level of integration to an order management system (OMS), an enterprise resource planning (ERP) system, and a warehouse management system (WMS) to rich media with audio and visual tools, customer product reviews, and social networking. But if a merchant wants to be involved in the international market place, there are a myriad of things or technology features to consider in addition to the basic e-commerce platform. Cross-border e-commerce has challenges of its own associated with language, currency, channel conflict, product restriction, export, customs, international payment fraud, and delivery hurdles. So the merchant for a cross-border e-commerce needs to ensure that the e-commerce platform includes important features to provide solution for channel conflict, product restriction management, export compliance, customs documentation, language translation, and currency conversion. E-commerce must provide means of protection against international payment fraud and ensure seamless processing, as well as delivery and tracking.

There are many forms of electronic transactions that have emerged with the advent of e-commerce itself. Their distinction depends on the kinds of players or parties involved in e-transactions. Or else it can be based on who is selling goods and services and who is buying or consuming those goods and services. This can range from those involving just consumers to those involving consumer/business and government. But the most common forms also in cross-border transactions are Business-to-Business (B2B) and Business-to-Consumer (B2C).

B2B involves 'companies doing business with each other; such as, manufacturers selling to distributors and wholesalers selling to retailers'[81]. B2B is by far the largest with respect to volume in transaction and dollar amount as this type of interaction can be multiple and continuous, e.g. supply chain. B2C involves online transactions between businesses and consumers or individual shoppers, and is the most prevalent online shopping activity. Various other types also exist, namely: Consumer-to-Consumer (C2C) for e-transactions among consumers, Consumer-to-Business (C2B) where individuals sell products and services to business, and even those involving government, for instance, for e-transactions between consumer or business and government (C2G) and B2G) respectively.

---

[81] As defined by DigitSmith Embroidery and Screen Printing, available at: http://www.digitsmith.com/ecommerce-definition.html, (last visited February 5, 2011).

iii.   *Global vs. National Characteristics of E-Commerce*

Rapid global expansion of e-commerce is attributable to the emergence of enhanced global networks of ICT which made the Internet technology possible. E-commerce has impacted the global economy and trade significantly with its ability to facilitate cross-border commercial transactions and to reduce transaction costs. With its potential to generate benefits for both producers and consumers by itself that exceed those of trade liberalization benefits provided by WTO, e-commerce has changed the landscape of cross-border trade involving consumer to consumer, business to consumer, or business to business transactions[82].

E-commerce has both national and global characteristics. It is national in a sense that some aspects of its transactions can be governed by national laws, whereas its global characteristics arise, among other things, due to certain aspects of it being not covered by national laws thereby being subject to international laws. The latter aspect exists because of the e-commerce's inherent cross-border nature. Traditional commercial transactions (those emanating from just a bricks-and-mortar business model) may be governed by direct regulations such as economic acts which provide certain "command and control" [83] capabilities. The problem; however, is that such direct regulation may not be feasible for every aspect of e-commerce transactions. Similar situations arise in other business transactions where traditional commercial laws do not provide sufficient coverage. Hence, some

---

[82] See Mitchell, supra note 79, at 3.

[83] Jane K. Winn, Electronic Commerce Law: Direct Regulation, Co-Regulation and Self-Regulation, CRID 30th Anniversary Conference Forthcoming, Cahiers du CRID, 3 (September 2010).

even argue with respect to such business transactions that the lack of direct regulation may have resulted in a displacement of traditional commercial regulations thereby paving the way for "self regulatory"[84] schemes. This tendency has similar implications for the e-commerce environment as well. Examples of self regulations are the Society for Worldwide Interbank Financial Transfers (SWIFT), Visa, and MasterCard[85], all of which have their own operating rules that have to be complied with and can be enforced.

iv.   The Need for E-Commerce Security in Offshoring

The involvement of computer networks and use of e-commerce in the FDI business process is of course not without consequences. Indeed, just as e-commerce faces security threats everyday due to the increasingly complex cyber attacks that affect all businesses, service FDI that uses e-commerce faces similar threats. Organizations engaged in e-commerce continue to have cyber attacks from both in and outside of the organization. The various cyber attacks equally pose imminent threats to all e-commerce users. For example, computer virus, malware attacks introduced by unauthorized Internet usage by employees, and denial of services attacks, to name a few continue to wreak havoc e-commerce infrastructure and cause substantial financial losses regardless of the nature or purpose of the e-commerce's use. These types of attacks require more than a single type of technology to counteract the attacks. The need for more technical

---

[84] In the case of the U.S., the term contextually could imply a system of co-regulation as similar laws in the U.S. simply delegate such powers to non-government agencies; see Winn, supra note 84, at 10

[85] Winn, supra note 84, at 5.

tools involving high cost of course complicates the level of efforts needed to protect against those attacks or to contain sustained damages.

These common e-commerce security issues have obvious security implication for offshoring service FDI. The reason is that offshoring service FDI transactions in the Internet era involve use of cyberspace or exchange of sensitive information using e-commerce platforms over cyberspace one way or another. Online trade or exchanging digital service products inevitably calls for extensive use of cyberspace, among other things.

While basic security issues of e-commerce remain the same for the most part as in all other business models facing information systems security threats, e-commerce is particularly susceptible to threats affecting online transactions. That is because global e-commerce relies entirely on the functionality and safety of the Internet architecture, as well as web browsers, both of which pose various security threats. The major issue with e-commerce is establishing trust and unfortunately there are plenty of security holes inhibiting this trust[86]. E-commerce transactions often involve online exchange of sensitive personal and financial information. A malware exploiting browsers, which is often brought about by a cyber attack known as 'man-in-the-browser'[87], for instance, is among the many threats faced by users during web browsing. Man-in-the-browser attack is especially a

---

[86] Ramanan R. Ramanathan; E-business: Trust Inhibitors, ISACA, JournalOnline, 1 (2008).

[87] See SafeNet, Inc, Understanding Man-in-the-Browser Attacks and Addressing the Problem, 6 (2010); available at http://www.safenet-inc.com/uploadedFiles/About_SafeNet/Resource_Library/Resource_Items/Whit e_Papers_-_SFDC_Protected_EDP/Man%20in%20the%20Browser%20Security%20Guide.pdf (Last Accessed August 10, 2012)

serious threat for users browsing e-commerce sites. An attacker would use social engineering methods before planting a malware on the user's machine, where the malware eventually controls the browser being used on the machine. Social engineering involves use of certain tricks by which users are easily persuaded or prompted via pop-ups to install software updates containing malicious code. For instance, the user is persuaded to install a piece of software that pretends to do good things while concealing real intentions. A good example is a Trojan horse, which presents itself as a useful program while in reality it can cause damages. A malware like man-in-the-browser, once successfully placed on the user machine, can activate itself and steal user credentials. Once user credentials like credit card or bank information is compromised, it becomes easier for the hacker (the perpetrator behind such attack) to steal financial resources and access other personal or proprietary information with a possible consequence of financial loss, as well as privacy violations.

In addition, there are other more prevalent issues affecting both consumers and vendors in e-commerce transactions as described in the following scenarios. For example, a user connects to a web server at an e-commerce site to buy some service product. The e-commerce vendor requires that the user completes certain forms to finalize the transaction. These forms require the user to include personal and financial information including personally identifiable information (PII)[88]. Meanwhile a single PII, e.g. social security number (in the U.S.), or combination of PII can be used to distinguish or trace an individual's identity;

---

[88] This includes social security number, user's physical/home address and phone, and other information; such as, driver's license number that can easily and uniquely identify the user as such.

such as, full name, biometric records, etc., which makes PII more vulnerable to online thieves for purposes of identity theft.

What are the security implications that could arise from such transactions?

There is a common misconception with regard to identity on cyberspace, where many people easily fall victim to various tricks while browsing or during online transactions. That is, many users presume identity of the source or other parties that they deal with without further verification and expose themselves to cyber attacks. Users should second-guess consequences of their action without hesitation when they open emails from unknown sources or click on pop-ups, then not all these sources are necessarily legit. In reality, while users can easily be fooled into clicking on spam emails or phishing links, it is also not an easy task to tell the legitimacy of the source with some certainty. Neither does a clear cut process exist to establish the identity of parties who transact online.

So in our example, both the vendor and user must be certain that they are transacting with parties whose identities are verified. To an extent possible, it must also be established that the parties intend to do what they promise. First, from the user's point of view, it is difficult for the user to know that the web server is owned and operated by a legitimate vendor. Secondly, the user cannot know with some certainty that the Web page and form contain some malicious codes or executable files. Finally, there is no way for the user to tell if the Web server will collect this information and distribute/sell it to unauthorized third parties.

From the vendor's point of view, there is no way the vendor knows that the user's identity is who he/she says who he/she is or he/she will not attempt to break into the Web server and make unauthorized changes on the site or do some other malicious act on the back end. One of the basic security issues on the Internet involves identity. The identity issue arises because on *"the Internet, the sender of information cannot necessarily be presumed to be who he or she is"*[89]. There is no way the vendor will be sure that the user will not try to disrupt the server by making it unavailable to others through a denial of service (DoS) type of attack.

On the other hand, both parties cannot know the network connection they are using for the transaction is free from eavesdropping by a third party who can listen and record the transaction and steal valuable information. Nor may both sides know their information exchange is free of alteration by a middle man.

v.   *Achieving Trust in E-Commerce*

Establishing reliable identity is the first step in ensuring trust, which is the key for parties in e-commerce transactions, even more so in cross-border e-transactions. So trustworthiness becomes the hallmark of e-commerce quality and security. Because of that, there is a need to implement tools and mechanisms which should ensure this thrust. And one way to accomplish that is through implementing appropriate network security, authentication, authorization, auditing, and non-repudiation during an e-commerce transaction. All or a combination of most of these security mechanisms can enable trustworthiness[90]. Trustworthiness ensures legal validity of the

---

[89] Vishnu Konoorayar, Regulating Cyberspace: The Emerging Problems and Challenges; Cochin University Law Review, 423 (2003).

transaction and is accomplished by implementing tools that account for at least authenticity, availability, and integrity of information during online transaction.

Authentication provides some assurance that someone or something is who or what it claims to be in a cyberspace. Proper authentication mechanism is an important security step for e-commerce transactions in particular. The notion of authentication in cyber security is slightly different from that used in paper based legal documents, e.g. contractual law. Regardless of a legal system, authentication in paper form document serves as the evidence of the document's authenticity, i.e. it provides evidence that the paper document or record is what its proponent claims it to be[91]. And authentication on paper is achieved, in most cases, using some form of signature with or without enhancement; such as notary seal[92]. However, authentication in electronic documents not only serves as the evidence for validity of the document, in which case also an electronic equivalent of signature; such as, a Public Key Infrastructure (PKI) based digital signature[93] maybe used, but it also provides a mechanism to control access to system, i.e. the same system that stores or contains the very document. The term authentication in e-commerce, thus, serves

---

[90] See Thomas J. Smedinghoff, The Legal Challenges of Implementing Electronic Transactions, UNIFORM Commercial Code Law Journal [Vol. 41 #1], at 22 (2008).

[91] UNCITRAL, Promoting Confidence in Electronic Commerce: Legal Issues on International Use of Electronic Authentication and Signature Methods, UNCITRAL 1996 Model Law on Electronic Commerce; UN, 14 (2009).

[92] Id. at 6.

[93] Digital signature refers to technological applications using asymmetric cryptography, also referred to as public key infrastructure (PKI), to ensure the authenticity of electronic messages and guarantee the integrity of the contents of these messages; See UNCITRAL, supra note 92, at 17.

two different purposes. For one it ensures that the identification source (person or system) identifying itself is valid while at the same time also verifying that the same person or systems is authorized: meaning that the identified entity is authorized to access the document. Authorization is part of an authentication process in an access control mechanism and ensures that only the entity authenticated in this way can access the electronic document or information in question. Both steps are done using an authentication system often utilizing authentication protocols. Among the most popular protocols for this purpose are RADIUS (Remote Authentication Dial In User Service) and TACACS+ (Extended Terminal Access Controller Access Control System). To perform the two step-process, RADIUS combines authentication and authorization in a user profile, whereas TACACS+ performs authentication and authorization process in two separate steps. TACACS+ uses the TCP, and, therefore, more reliable than RADIUS, which uses UDP.

On the other hand, authentication also provides assurance, in the case of electronic document being accessed, that the document or information being accessed, which bears digital signatures is valid.

An authentication system, in the case of electronic authentication, has a subject, e.g. a person or group to be authenticated and a distinguishing characteristic that uniquely identifies the person or group. It should have a mechanism for verifying the presence or absence of the differentiating characteristic available on record, and an access control tool that determines the authorized actions performed by the person or group being authenticated. Authentication is achieved using an authenticator based on a distinguishing factor such as something one has (e.g. a security token, ID card), something one knows (e.g. password, pass phrase, PIN), and something one is (e.g. biometric[94] features: fingerprint, DNA, voice recognition).

The best approach is to use some combination of all three also called multi-factor authentication (using two or more authentication mechanisms). However, even this combination is not always spared from sophisticated attacks. An attack called phishing[95] usually initiated with an email purporting to come from a legitimate source such as the user's bank or e-commerce site can be one such complex attack that can circumvent strong authentication systems. In a phishing attack an unsuspecting user is often lured to click a link on the email. The link takes the user to a look-alike but fake website, which is nearly identical, i.e. has a look and feel of the legitimate site[96]. Once on the site, whatever the user types including authentication credentials for the legitimate site could be compromised - meaning covertly recorded in the background by the phishing website.

In addition, a Trojan[97] or more sophisticated worm installed on the user computer also initiated through spam emails can even defeat the purpose of the secure connections that use encryption based on tools like secure socket layer (SSL) and Virtual Private Network (VPN). Even when the user is browsing via an encrypted

---

[94] Biometrics is a measurement used to identify an individual through his or her intrinsic physical or behavioral traits.

[95] It means deceiving individuals into disclosing sensitive personal information through deceptive computer-based means. It includes a method called 'baiting' where the scammers use email bait to phish for passwords or financial data. For more on this, see Marco Gercke, International Telecommunication Union – Understanding Cybercrime: A Guide for Developing Countries, 59 (Draft 2009).

[96] Ramanan R. Ramanathan, E-business: Trust Inhibitors, ISACA, JournalOnline, 2 (2008).

[97] A program that overtly does one thing while covertly doing something else, see PFLEEGER ET AL., supra note 36, at 15.

connection from user's computer to a server, since the Trojan horse, an example of which is a "key logger"[98], can listen and record any input user is making on the key board of the compromised computer, the key logger is able to capture everything including passwords, session keys, etc. that allow that attacker to decipher the real data being exchanged between the server and client. The key logger captured inputs could either be automatically relayed to the hacker or recorded for later access and use by the hacker for impersonation purposes. In cases like this, thus, SSL or VPN secure channels are as good as the security of the computer on the client side.

As I stated earlier, authorization is another important step in access control security measure which helps enhance trust in e-commerce. From the cybersecurity point of view, authorization ensures that a person has the right to access certain information. However, from an e-commerce point of view, authorization further answers the question whether the transaction is allowed to take place electronically[99].

Other technical measures for securing e-commerce include network perimeter protection tools and tools for transmission and session encryption; such as, virtual private network (VPN) and secure socket layer (SSL). Firewall is a perimeter security tool that comes in software or hardware versions. Firewalls must be

---

[98] A key logger is a piece of 'software that record every keystroke typed on an infected computer's

Keyboard'; see Gercke, supra note 135, at 25

[99] See Thomas J. Smedinghoff, The Legal Challenges of Implementing Electronic Transactions, UNIFORM Commercial Code Law Journal [Vol. 41 #1], at 6 (2008).

implemented at a network perimeter to protect front-end and backend systems for e-commerce applications, servers, and files within the network. A hardware based firewall, for instance, is a network node consisting of both hardware and software that isolates a private network from a public network and monitors incoming and outgoing electronic traffic on the network.

VPN is another security solution that encrypts the link between the e-commerce site or network and a consumer workstation or network. An implementation option relevant to a service FDI would be a VPN deployment to encrypt the link between an e-commerce network at the branch/affiliate FDI location abroad and the home office network. VPN is used to create a virtual secure tunnel over a public network; such as, the Internet. It uses encryption protocols like point to point tunneling protocol (PPTP) or newer protocols, e.g. IPsec, to create encrypted tunnels. VPN creates a private tunnel over the Internet and uses encryption to scramble the communications.

Another vital security tool to consider for online transaction between client (e.g. a web browser at an FDI site) and web server at home office site is SSL. If the FDI business process involves web applications, there is a strong business case to implement SSL. SSL is used to encrypt web communication sessions between a web-client and web server using signed certificates that must be validated before establishing connections. Again SSL provides an added security measure for cross-border web-based transaction by ensuring that clients and servers must authenticate themselves before exchanging any sensitive data traffic between each other. Use of SSL and its verifiable certificate ensures, among other things, that the communication may not be hijacked by an unauthenticated client and user behind that client thereby limiting unauthorized access.

In practice, not only communication session, but data itself can be encrypted, meaning the data can be converted from clear text, graphic, voice, etc. type data into scrambled, unreadable cipher text using some form of encryption algorithm. Encryption helps meet the confidentiality objectives within the information protection triage confidentiality, integrity, and availability (CIA)[100]. However, since encryption per se cannot guard against modification of a cipher text or encrypted message itself, integrity will still be an issue. Therefore, additional integrity checking mechanisms like message digest are needed. This counter measure should be used with VPN or SSL to ensure that information has not been tampered with. This should also accompany an authentication process to verify the identity of anyone using the VPN client to access the server through an access point, e.g. a firewall containing VPN concentrator, on the e-commerce network.

Information security demands a defense in-depth strategy in majority of circumstances and there is a need to implement more tools in e-commerce platform in particular. Defense in-depth is an information assurance concept in which multiple layers of security controls are implemented. For the e-commerce provider this sounds rather cost ineffective. But cost can be justified by the fact that e-commerce by its very nature is more susceptible for online security exploitation on cyberspace through remotely accessing users including bad guys. Such layers of defense require further data and transaction protection mechanisms, especially useful in e-commerce and include audit logging, network monitoring using IPS/IDS tools, web traffic filtering, and ensuring non-repudiation. Auditing is the process of collecting information (usually by an operating system or Intrusion Detection as well as Prevention Systems (IDS/IPS)) that must be

---

[100] See PFLEEGER, supra note 36, at 10.

maintained unchanged in an edit-protected manner or with no privilege to make changes by anyone. While both IPS and IDS are systems or a special category of software that can be configured to monitor activity across a network or on a host computer, watch for suspicious activities, and to take automated actions including averting the intrusion and logging the incidents for later auditing, they also have the ability to alert administrators. An audit log tool captures any attempts to access particular electronic resources, use particular privileges, or perform other security actions. Finally, non-repudiation limits the ability of parties to deny that a legitimate transaction took place. There are tools on the marketplace which provide this capability usually by means of electronic signature.

In sum, it is safe to say that an investor planning to utilize e-commerce solutions in support of an FDI project needs to be aware of the need to account for security through use of any number of these technical safeguards to make sure the exchange of data across borders, over cyberspace is made relatively safe. Investors need to be willing and prepared to analyze the threat landscape on cyberspace, and assess the pros and cons of various e-commerce implementation options, as well as technological security tools before implementing an e-commerce platform. Clearly, while no suggested tool guarantees full protection, digital investors in the global market place are much better off when they include an appropriate number of these solutions into their portfolio of protection mechanisms. The implementation of these solutions and adherence to other security standards will also allow them to come close to meeting their goals in terms of ensuring security for their digital data and ultimately assuring trustworthiness for their clients.

B. *Security Risks for Digital Assets in Offshoring*

1. Types of Risks Specific to Offshoring

When it comes to risks in FDI undertakings, of course, it is not only the financial risk that becomes more visible, but there are many other types of risks particularly associated with offshoring service FDI. In terms of risk target, one can broadly categorize offshoring service FDI risks into three. First, there are risks directly impacting the offshoring firm itself or its financial assets. Secondly there are those affecting individuals (employees and third party victims). These could include threats against individuals in the form of privacy violation and loss of life, as well as financial wellbeing. Finally, there are those threatening national security and economic welfare of nations.

Few of these risks are unique to IT offshoring per se, while many others are generic in nature and common to all FDI[101]. Generic risks range from socio-economic and political incidents to those emanating from individual investment projects mainly confined to business enclaves abroad but affecting nation-states. In terms of IT and IT-enabled service offshoring, some consider two broad aspects of security risks: one associated with loss of control over business process – outsourcing risks; and secondly, risks associated with computer systems – systems intimacy risk[102]. All the same, control over business process is not limited to

---

[101] Jean Camp et al., Offshoring: Risks And Exposures, In the Globalization and Offshoring of Software, A Report of the Association for Computing Machinery (ACM) Job Migration Task Force, ACM 0001-0782/06/0200, at 6-2 (2006).

[102] Id. at 6-3.

outsourcing. Investor controlled offshoring (FDI) can entail business process control risks as well, which may be caused by factors affecting management control. These factors could include changes in legal, political, and socio-economic environments or legal barriers causing hidden cost of offshore contracting, litigation, and issues in international trade, tariff, as well as taxes. Thus, the overall risk factors affecting offshoring service FDI can be categorized as those affecting management control and business process (e.g. legal concerns), and those directly or indirectly emanating from computer and communication security weakness. Computer or data communication risks are primarily information systems security risks. An offshoring IT business process, therefore, is especially susceptible to these kinds of risks due to the distance in data communication involved and the diversity of computer networks that relay sensitive information back and forth. The longer the chain of communication or the more complex and diverse the networks involved are, the more susceptible and vulnerable to attacks the communication becomes between two points on cyberspace[103]. The same is true with longer supply chain, where multiple vendors are involved in supplying service products or processing online transactions. There are many kinds of data communication related risks associated with IT offshoring business model. Among some of the specific risks associated with IT offshoring primarily are loss of control over network perimeters, non-controllable data communication channels that may be vulnerable to network attacks, vulnerable ICT platforms/network backbones, and conflicting policies or incompliance with standards, as well as

---

[103] See Jean Camp et al., Offshoring: Risks And Exposures, In the Globalization and Offshoring of Software, A Report of the Association for Computing Machinery (ACM) Job Migration Task Force, ACM 0001-0782/06/0200, at 6-2 (2006).

protocols, just to name a few.

2. What Needs Protection?

a) Software, Hardware, Data, and Information Systems

From an offshore investor's point of view, there are relatively distinct types of investment assets that may be subjected to threats of all kinds. These assets can generally be divided into tangible and intangible assets. In terms of computer security and associated threats; however, these assets can be narrowed down to just software, hardware, data or information, and information systems owned or operated by the investor. Nonetheless, seen from a different angle, what can be considered an investment asset could sometimes depend on what is specified on an investment agreement (bilateral or multilateral), or other instruments that have been ratified by home and host states, with which the investor has FDI deals. If a bilateral investment treaty (BIT), for instance, specifically lists types of assets covered under the agreement and, thus, protected by the BIT, and assuming digital assets are explicitly included or implied in the text, then the investor's digital assets may be considered as covered under the protection scope. This does not necessarily mean that the investor has no other means for protection absent such protection mechanism provided under whatever BITs the investor's home country may have with a forum. The investor may still have additional instruments; such as, the International Center for Settlement of Investment Disputes (ICSID) for dispute resolution in addition to applicable host and home country investment related regulations. If the ICSID center is invoked, tribunals could apply international standards in determining what should be considered protected as an investment asset. This means absent specifics in investment law or agreements as to what is considered investment asset, international minimum standards will apply. These standards allow the investor to seek remedies and recover from loss of intangible assets including damages to computer systems and sensitive information.

Notably, most BITs include general statements using phrases like 'all assets', e.g. a BIT between Ukraine and Denmark[104] , in which case it can be argued that the phrase 'all assets' includes digital assets. But it all depends on how those phrases are interpreted in individual situations.

Nonetheless, in terms of a digital investment in an offshore setting, the three broad categories: hardware, software, and data maybe common to most IT offshoring investment assets. Or these asset categories may even be clearly enumerated on specific investment concessions or project agreements so that protection coverage for investor assets will not be a problem.

With regard to risk management for protecting these assets, the investor has to identify and categorize information assets. Such a risk management approach allows the information owner to properly manage information asset, and implement adequate and targeted protection mechanisms. An additional benefit of this process is that it will help determine monetary value of each type of asset in case of loss or not being able to access such information asset in useful format. While all assets warrant some

---

[104] David Collins, Applying the Full Protection and Security Standard of Protection to Digital Investments, Journal of World Investment and Trade, Vol. 12. No. 2, pp. 225-243, 2011, at 3 (September 6, 2010), also available at SSRN: http://ssrn.com/abstract=1672709, (last visited December 10, 2011).

form of protection, the big difference lies in the importance or priority placed in each type of information asset needing protection. In other words, a sliding scale may be established in terms of importance from one information type specific to a certain business environment to another depending on business objectives. This in turn depends on the business process or type of offshoring service engagement. If an investor is engaged in developing software, for instance, the bulk of data may involve software products. Protection for this software with regard to intellectual property could be more important than other types of information in the business process. For an investor dealing with e-commerce, again, although, the business process entails IP rights, protecting e-commerce transactions and client data (financial, privacy, and so forth) both legally and by means of information security mechanisms becomes very important.

As stated earlier, categories of software, hardware, and information warranting investment protection heavily depend on the nature of a business process. They can be classified as those that support or are part of the business process and those that are products of the business process. So, information or data types (e.g. software program design and instruction) involved in the business process need information security protection as much as those data types that are results of the process, e.g. software programs.

The occasional blur in terminology makes it worthwhile to describe a little more in detail the three most common categories of investor's digital (software, data) and non-digital (computer and communication hardware) assets in IT offshoring mentioned above. Software, depending on the nature of a business activity, could be any program or application system owned or operated by the investor to support the offshoring business process. It may include back-end and front-end systems (enterprise and web applications, database systems, and operating systems or servers) and network appliances. Hardware can be any tangible platform used to host or house systems and software modules supporting the offshoring business. This can also include devices supporting networks and telecommunication that are owned by the investor. It can include outsourced hardware that supports the business as long as the investor has contractual rights to control the security of the outsourced equipment. Conceptually though, when we refer to hardware, for the purposes of understanding information security, the focus here is only on the hardware that hosts, processes, stores, transmits, or houses valuable information belonging to the offshore investor or its clients. The value of hardware itself may not be as important as the value of information being, for instance, stored on such hardware and, thus, the protection of this hardware really is relevant only to the extent that its protection ensures the safety of the data from the information protection stand point.

While the third category for the purpose of relevance here consists of data, in any business process involving IT and IT-enabled services, there is another important set of assets: information system that equally needs information security protection. Information system is defined as a 'discrete set of information resources (people, technology, processes) organized for the collection, processing, maintenance, use, dissemination, or disposition of information'[105]. Hence as information systems are involved in processing, storing, and transmitting data, there is the need to protect them as much as the data itself. In other words, the information system, the information resources involved in

---

[105] See Committee on National Security Systems (CNSS), National Information Assurance (IA) Glossary, CNSS Instruction No. 4009, at 37 (April 26, 2010).

processing storing, and transmitting the information, must also be protected. The reason is that these resources either contain or process valuable information, or are involved in being transmission media for such valuable information or data. Hence, they too become an important asset category, which needs to be safeguarded from unauthorized access or destruction.

In the meantime, data and information are sometimes interchangeably used, hence misunderstood despite an important difference. Data is a subset of information in an electronic format[106] and is the lowest level of abstraction, whereas, information is the next level. Data in computing can be anything in its primitive form of abstraction, e.g. image, number, symbol, character, etc. that can be stored, processed, or transmitted in digital format using computing devices. Information is defined as data organized in such a manner as to be useful and relevant for business decisions[107] . As applied in the field of information systems, information in unorganized state is referred to as data, whereas, such data becomes information when organized to be meaningful. For an investor, such unorganized data could be any raw text, measurement, and codes in digitized format. But when this digital data is organized in some meaningful manner, for instance, to be an executable software code, then it is information.

Information that can and needs to be secured using information security tools and technique for an investor, thus, may include anything valuable and meaningful in the FDI business process that resides in an electronic format. By being able to be processed, stored, or transmitted by a computing or electronic

---

[106] CNSS, id. at 26.

[107] Marakas, George M., Decision Support Systems in the Twenty-first Century, 263 (1999).

device, this information, thus, takes a digital form of asset for the investor, where the digital asset now requires legal and technical protection.

b) Location of Information and Information Systems Subject to Cyber Threats

In any offshore business process, electronic data and information systems belonging to the business can be in one of three different states at a given point in time. Data can be in process, i.e. it can be in a state of being processed involving three distinct steps: input, process, and output before being stored in the form of meaningful data also known as information or as another form of raw data. Data or information and systems can also reside in a storage state. Information systems containing data can be located in an offshore facility or can be stored in an outsourced facility and equally subject to serious cyber security breaches. Data in storage is also known as data at rest; meaning it is saved or stored on storage media. Data at rest may not include data stored in a volatile storage environment; such as a random access memory (RAM). Both data in process and at rest can be protected using physical and environmental, as well as technical controls; such as, encryption and input/output controls. There are various storage media and technology including disk, tape, and external storage devices.

Information systems and data in an offshore business process can further be in a transition state at any given time. Data and information systems may be transferred either electronically or physically from and to the offshore facility thereby being exposed to further physical, environmental, and network based potential security breaches. Regardless of the state the data and systems find themselves anywhere in cyberspace or geographical location, they need to be protected against unauthorized disclosure, modification or destruction, and denial of service. However, protection mechanisms need to be tailored to meet the security needs of information assets. The security dynamics to protect this data can change depending on the status of the data. For example, when stored data is set in motion, the level of security risks change and so too are mechanisms to protect the data in motion. That is why it is critical to know in what state or where the data finds itself at a given time. Implementing appropriate, tailored counter measures for data during processing, storage, and transmission reduces the risk of the data being exposed to or compromised by unauthorized parties.

c) Confidentiality, Integrity, and Availability of Sensitive Digital Assets

The three important aspects of protecting both information and information system, also known as security states or objectives as defined by Federal Information Processing Standard 199 (FIPS 199)[108] in the U.S. are confidentiality, integrity, and availability (CIA). Confidentiality (privacy) is keeping private or sensitive information from being disclosed to unauthorized entities or processes[109]. Integrity is the ability to protect data from

---

[108] Federal Information Processing Standard 199 (FIPS 199) which is a mandatory standard for the federal government in the U.S., see FIPS 199, Standards for Security Categorization of Federal Information and Information Systems, 2 (February 2004).

[109] See CHARLES PFLEEGER P. & SHARI PFLEEGER L., SECURITY IN COMPUTING 10 (3rd Ed., 2003).

being altered or destroyed in an unauthorized manner or accidentally. Availability objective, on the other hand, ensures the ability of a person or a program to gain access to the data in a timely manner and useful format when needed[110]. FIPS 199 describes the nature of loss of each of the triage or the security impact when the objectives are not met while Federal Information Systems Management Act (FISMA) again in the U.S. defines the three security objectives as summarized in the following table [111].

---

[110] See PFLEEGER ET AL., SECURITY IN COMPUTING 11 (3rd Ed., 2003).

[111] NIST Special Publication 800-60 Volume I Revision 1, Guide for Mapping Types of Information and Information Systems to Security Categories, p. 9 (August 2008)

Security Objective	FISMA Definition	FIPS 199 Definition	Vulnerability Examples (for Network based attacks)
Confidentiality	Preserving authorized restrictions on information access and disclosure, including means for protecting personal privacy and proprietary information...	A loss of confidentiality is the unauthorized disclosure of information.	Eavesdropping Passive Wiretap Mis-delivery Traffic flow analysis Cookie
Integrity	Guarding against improper information modification or destruction, and includes ensuring information non-repudiation and authenticity...	A loss of integrity is the unauthorized modification or destruction of information.	Active wiretap Impersonation Falsification of message Noise Website defacement DNS attack
Availability	Ensuring timely and reliable access to and use of information...	A loss of availability is the disruption of access to or use of information or an information system.	Transmission failure Component failure Connection flooding e.g. ping of death Traffic redirection DNS attack DDoS attack

Table 2: Summary of Sample Vulnerabilities & Information System Security Objectives

According to NIST, the analysis of the CIA objectives should include impact assessment. The impact analysis is conducted on information categories using NIST standards to determine adverse impact levels as high, moderate, or low of potential security breaches on assets or human lives[112]. Accordingly, depending on the environment or level of importance to stakeholders, a given information type can be determined to be critical based on the

---

[112] NIST Special Publication 800-60 Volume I Revision 1, Guide for Mapping Types of Information and Information Systems to Security Categories, 12 (August 2008).

impact level assessment with regard to expected negative consequence on humans or properties when such information types are disclosed to unauthorized parties, made unavailable, or altered. In other words, for any information category to be assessed as having high impact or classified as critical, its compromise should result in severe consequences for human safety, major programs, or critical infrastructure.

More importantly identifying and classifying what is considered sensitive information in a business process will ultimately help the organization in selecting the right security controls and determining the rigor of such safeguards.

Meanwhile, NIST's CIA objectives have been expanded recently, where the revised model now includes non-repudiation and authenticity, which are also adopted by the International Standards Organization (ISO). Nonetheless, others disagree with this revision arguing the two additions still are either not comprehensive enough to cover security states that may be missing or misplaced in the original concept[113]. The descriptors, CIA, as originally defined by NIST represent the security state of information not the source of an action or the action itself.

Yet one of the most recent approaches has proposed a new model to include utility, possession, and authenticity (originally rejected).[114]. The new model adds possession to the confidentiality definition to account for an unauthorized observation (e.g. shoulder surfing)[115]. The NIST's definition of confidentiality protects against disclosure but NIST did not

---

[113] Donn B. Baker, Our Excessively Simplistic Information Security Model and How to Fix It, the (ISSA) Journal, 13 (July 2010).

[114] Id.

[115] Id. at 14.

specifically consider counteracting violations through observation, for example, via espionage. This aspect of a potential security breach was not considered to be explicitly defined as a component of the confidentiality objective. The new model also requires availability to include utility since information assets when available in a non-useable state arguably are of no use or importance for the stakeholder[116]. Therefore, protection of the availability objective in a narrower sense per se may not suffice to meet the information protection needs of the stakeholder. The information asset has to be available or accessible in a useful format.

The above three security states/objectives in an expanded format are also important to consider when it comes to attempts to safeguard digital assets in IT services offshoring. For offshore transactions, what this means is that there should be information security mechanisms in place at all locations and network enclaves regardless of these network premises being controlled by the information owner/investor as long as the networks are being used by the investor. This is to ensure that all three objectives are met to protect information and information systems no matter in what state or where the information finds itself at a given point in time.

Therefore, it is prudent to use risk based decisions for information security even in an offshore settings. It also means that information assets need to be identified, categorized based on criticality, and analyzed for implementing control mechanisms that ensure protection according to the modified CIA triage. To that end security risks should be assessed at least using approaches similar to what NIST lays out as a minimum standard. This involves the following more expanded steps at a minimum:

---

[116] Id. at 13.

identify digital asset types, determine their sensitivity, categorize those assets, and finally rate the assets in terms of adverse effects if the security of these assets is compromised during offshoring. Information systems (technology, people, and processes) that contain or process, store, and transmit data and information, as well as the data and information themselves that belong to the investor should be protected in such a manner that all three security objectives are satisfied. There are industry standards and best practices to be followed in order to meet these objectives. One such standard applicable to any business environment with some adjustment is the ISO 27001 based Information Security Management System standard. It defines a management process that can be used to identify digital assets and allow the information owner to assess the information risk and implement controls to reduce those risks.

In practice there are several information security management approaches applied by different organizations. It is prudent that no matter what program is being selected, information security should be planned in an enterprise information security architecture (ESIA) format and mapped to organizational enterprise architecture. This will ensure, among other things, seamlessness in any change affecting information systems. The integration of IT security with the enterprise architecture also promotes the level of involvement and conceptual understanding of security portfolio and needs by all levels of management.

As far as implementing security programs is concerned, important thing to keep in mind is that choosing any given approach should depend on organizational security needs and budget. However, a good security program should define organization-wide IT security policies and goals first. An IT security policy is the most critical element of a security program. The coverage and depth of a given security policy will determine a make or break in security posture of any organization. Moreover, without first determining security goals, you cannot make informed decisions about security. The security decisions an organization makes or fails to make solely rest on the type of IT security goals and polices the organization has in place. However, securing information assets demands the implementation of at least a minimum set of security controls prescribed by security policies and procedures. Furthermore, security policies have to be communicated at all levels of the organization to reinforce the need for implementing those controls.

A security program can be designed, for instance, based on an approach that includes the following minimum categories of security measures. Organizations should start a security program implementation with well defined and communicated set of security policies applicable to all systems organization-wide. These policies discuss all aspects of security requirements at all levels of the enterprise. They also need to mandate development of procedures at both enterprise-level and/or system level. The next step is to take measures geared to help raise awareness among all members of the organization of the need to account for information security. That includes a security awareness training program, which needs to be planned as vital component of the overall security program. Everyone in the organization should be made aware that they have the responsibility to protect information assets of the organization. This can be done in a variety of ways including planning a periodic training for all, requiring all members of the enterprise to sign an agreement, i.e. some kind of rules of behavior that specifies what actions the user is allowed or not allowed during the use of organizational computing resources. This agreement should also define sanctions for not abiding by this agreement. The fact that users can be held accountable for any action or failure to act, which results in a compromise of confidentiality, integrity, and availability, will more likely promote user adherence.

The second set of security measures is concerned with users' identification, authentication, and access controls. This set of controls will ensure that users have a proper way of identifying themselves when attempting to access digital assets owned and operated by the organization. Users must use appropriate identification mechanisms as specified in policies and procedures. The same applies to authentication process where users and user devices must be provided with appropriate authenticators. These authenticators uniquely identify user entities – meaning verify identities or other attributes claimed by all entities based on entities' IDs stored in specific systems and grant them primary access. Access control measures, again based on the specific access control mechanisms implemented, specify how user privileges are provisioned, and what actions users can or cannot perform logically (on the system) or physically (to access system location/site). But the type of tools implemented for each of these control measures entirely depends on the level of security needs and requirements at each system level.

A final set of control measures can be grouped under infrastructure based controls. This control group includes control measures that provide defensive mechanisms at perimeter/network and hosting/housing platform levels. Infrastructure level control measures require the implementation of layers of security to include network security tools and system hardening techniques. For instance, implementing firewalls at both network and host levels coupled with the use of IPS/IDS network monitoring tools will provide extra layers of protection. If platforms and network appliances are scanned periodically and to identify vulnerabilities including missing patches along with mitigating all identified vulnerabilities will enhance the security posture as a whole. If the organization accurately tracks the inventory of all organizational system assets and components, and prevents addition or removal of the same without authorization, this measure will improve security. If the organization audits actions from users, user devices and applications, and monitors unauthorized actions, as well as takes appropriate security actions based on reports of security relevant incidents, these capabilities along with all of the above constitute defense in-depth. These capabilities more likely put the organization in a better position to respond to all internal and external security threats.

The offshore investor will need to implement security safeguards at all levels, if possible, of the offshore business process and supply chain. It also means information systems and supporting tools, software, hardware, and firmware have to meet security standards. Software and systems development lifecycles should follow the industry standards in terms of embedding security controls in the life cycle. System components must be tracked for available updates and patched with appropriate updates or firmware upgrades, as well as periodically assessed for vulnerabilities. Network enclaves and perimeters should be protected using appropriate protection mechanisms.

Several security tools and risk management approaches contribute to meeting the security objectives. It is possible to make a network environment and system components more resilient to security breaches using tools and techniques available today as long as one has not only funds available to do so, but management control over such network enclaves and system components. For example, information and systems that process and store the information in an offshore location can be made safe applying proper security mechanisms as long as the data or information remains within the premise of the offshore facility. If the same data needs to be electronically transmitted to another location or network, this will usually involve the Internet. The problem with the use of outside networks; such as, the Internet is that there are certain security and management aspects that fall beyond the control of the offshore investor.

In other words, even though the investor can comply with standards and best practices within the investor's network enclave by applying best tools and proven methods, the security objectives may still not be met due to access to the Internet and the very transnational nature of networking involved in offshore transactions. There may be other network environments and systems involved to handle or at least help transmit information belonging to the offshore investor or its clients. Such outside networks may not be up to par in terms of security and may not meet the security needs of the investor. And yet the investor cannot control these networks and systems, nor can the investor force or require those networks to comply with security best practices. Simply put, the security of the networks outside the offshore facility is most likely beyond the investor's reach. In fact, the investor may or may not even know whether these networks and systems are safe and secure to be used in the first place. Indeed, in many cases, there is no way anyone can identify with certainty which network or system nodes a given piece of information/data packets traverse through on the Internet and which node or network exhibits the weakest link.

The Internet is the network of networks as it connects many other networks some of which are secure, whereas others are not. Many networks may not even use similar tools or protocols, or follow industry standards. Yet they are able to talk to one-another thanks to the Internet technology called router, which makes the internetworking possible. Routers, in particular those equipped with gateway protocols, enable diverse and heterogeneous networks send and receive data and are the most important device within the Internet technology in this regard.

There are many gray areas in the Internet that make it unsafe, the most notable being the elusive nature of the identity of user. In some cases, the Internet makes attribution nearly impossible. So the use of global cyberspace for conducting cross-border business transactions has its own advantages and drawbacks. Overall, the global security threats posed by illicit actors on the Internet are more pronounced and peculiar to IT offshoring. These threats make information security for offshore transactions in IT and IT enabled business models more relevant.

But implementing security safeguards in global cyberspace becomes even more challenging and yet a necessity.

3. Mitigating Risks via Regulatory Means of Data Protection

a) The Need for Legal Protection in General

As stated earlier, among the major categories of information in offshoring that need both legal and non-regulatory security safeguards range from intellectual property[117] to financial transactions, proprietary (e.g. business communication about service products), to Personally Identifiable Information (PII). Even though all kinds of information associated with an offshoring business process require some degree of protection both legally and by means of non legal information security mechanisms, the above categories demand more protection. Hence, the suitability of any type of protection mechanism for these categories warrants most scrutiny in terms of availability and sufficiency of such mechanisms. This is due partly to severity of potential consequences of lack of such protection. A possible consequence could include a significant loss or damage in terms of financial assets, reputation, and proprietary information, and that not just in a short term but in the long run as well.

Theft of intellectual property, for instance, costs U.S. businesses a substantial amount financially (about $250 billion annually[118]) and even results in a collateral damage; such as, loss

---

[117] Includes trade secrets, trade symbols, copy rights, and patents; see RICHARD A. MANN, SMITH AND ROBERSON'S BUSINESS LAW, 850 (11th Edition, 2000).

of jobs.

Another often associated concern is the impact of personal privacy due to offshoring, where medical and financial records become available to third parties, in foreign countries in particular, who have no need to know or to access such information. This sensitive data is easily made available through offshore transactions with no sufficient security safeguards[119]. The reason is that there may not be adequate regulatory frameworks requiring security of personal data or even if there are regulations, it is often possible for certain regulations to be riddled with ambiguities and loopholes that can be exploited by business entities and individuals. For example, depending on offshore locations, there may or may not be legal frameworks similar to Health Insurance Portability and Accountability Act (HIPAA) for medical patient data or Gramm-Leach-Bliley Act covering privacy of financial information, which could help protect sensitive information in cross-border transactions. Carefully designed legislations provide security frameworks in such a way that software and application developers ensure that their products are built with adequate information security mechanisms in place to comply with the legal requirements.

It is also important to note that information security measures can only mitigate risks. They cannot eliminate risks; therefore, there is always the likelihood that any of these information types can be exposed to threats despite technical security measures. The question is what needs to happen in case a security breach takes place and proprietary information is lost or compromised, altered, or made unavailable? This is where legal

---

[118] Steve Luebke, Trade Secrets: An Information Security Priority, The ISSA Journal, 28 (December 2006).

[119] See GAO, supra note 55, at 39.

protection, particularly norms that allow legal recourse for sustained damages, comes in wherever possible, if applicable, and available. That is because consumers, producers, and technology alike should be able to rely on the power of law for enforcing rights and obligations, as well as for obtaining equitable remedy. Thus law becomes as relevant for protecting the technology itself as it is for protecting consumers and environments from technology born dangers[120]. That is sort of the intersection and collision point at the same time of law, technology, and security.

b) Effectiveness of Legal Instruments to Deal with Cyberspace

We noted that legal instruments are needed to safeguard cyberspace with their deterring abilities or at a minimum to ensure that breach in cyberspace is accounted for with appropriate legal injunction. But the question is - how effective is the current regulatory environment to deal with cyber born criminal and civil offences? Legal efficiency on cyberspace demands that there be cyber regulations that are sufficient, relevant, and enforceable. However, it turns out the availability, let alone efficiency, of effective regulatory norms often becomes an issue in many jurisdictions.

Evidently, the legal avenue for cybersecurity is beset with various hurdles. Normally, once security breach occurs, some

---

[120] There is a clear interaction among science, technology, and law as they all impact one-another. Progress in science and technology necessitates adjustments or changes in legal norms to ensure coverage, and law also makes use of science and technology to enforce its norms, hence "science and technology need law just as law needs them". For details on this, see Okeke, supra note 19, at 6f, 40f; also available at: http://digitalcommons.law.ggu.edu/lectures/2, (last visited May 18, 2011).

remedy under tort and criminal liabilities, inter alia, could be sought for depending on a forum by the party sustaining a data breach. But then, the applicability of law, or rather its availability to account for the liability may even be an issue in cases involving cyberspace. That is because, for one although there are jurisdictions that regulate information security more granularly, e.g. Nevada, Oregon, and Massachusetts in the U.S.[121], there are others which do not address cyberspace at all. Secondly, the concept of cyberspace is still elusive and legal questions emanating from it may not find homogeneous interpretation or resolution across national boundaries. One of the more contentious issues in cyberspace, for example, involves the territoriality principle, on which the state and its laws are based[122] (though the importance of this principle in terms of judicial jurisdiction is diminishing[123]). This principle is contentious with regard to jurisdiction on cyberspace because cyberspace has no physical boundary that could relate to a given nation. So, while many aspects of cyberspace are covered under national laws, under certain circumstances, there are occasions, where few cases emanating from cyberspace may not even be covered under any law.

Certainly the legal environment for cyber security is evolving globally as the trend in national legal provisions, for

---

[121] Randy V. Sabett, The Evolving Legal Duty to Securely Maintain Data, the (ISSA) Journal, 14 (January 2011).

[122] Joanna Kulesza, Internet Governance and the Jurisdiction of States, Justification of the Need for an International Regulation of Cyberspace, 1 (2003).

[123] There is a shift from territoriality to reasonableness in international law; see GARY B. BORN; INTERNATIONAL CIVIL LITIGATION IN U.S. COURTS: COMMENTARY AND MATERIALS, 90 (4th Ed. 2006).

instance in the United States shows (starting from a rather reactive legislation in California to proactive ones to much granular laws in the states; such as, Nevada and Oregon mentioned above). Reactive cyber laws are usually promulgated after the fact, i.e. after certain bad cyber security incident has taken place. These laws don't always have amorphous deterrent effects on cyber crime[124]. So, evolving legal environments leave plaintiffs in cross-border cyber security disputes with little or no options to seek injunctions. That is, even if they may obtain remedies under the laws of certain forums, the same is nearly impossible under laws of some other forums where these plaintiffs sustain similar damages. Another potential problem is that, even if the forum is identified as a source of applicable legal norms for cyber incidents, there may still be various conflicting norms and circumstances that negatively impact or hamper such injunction.

A further contentious issue on cyberspace that leads to legal confusion and, hence inability of law to effectively resolve cyber disputes involves the question of jurisdiction. On cyberspace as in many other instances of conflict of laws, there is the possibility that an issue at hand may or may not be governed by forum or national laws due to lack of jurisdiction. While most cases on cyberspace are beset with legal ambiguity or loopholes, the situation with jurisdiction becomes a point of contention even if forum laws substantively deal with the issue of cyberspace. So in global cyber conflicts one thing is certain. That is, there is the possibility to loop around endlessly looking through legal regimes and norms in hopes to identify source of law whether it is international, intra-national, or foreign law that may govern the

---

[124] See Randy V. Sabett , The Evolving Legal Duty to Securely Maintain Data, The (ISSA) Journal, at 14 (January 2011).

issue at hand, and to determine its applicability, validity, sufficiency, etc.

Similarly, some cases may be addressed or issues may be regulated and governed by legal norms at multi-national and international levels simultaneously. Thus, there is a bit of legal pluralism to deal with. These legal norms may exhibit normative conflict and may even turn out, in some instances, to be contradictory to one another. Therefore, in the case of cyberspace born criminal incidents or an Internet related legal dispute, one faces not only the challenge of legal plurality, the fact that there is the need to carefully approach multiple legal systems to choose from, but the same case maybe dissected into pieces and fall under multiple legal systems. That is, one forum may govern one aspect or portion of the case, whereas, the rest of the case may be resolved using legal norms from various other jurisdictions. Needless to say, such legal uncertainty poses a financial risk for both a plaintiff and defendant in cross border disputes. From the defendant's point of view, especially when the defendant is a juridical person (a firm) with a world-wide or offshore presence, e.g. through an e-commerce, chances are the offshoring firm can be sued at multiple forums for the same data security breach. Such lawsuits can include a class action, which, as the privacy breach case against Amazon.com, Inc[125] proves, can involve plaintiffs from multiple jurisdictions. Though this particular lawsuit involving Amazon.com, Inc was brought by the U.S. plaintiffs, it implies a far reaching impact as other similarly affected individuals from around the world could either participate in the class action or bring their own lawsuits and file such suits in any forum that Amazon.com, Inc does business. And

---

[125] See Del Vaccio vs. Amazon.com, Inc; Case # 2:11-cv-00366-RSL Document 1 Filed 03/02/11; U.S. District Court, Western District of Washington at Seattle.

since Amazon.com does business by default worldwide (through its online or e-commerce presence), it can be sued in any forum worldwide as well. This is a proof that cases like this not only pose the risk of compliance requirements with multiple legal systems for the offshoring investor, but any non-compliance will end up ensuing worldwide litigation.

So it is not surprising that offshoring firms today must look into ways to minimize such risk exposure. This often leads to the fact that investors get more interested in knowing whether they are compliant with legal requirements at a given potential investment destination in terms of information security right from the outset, i.e. in some cases even before the start of their investment undertakings. They will have to also know if their security choices are legally defensible to ensure that security mechanisms implemented are justifiable in legal contexts[126].

A similar situation arises in which not only cyber security converges with the need for legal protection but sometimes there is an implication for a dwindling possibility that a security breach itself can be inadvertently sheltered with legal norms per se. It may also be the case that certain regulatory regimes create law enforcement hurdles by making at least the prosecution of data breaches almost impossible. For instance, a legal shelter of a security breach can occur when a legal system makes it harder for transnational law enforcement in terms of the cost of enforcing the law. A case where a legal system or a combination of legal regimes making law enforcement harder may arise as an outcome of distributed computing. This situation is better illustrated in cases originating from or incidents taking place in distributed network of computers (a DDoS using a BotNet being a good

---

[126] David Navetta, The Legal Defensibility Era the (ISSA) Journal, 12 (May 2010).

example), where a distributed cyber attack is often made possible by the hallmark of cyberspace itself.

A cyber security breach can be initiated somewhere in cyberspace but enhanced by various orchestrated networks where the attacker uses multiple targeted nodes from independent network enclaves to launch an attack. These unintentionally participating networks may be based on various jurisdictions around the world. For one single attack, there is the implication for software developers, vendors, system owners/users, and actual hackers that they can be liable or subjected to lawsuit alike in a chain of event. A good example is a distributed denial of service (DDoS) attack, which involves multiple parties – victims and actors, resulting in possible negligence lawsuits for unintentionally participating parties owning zombies[127]. DDoS is discussed in more detail with regard to the availability objective of the information security below /infra chapter II, B, 5, c)/. DDoS cases can easily invoke multiple legal regimes and forums thereby complicating the legal proceeding for the parties involved.

Meanwhile, not only are participating networks and zombies subject to law suits, but the software and application developers may be sued as well for design flaws that allow unauthorized manipulations on computers that become zombies. The problem with that; however, is it is not always easy and obvious to establish duty of care, which is the basic element of negligence, among other things, in tort as *Cooper vs. Hobert* shows[128] demonstrates. Duty of care could be established for

---

[127] Computers infected with malicious code for purposes of manipulation, where the infected computer becomes a tool of attack or at least a participant; also see Jennifer A. Chandler, Security in Cyberspace: Combating Distributed Denial of Service (DDoS) Attacks, University of Ottawa, 236 (2004).

DDoS cases analogously using the two-step test: proximity and foreseeability as argued by the Canadian Supreme court in *Cooper vs. Hobert*[129]. Duty of care must exist along with its breach and damage caused by such breach[130]. Bottom-line is in the context of DDoS, if an offshore investor is a target of a DDoS attack, the investor too can and should be able to hold the vendor of insecure software accountable in addition to going after all other participating perpetrators. However, in reality, it is hard to establish such duty of care against the software vendor, and even much harder to attribute a given source of DDoS to a specific perpetrator.

The networked world and the Internet multiply liability, as well as blur the link between victim and perpetrator[131]. Thus, there is the possibility for an offshoring investor to sustain cyber attack and yet not being able to recover the damage even with the help of legal protection. Simply put, this proves that even if a normative source is identified for legal injunction, the above circumstances complicate the application of the identified legal source.

Finally there is an issue of enforcement. The already weak international legal regime in terms of judgment enforcement becomes even less effective in enforcing cyberspace born legal disputes and crimes. Therefore, to protect digital assets in offshoring, relying on cyber security measures is perhaps more

---

[128] Canadian Supreme Court Decision 111601 - June 20, 2001, available at: http://www.eron-pwl.com/order9.html, (last visited March 7, 2011).

[129] Canadian Supreme Court Decision 111601 - June 20, 2001, supra note 175, at 1.

[130] Chandler, supra note 121, at 256.

[131] See GERALD R. FERRERA ET AL., CYBER LAW: TEXT AND CASES 293 (2000).

predictable than reliance on legal protection by way of legal remedies.

4. Sources of Cyber Security Threats and Attacks

a) Threat Types & Sources

i. *What is a Threat?*

Whatever computer security risks (inherent or unexpected) organizations end up being exposed to, there is a potential that these risks turn into incidents mainly in two ways: through accidents and intentional acts. All computer security risks pretty much involve threats and threat sources. The level of risk and likelihood of incident occurrence hinge on the vulnerability to the types of impending threats. But what is a threat? Threat can be defined broadly but with regard to offshoring, it can be any circumstance or event (natural, man-made, environmental) with the potential to adversely impact business operations, and assets, as well as employees in an offshore location. These threats can be narrowed down to just those that have roots in cyberspace, 'cyber threats'.

ii. *Advanced Persistent Threats*

Cyber threats range just as widely as their impacts and can be grouped by source or effect to include those caused by foreign or national origins, or errors in computing devices. More serious cyber threats include those involving foreign governments also called advanced persistent threats (APT) and terrorists. No terrorist sources have been identified as of yet to pose imminent threats with such an advanced capability. The reason appears to be that terrorist cyber attackers usually lack resources in terms adequately trained human capital and financial means to be well organized and be in a position to launch more resilient attacks, but the potential is there. On the contrary, states have the means, the intent, and resilience as well as technical and human resources. While APT poses especially serious source of threats for both nation-states and organizations, its capability is not limited to foreign government sources. Any organization that has the funding and technical know-how to sufficiently equip itself and persistently launch an attack can pose as a source of APT. Non-state sponsored sources of APT are said to specifically target other organizations, especially companies in the U.S. and Britain for economic reasons. The multi-billion dollar loss suffered each year by many companies in these nations in particular is attributable to the theft of intellectual properties through such targeted attacks often referred to as economic espionage. For instance, business sources from other nations, China in particular, have been reported to consistently and persistently prey on U.S. technology companies to dig into proprietary assets, e.g. software codes, licenses, patents, trade secrets, etc. APT originating from government sources can also target businesses with the intent to disrupt operations in retaliation for different government actions in the nation where business targets are located. Iran for instance was believed to have been behind the massive DDoS attacks against U.S. banks in the late 2012 in an apparent retaliation attempt for the previously unleashed attack against Iranian nuclear facilities. The incident involved a malware called *Stuxnet*, which the government in Iran is said to have believed to come from the U.S.

Meanwhile, with regard to APT from nation-states whether a cyber attack can qualify as a cyber or 'kinetic' war if a government is a perpetrator has been hotly debated. More recent assessment by experts suggests real possibilities of cyber warfare or even its defense involving active government actions given the tools available to unleash such attacks at a high level[132]. Serious attacks can also emanate from cases, where foreign government backed cyber-spies actively or passively prey upon national security relevant data. Such serious attacks can target critical infrastructure like industrial control systems (ICS) (e.g. power grid controls) that could severely impact all or parts of a country. A good example of an attack with a far-reaching effect that could debilitate an entire nation is the 2007 cyber incident that paralyzed the emergency response capability of the nation of Estonia for weeks clearly illustrates[133].

At the same time, there is still no clear international legal precedent or authority when it comes to legal treatment of cyber war. However, under international law the fact that states must respect other states (their sovereignty), refrain from provocation by any means to avoid violating the laws of war, or adhere to principles of non-intervention could be construed to cover the situation with state-sponsored malicious cyber incidents. In other words, the state's obligation for non-interference under international law could imply the possibility that this norm can be broadly construed so that international laws, laws of war specifically, apply. Accordingly, it is persuasive to argue that the existing international laws – norms under the law of war can be

---

[132] See Duncan B. Hollis, An e-SOS for Cyberspace, 4 (2010).

[133] Id. at 2.

applied under circumstances where a state sponsored provocative cyber attack is analogous to a war inducing act by the state. This position has won some consensus among scholars, so too argue most recent views[134].

iii.   *Insider and Outsider Threats*

With regard to intentional human acts, cyber attacks take place almost always using malicious codes that can alter, disrupt, usurp, or destroy computers and networks. Such codes allow the perpetrator to access a target system or data and perform a variety of unauthorized actions.

In term of actors (threat agents), many computer security threats originate from humans. Those directly originating from humans can be divided into two categories: Insider and outsider (mainly hackers) threats. Since the context here is for actively engaged threat sources, threat sources originated from unintentional human actions do not belong to this group. Unintentional actions committed by, e.g. inept employees who fall victim to social engineering[135] yet contribute to security breaches by inadvertently disclosing sensitive credentials, will be discussed later (see infra section b), ii below). Neither do the categories discussed here include actions caused by human errors (e.g. a system administrator wipes out a database by mistake while re-provisioning a server thereby causing a major outage).

Human actors in this context are those who commit security

---

[134] Id. at 19.

[135] Defined as an attempt to trick someone into revealing information (e.g., a password) that can be used to attack an enterprise, see Committee on National Security Systems (CNSS), National Information Assurance (IA) Glossary, CNSS Instruction No. 4009, at 69 (April 26, 2010).

breaches or criminal acts on information systems with clear motives. Active threats caused by humans usually are based on various motives. Such motives range from simple hacking for challenge by thrill seekers (usually hackers), to criminals whose intention is to gain unauthorized access and steal information, to those who systematically infiltrate into systems with much more destructive motives to either cause loss of data or for intelligence purposes.

Insiders are internal users who may be disgruntled or rouge employees, or employees with financial troubles or criminal history. These employees can either be easily fooled into an action with some financial or other incentives from hackers or act on their own with the intent to inflict damage or gain other benefits. Contrarily, non-internal perpetrators include hackers of all kinds and levels of complexity, as well as perpetrators acting as or backed by foreign government agencies.

iv.   *Insiders & Outsiders: Methods, Opportunities, Motive*

No matter what the source is for an attack, a malicious attack requires the following elements in order for the attack to take place: Method (skills, tools, and other means), opportunity (time and access), and motive (reason for the act)[136]. Though there may be some difference in methods, opportunities, and motive for both categories of attack sources, i.e. insiders and outsiders, the potential consequence for the targeted organization is similar in a majority of cases. Attackers have a motive to cause a system failure or to access the target information and often times know the possible consequence of their action. And that, of course, makes the determination of a

---

[136] See PFLEEGER ET AL., SECURITY IN COMPUTING 8 (3rd Ed., 2003).

criminal intent in litigations involving computer crime much easier.

In terms of potential for security breach and causing harm or damage, insiders are said to have more opportunities and lesser constraints or barriers. This is due to their ability to have access to internal resources that might otherwise be unavailable for non-insider. Insiders do not face the same level of rigor for defense from inside as attackers from outside would due to added security countermeasures at network perimeter to fence off much of outside hacker activities.

While insiders acting intentionally or unintentionally are responsible for the majority of confidential data loss or damage, about 80 percent of all incidents[137], negligence is the primary driver of data breach (about 80% in 2008)[138], where again insiders (at least those acting unintentionally) still play a major role. For those insiders and outsiders acting intentionally, a survey by the FBI in 2005 entitled the 2005 Computer Crime Survey revealed that insiders pose the greatest number of threats to IT

---

[137] See Steve Luebke, Trade Secrets: An Information Security Priority, The ISSA Journal, 28 (December 2006).

[138] Paul E. Paray, Cost Effective Risk Management of Health Information, the (ISSA) Journal, 13 (February 2011).

[139] Ronald L. Mendell, Dealing with the "Insider Threat", the ISSA Journal, 16 (May 2006).

[140] A method of isolating information resources based on a user's need to have access to that resource in order to perform their job but no more. The terms 'need-to know" and "least privilege" express the same idea. 'Need-to-know' is generally applied to people, while 'least privilege' is generally applied to processes; see Committee on National Security Systems (CNSS), National Information Assurance (IA) Glossary, CNSS Instruction No. 4009, at 49 (April 26, 2010).

infrastructure[139]. The reason is that insiders, especially those with more privileges, could not only gain access to more system resources and information based on elevated privileges (a good example being a root user in UNIX environment), but also they could easily exploit a weakness caused by lack of separation of duties.

Certain environments may allow users to share or perform cross-functional duties thereby disregarding rules for separation of duties. Separation of duties is critical in processing, for instance, financial transaction to ensure accountability. A payment transaction needs to be authorized by one person and processed by another. The principles of separation of duties and least privileges that limit access to information based on need-to-know[140] only are often ignored in information security management. These principles, if applied consistently, could help mitigate insider threats.

v.   *Technical vs. Non-Technical Attacks*

With regard to the nature of attack, threats originating from humans can be either technical or non-technical. Technical attacks are perpetrated using software and systems knowledge or expertise and usually occur through methodical approaches. There are plenty of software tools that are readily available for use over the Internet. Hackers are often able to easily access such tools by merely searching for or locating them on public domain; such as, the Internet and peer to peer file sharing networks. These tools can enable hackers to easily exploit vulnerabilities in a given system. Once hackers are successful in compromising the system security safeguards with the hacker tools, then they can expose the system for further attacks. Alternatively, they can access the system and manipulate, steal, modify, or delete information maintained by the system.

Non-technical attacks, on the other hand, mostly occur through human interactions. These attacks use, for instance, deceit to trick people into revealing sensitive information or performing actions that compromise the security of a system or network. Deceiving people into revealing sensitive information takes place through social engineering. It can be accomplished by means of traditional mode of communication; such as, phone conversation also known as pretexting or other means including email. Pretexting is the most prevalent social engineering method, where a hacker calls up and imitates someone in a position of authority and relevance to gain sensitive personal or company information.

Humans, e.g. employees in an organization, are the weakest link in this attack. This weakness can be mitigated with raising security awareness through training and clearly defined rules of behavior that user can sign before accessing the system. Periodic and consistent security awareness training for employees can help curb threats posed by social engineering while requiring employees to acknowledge understanding the threats and consequences through rules of behavior will make employees responsible and accountable. In addition, system specific or programmatic policies that include sanctions will greatly improve the overall risk management process and curb social engineering.

b) Security Threats Emanating from Unintended Sources

i. *Weakness in Communication Network and Infrastructure*

Information security vulnerabilities can be caused by a weakness in infrastructure supporting information systems while such weaknesses can stem from intentional or unintentional sources. Infrastructure weakness can be exploited by threat sources targeting weak links that by itself also becomes a root cause for further collateral damages to unexpected targets. Weakness in computing infrastructure can also result in accidents or any other unintended consequences. Weakness in communication network backbones can by itself lead to security issues ranging from loss of connectivity to availability issues to data leak or loss. Especially when this weakness is associated with computer network infrastructures, it can severely undermine perimeter protection and eventually lead to unintended consequences in the integrity of networked information and systems. Both unintentional factors and intentional actions equally threaten computer networks and critical infrastructure. Nevertheless, studies show that the majority of failure incidents in physical and environmental systems supporting computer technology are not attributed to intentional actions. For example, computer systems supporting a Supervisory Control and Data Acquisition (SCADA) fail for the most part due to human errors (about 75% of all incidents worldwide[141]).

Apart from human errors, failure in equipment or communication devices caused by an obsolete system support environment partly due to changing technological landscape can

---

[141] See Erwin van Zwan, Security of Industrial Control Systems, in ISACA Journal Volume 4, at 1 (2010).

be a good example of infrastructure weakness. Vulnerabilities in this category can also be caused by acts of nature or natural disasters and accidents. Lack of physical and environmental safeguards that must carefully be built into computing infrastructure can lead to accidents from physical and environmental factors eventually causing severe damage to a data center. It could be a male-functioning water sprinkler system or failed power surge controller in a server room that can cause serious damages. Due to the heavy dependence of Industrial Control Systems (ICS), e.g. SCADA on ICT nowadays, a single failure in anyone part of environmental and physical controls can result in a chain of failure reactions. A loss of an underlying infrastructure often results in a system-wide downtime. But if such a system failure happens in an environment supporting a critical infrastructure or SCADA, the consequence will be severe. In other words, the effects of a failure in critical infrastructure; such as, ICS could be more catastrophic than system failures in non ICS environments.

One of the distinguishing characteristics of unintentional source of threats is that they are, unlike intentional sources; such as, hacking, not well planned and orchestrated to cause an at most damage. Actions from intentional threat sources can cause significant damages as they can be carefully planned with respect to a targeted victim[142]. Thus, even with regard to a critical infrastructure, cyber attacks originating from intentional sources could carefully target the weakest point in control systems like ICS to cause the severest possible damage. Carefully planned intentional attacks to critical infrastructure assets when successful

---

[142] See Jean Camp et al., Offshoring: Risks And Exposures, In the Globalization and Offshoring of Software, A Report of the Association for Computing Machinery (ACM) Job Migration Task Force, ACM 0001-0782/06/0200, at 6-8 (2006).

can inevitably lead to a catastrophic failure in those systems with the possibility for loss of life and valuable resources.

ii.   *Human Factor (Lack of Awareness, Misjudgment)*

As stated earlier accidents involving human errors account for the majority of incidents in terms of systems failure. System failures attributable to human factor can be caused by either an erroneous action or inadvertent omission by humans. Unsuspecting employees or computer users falling victim to a social engineering attack fall under this category as well, for their unintentional exposure of data depending on circumstances can be considered a mistake.

Social engineering persuades victims to reveal essential security credentials that will later help the attacker to gain access to information and systems to do whatever can be done. Social engineering victims reveal security relevant information without intention to do so usually thinking that the requesting party is legit. But such victims can also expose unauthorized information to third party with some gross negligence, where they grossly disregard very basic security steps. This may be inexcusable as it could be attributed to the victim's unwillingness to participate in security awareness training or victim's negligent disregard of security awareness training. In any event users fall victim to social engineering by mistake or negligently.

Meanwhile social engineering has become a prevalent method of compromising security credentials leading to major cyber security breaches as internal users whether acting with good intension or gross misjudgment can become a valuable target for cyber criminals. The global proliferation of social networks; such as, Facebook, and use of smart phones exacerbate the situation. Moreover, these media easily allow malicious collection of private and even business proprietary data by hackers. They become easy and valuable target for data mining as these devices and sites hosting social networks become sources of valuable information links from both users and their associates or friends.

Accidents caused by human errors; such as, those committed by well-intentioned employees are an essential part of vulnerabilities caused by an unintentional human action or omission. Human mistakes can have grave consequences, especially when mistakes are made in computer systems that support critical infrastructure discussed earlier. The impact of mistakes resulting in failure of such systems can be far-reaching ranging from financial crisis to loss of life.

Human errors play roles at all phases of a system life-cycle. Users and developers at all levels of this cycle can become responsible for errors. Erroneous codes can be inadvertently embedded in a software program during system development. Programming and development errors also called bugs can be benign at times, but can also be severe that can result in a catastrophic incident.

For systems that rely on input accuracy, an input validation mechanism is critical to avoid negative consequences. Such a validation takes place through checking errors and omissions during data entry if this capability is built into the system's functionality. Some errors and omissions directly result in security alerts and so an input validation capability helps avoid security incidents that could negatively affect one or more of the CIA triage (confidentiality, integrity, and availability) for information and systems. Yet many programs, especially those designed by users for personal computers, lack such capabilities or steps for quality control. Even the most sophisticated system may lack error checking capabilities.

Lack of security awareness and lack of accountability generally contribute to lax in employees' responsibility. Employees with inadequate exposure to awareness training do not clearly understand their responsibilities, and in some cases may not have been given the opportunity by management to acknowledge such responsibilities by signing a set of rules of behavior. These employees tend to pay less attention to due diligence in dealing with sensitive data or critical systems. Lack of awareness to safety and security can be the root cause for committing errors both through inadvertently revealing protected information and not following standard procedures when dealing with critical system processes. Security awareness training and clearly defined rules of behavior that can be enforced with the help of a security policy or law are said to improve user behavior.

There is no doubt that, as stated earlier, a carefully crafted security training program and its implementation through periodic mandatory training will improve employees awareness of safety and security in whatever system they handle. Furthermore, in order to reduce insider security breaches, rules of behavior should be developed which must state that violations could result in adverse actions ranging from verbal reprimand to termination to criminal or civil prosecution. It should be crafted in a way that it enhances understanding of system specific security procedures by internal users. Employees or users should acknowledge and sign such rules so there is an established accountability.

Mistakes and accidents cannot be totally avoided but appropriate, mandatory, and enforceable user security training will help minimize them. Employees and all other internal users immensely benefit from security awareness training tailored to address system specific rules of behavior, security issues, standards, and procedures.

iii. *Lack of Systems Security Standards*

Generally, standards in computing and network connectivity environments facilitate interoperability. It is due to the existence of protocols developed based on certain standards that the interconnection among independent segments of networks is possible. The functionality of network devices such as routers, without which the Internet would not exist in its current capacity, heavily depends on such standardized protocols. Security standards likewise account for interoperability of computer networks, security devices, and methodologies developed based on security best practices. In the big picture; however, security standards tend to reflect applicable policies just as policies reflect governing regulatory frameworks.

As one can imagine, the diversity in regulations around the globe can result in a stark variance in policy frameworks, which in turn affect the development and content of security standards. Security policies can help establish standards as they proscribe security compliance norms and user behaviors in general terms. But policies can also take advantage of existing and more established standards to come up with and determine policy statements. This is the case, for instance, with the U.S. government agencies, which for the most part utilize NIST standards and common criteria (CC)[143] evaluation requirements developed by the International Organization for Standardization (ISO)[144] to establish internal, agency level IT security policies.

---

[143] See the Common Criteria version 3.1 release 3, available at: httn://www commoncriterianortal org/cc/ (last visited October 2. 2011)

Globally, there is a heterogeneous source of security standards applicable to IT systems[145]. We have security standards developed by national organizations that are applicable at national territories, and there are those intended to work at international level but not exactly meet this goal everywhere due to various other factors. Security standards whether international or national, when applied as prescribed, might help meet the security needs of a given network or system. Common Criteria (CC) are used, for instance, to ensure that products implement commonly accepted set of security features. To this end CC require use of certain evaluation and certification schemes. CC evaluation thereby ensures interoperability and assurance for security of products.

Historically, the CC standards themselves have a national origin. They are said to have stemmed indirectly from the U.S. standard named 'the Orange Book' developed by the National Computer Security Center (NCSC) in 1983[146]. The Orange Book had set off similar efforts within various countries resulting in a variety of national standards until they all later merged to a single standard called the Information Technology Standards Committee (ITSC) based on the ITSC committee formed in 1990. ITSC later got combined with the U.S. standard called Information Technology Security Evaluation Criteria (ITSEC) to eventually become CC, a *de facto* international standard.

---

[144] Governmental organizations from various countries including the U.S., Canada, Germany, etc. contributed to the criteria; see Common Criteria for Information Technology Security Evaluation, Part 2: Security functional components, 3 (July 2009).

[145] Few other examples include green book (Germany) and CLEF (British), in addition to the orange book and CC; see Charlie Kaufman et al., Network Security; Private Communication in a Public World, 36 (2002).

[146] Id. at 34.

With regard to these multifaceted standards, the problem; however, lies not in the existence or use of such standards per se. Nor does the diversity of security standards alone significantly impact network security. The fact that there are sometimes contradictory rules of standards or policy norms per se might not hugely affect the security posture of segregated network enclaves either. The issue may arise when various security standards collide while attempting to combine/connect different sets of independently managed computer network environments that are built based on different sets of security standards. Such diversity in architecture and protocols may introduce interoperability issues with respect to both security and functionality. Interoperability issues can be resolved at least from the network connectivity point of view using tools like gateway protocols.

But in terms of the effectiveness of security, such interoperability cannot be guaranteed. To begin with, different networks using different sets of security standards may not always work as expected when interconnected and one or more segments can become the weakest link.

Even much more problematic is the case where no security standard is adhered to by a given computer network. If the network has no policy prescribing security and other operational requirements, it won't necessarily attempt to build security into the enclave. Neither will it be in a position to buy into industry standards with respect to security and implement the same to accommodate everyone else attempting to establish connection with it. Put differently, if a computer network does not have a security policy to comply with or does not follow a certain set of security standards in order to ensure perimeter protection and network interoperability, then this will result in internal and external security and connectivity issues.

A network enclave that doesn't adhere to any established security rules and standards will also cause a spillover effect on security of other networks and systems as stated in the previous paragraph. Such cases generally undermine the security functionality of the whole network environment to include the Internet. Incorrect, inadequate, or non-existent security configuration or insufficient use of security tools of one or more network segments within a larger network setting could defeat the security of the whole network. That is because when data from a relatively secure network enclave passes through the secure perimeter and traverses across insecure network segments, which is the case on the Internet, the data may be exposed while in transmission to security breaches like unauthorized access via tapping into wires or sniffing.

Data in transmission can generally be secured using methodologies like session or data encryption to avert the security breach posed by the weakest segments on the Internet. But this is not to say that encryption alone suffices to secure such data in transmission since even encrypted data can be modified or lost, and thus, become unavailable. Experience also implies that not every user or data owner is proactive enough to utilize available confidentiality tools to even just encrypt data.

Therefore, at least regarding network segments that organizations control, they need to make sure their individual enclaves comply with existing standards both in terms of functionality and security to avert interoperability issues in general and security impact in particular.

On the same note, offshoring organizations should not only configure their networks in compliance with generally accepted security standards; such as, CC, but when they choose to outsource this capability to a third party, they need to assess third party's adherence to security standards. This is especially relevant when an offshoring business leverages network and computing resources or services from contractors including cloud providers.

Meanwhile cloud computing has certainly a huge potential to attract offshoring service FDI as well due to cost benefits. Cloud computing by the way has nothing to do with bunch of computers floating in the sky/cloud. Rather, cloud is the term adopted due to the use of an abstract cloud-shaped diagram to denote shared resources in such a computing environment. Cloud computing involves the use of computing resources (hardware and software) that are delivered as a service over a network - typically the Internet. Offshoring service FDI can take advantage of shared, but inexpensive services in a cloud to not only utilize application systems for processing offshore data, but leverage storage media to store the data and platforms to host or house systems. The cloud provider needs to be aware of specific security and privacy needs of the offshore investor so they can make adjustments to the nature of the subscription as necessary in the cloud computing environment. It is warranted that the offshoring company outlines specific requirements even from the outset that any selected public cloud computing solution is configured, deployed, and managed to meet their specific security, privacy, and other requirements.

5. Offshore Digital Transactions Prone to Cyber Attacks

a) Infringement of Copyrighted Content

Technical or non-technical attacks common on cyberspace today can vary depending on source or target. Their frequency varies as well. Proprietary information like copyright as a target of such attacks is one of only few examples (selected based on relevance to offshoring) discussed in this section. Attacks targeting intellectual property rights (IPR) or causing infringements of intellectual property in general and copyright in particular can be considered as one of the most frequently occurring category of cyber attacks today. In terms of relevance to offshoring, it can be argued that the IP infringement during global digital transaction is among the most frequent cyber incidents. The level of exposure for intellectual property contents to possible infringement through IT and IT-enabled offshoring continues to rise. The IT service offshoring business model is more inclined to make intellectual property assets widely available electronically and that online sometimes on the Internet due to its intensive use of IT resources thereby making this business process a target for IP infringement.

Providing better protection of IP to investors or outsourcing clients in IT offshoring becomes, thus, an important aspect of protection for investor digital assets. However; any protection effort falls short primarily for two reasons. First, many nations either do not recognize or respect IP rights and regulations provided by other countries like the U.S.[147], and even if they recognize the value of IP rights and even have laws to that end, they have very lax enforcement mechanism in their territories. Secondly, the IP asset can easily be stolen in most cases due to lack of cyber security mechanisms on investors' networks or systems that enable an involuntary sharing of this asset. And this

---

[147] See Jean Camp et al., Offshoring: Risks And Exposures, In the Globalization and Offshoring of Software, A Report of the Association for Computing Machinery (ACM) Job Migration Task Force, ACM 0001-0782/06/0200, at 6-7 (2006).

type of theft is even more prevalent and easier on larger sets of networks, the Internet or cyberspace for the apparent reason that the Internet is the weakest link in data communication. For example, a software code made available for an offshoring facility can be accessed by unauthorized party either during transmission via the Internet or while residing on the onshore or offshore facility network.

Copyrighted content is more susceptible to cyber theft than other IP rights. When it comes to the regulatory protection for copyright, legal system grossly vary and sometimes vague. The U.S. law, for instance, appears to be less clear with regard to software program protection. That is, with respect to copyright protection for software itself in U.S., the legal system appears to still grapple with the interpretation of the law. The U.S. copyrights law was originally enacted to enable protection of paper-based expression of ideas. The software program consists of algorithm (could be concept/idea) and the statements of the program (lines of the code). There is no clear legal precedent from the U.S. point of view in terms of whether the U.S. copyrights law should apply to algorithm. The reason is that it is still unclear if algorithm should be considered not just idea but copyrightable material. The algorithm of the code based on the current interpretation of the U.S. copyright law may not be protected because copyright law applies to only the expression (only statements in this case)[148]. Thus copying the entire code but not implementing the idea, the algorithm alone, seems to be protected. Nonetheless, the software program code in the hypothetical case above can be copied in its entirety and that is protected at least under the U.S. copyright law and also as a literary work under the Berne Convention[149], as well as the copyright treaty of the WIPO, which

---

[148] PFLEEGER ET AL., supra note 130, at 559.

extends Berne Convention to include computer software. That said, as far as unauthorized access to an IP asset, e.g. a software code, is concerned, methods and tools used by hackers depend on the location or computing state the software finds itself. Man-in-the middle attack and network sniffing are good examples of network based methods used by hackers to catch copyrighted material place in a network. Network based attacks allow to hackers to steal data thereby eventually making the action a data theft with the consequence that the same action also qualifies as a possible copyright infringement. Regardless of tools or methods used, stolen IP data is not only consumed by hackers but copied and redistributed to others thereby causing an influx of unfair use of copyrighted materials. Studies find that younger generations are operating online overwhelmingly ignorant of any copyright laws[150]. This has resulted in international trends involving an influx of illegal copying of digitized copyrightable materials. Unauthorized use of copyrighted materials is sometimes termed as piracy. The frequency in digital piracy can be attributed to the existence of much more capable tools for copying and transporting of electronic data. Users take advantage of easily accessible technologies and networks like peer-to-peer sharing medium for their illegal copying or redistributing copyrighted items. Copying music from a CD used to require a disc burner and so normative control of copyright infringement through such a disc replication was relatively easier. Thanks to rapid changes in technology, MP3 has allowed friends to share music among each

---

[149] Rao, supra note 72, at 18; Berne Convention for the Protection of Literary and Artistic Works 1886, opened for signature 4 May 1886, ATS 1972 No 13 (entered into force 5 December 1887).

[150] John Palfrey et al., Youth, Creativity, and Copyright in the Digital Age Research Publication No. 2009-05, at 79 (June 2009).

other very easily. Suddenly, this type of sharing seems nothing like copying and, thus, consumers (mostly young people) tend to think it is not a copyright infringement at all. The dramatic reduction of costs in computation spurred availability of digital content in an unlimited proportion, which in turn has galvanized unlimited access to this content for both legitimate and illicit purposes[151]. Thus, piracy has become an epidemic in itself and a prevalent way of infringing copyright, and as such a challenge for owners and legal community. There is some disconnect among legal, social, and technical norms, as some argued, that needs to be addressed with some sort of non-legal recourse[152]. Without such non-legal means, the day to day copyright infringement by young people, in particular cannot culminate anytime soon. Many users think that they are almost entitled to download digital content (music, films, software, broadcasting, books).

From the U.S. users' perspective, the 'fair use' doctrine, which is already blurry,[153] is not understood among many people let alone younger generations. The fair use statute of Section 107, 17 USC states four limitation factors, but those factors are said to contradict to each other when applied[154] to digital content and could lead to an unfair outcome. The new digital networked world enables young generation not just to copy and consume other's works but to utilize their skills and manipulate those materials for further innovation. So the question of fairness gets

---

[151] Sacha Wunsch-Vincent, IP's Online Market: The Economic Forces at Play, WIPO Magazine Issue #6, at 5 (2010).

[152] See Palfrey et al., supra note 144, at 82.

[153] See John Palfrey et al., Youth, Creativity, and Copyright in the Digital Age Research Publication No. 2009-05, at 82 (June 2009).

[154] See Bit Law Legal Resources, available at:
http://www.bitlaw.com/copyright/fair_use.html, (last visited May 4, 2011).

raised often times but the line between what is fair and what is not remains blur. Indeed, in the digital age, any copyright infringement claim against such innovative use is bound to trigger a fair use defense. The attempt to balance the rights of copyright owners and users through the 'fair use' doctrine (first developed through case law[155]) continues to be debated. But there is no doubt that a reasonable use of copyrighted materials could allow tech-savvy users to explore and exploit the fastest growing sophistication of technology and create new products. And such free innovation can only be possible if the first factor, the purpose and character, in the U.S. Copyright Act is more liberally applied in an expanded manner. The expansion approach seems to be reasonable to uphold the position that innovation by way of access to copyrighted content should be promoted as long as the main goal is not to use the material itself for commercial purposes.

On the international arena, the diversity of legal systems and multitude of varying interpretations make things more complicated. While there are some similarities in a few legal systems, in part as a result of some minimum standards set by multilateral treaties; such as, WIPO's copyright treaty[156] and TRIPS[157] agreement, there are stark differences in conceptual

---

[155] Developed over the years as courts tried to balance the rights of copyright owners with society's interest in allowing copying in certain, limited circumstances; see Bit Law, id.

[156] This extended IP protection provisions in the Berne Convention to include computer software; see GERALD R. FERRERA ET AL., CYBER LAW: TEXT AND CASES 359 (2000).

[157] Agreement on Trade-related Aspects of Intellectual Property Rights ('TRIPS Agreement'), opened for signature 15 April 1994, 1869 UNTS 299 (entered into force 1 January 1995), id.

implementation and enforcement. So the somewhat broadly interpreted U.S. statutory fair use exception and the Australian 'fair dealing' approach, just to name a few, among other things, differ in terms of enforcing the copyright laws[158].

IP protection is still a gray area in legal systems of many other nations[159], and of course such an imperfect protection has a negative effect on offshoring FDI decision. One can also imagine similar effects on investment promotion as well. That is, from the perspective of a given foreign jurisdiction, lack of IPR protection in the jurisdiction will more likely discourage potential investors, as well as hamper technology transfer thereby defeating in some cases all other FDI promotion efforts. Technology transfer is negatively impacted because firms with technology vulnerable to imitation are generally reluctant to let a free flow of technology transfer in an attempt to limit possible leak in knowledge to competing firms. On the potential impact side, the overall economic effects of IP infringement can be immeasurable from the owner's perspective, not to mention the high cost of litigation. The cost of infringement just for U.S. businesses is in billions every year[160].

Thus, while it is prudent for an investor to closely examine IP protections, copyrights in particular, afforded to investor's digital assets by any territory before making an offshoring move, there is a need for the national policy regime to ensure copyrights protection is fully considered in incentive packages for offshoring

---

[158] Chris Dent, Copyright as (Decentred) Regulation: Digital Piracy as a Case Study, the

Monash University Law Review, Volume 35, Number 2, at 358 (2009).

[159] See Rao, supra note 72, at 17.

[160] See Steve Luebke, Trade Secrets: An Information Security Priority, The ISSA Journal. 28 (December 2006).

FDI.

b)   Cyber Espionage and Attacks
Targeting Critical Assets

Western governments and private sector in technologically advanced parts of the world have spent years building information infrastructure, more aptly known as 'information highways'. More focus had been on the interoperability, ease of access, as well as use, and to some extent also speed. Information highways were built with openness and communication efficiency in mind, but less so on the security side. Security was never an essential attribute of this at least initially. The fact that security was not built into such infrastructure from the outset has made lots of network infrastructures as they exist today vulnerable to today's cyber attacks. These networks rely on TCP/IP protocols for communication, which has inherent weaknesses. Critical assets; such as, complex financial systems and networks, e.g. clearing houses for national and international banking transactions, rely on use of such networks. The U.S. Federal Reserve system known as Fedwire, for instance, processes transactions worth trillions of dollars daily[161]. If the weakness of the TCP/IP based networks used by such important financial systems is exploited by illicit users, one can only imagine the consequences on financial systems both nationally and globally. The Internet uses the same infrastructure and, therefore, is also vulnerable in the same ways as many network infrastructures currently in place within national boundaries.

---

[161] It processed around 521,000 payments on average in 2008 worth about 2.7 trillion dollars a day; see also Gable, supra note 17, at 26.

Both government and private sector information systems are at risk due to this weakness. Critical assets owned by governments and private sector can be equally exposed to more potent threats; such as, information warfare[162] or cyber espionage, which could result in cyber attacks that can steal valuable proprietary information assets or debilitate critical system operations. Cyber espionage is a potential attack using cyberspace as a tool that can be based on various motives, but could also be orchestrated by a foreign government targeting either another government (e.g. information warfare) or a corporation for economic espionage. A target could also be proprietary business information in an offshore undertaking.

The real possibility for corporations to lose trade secrets with dramatic economic consequences through economic or electronic espionage was recognized early on by the U.S. congress, which promulgated another cyber security type of law, the Economic Espionage Act (EEA) which became law in 1996. The law was supposed to deter the rising tide of loss of corporate intellectual property due to international and domestic economic espionage[163]. The Taxol (an anti cancer drug) case[164], which was the first case to be adjudicated under the EEA legislation, underscores the importance of such legislation in the information age. The EEA criminalizes theft of trade secrets with the intent to primarily benefit foreign governments, though its second part deals with generic reasons. However, the Taxol case shows that

---

[162] Governments around the world today are actively participating in information warfare against each other both offensively and defensively using cyberspace weapons (cyber attack tools) like sniffing, Trojan horse, DDoS, logic bomb, etc.

[163] GERALD R. FERRERA ET AL., CYBER LAW: TEXT AND CASES 319 (2000).

[164] United States vs. Hsu 155 E3d 189 (3rd Cir. 1998).

such espionage does not always occur to benefit foreign governments. It benefits private sector, i.e. businesses, as well.

Theft of proprietary information can occur online or offline through traditional means of espionage. Clearly firms, especially those active in cross-border business undertaking are more vulnerable to such attack that can take place through theft of sensitive electronic information by means of exploiting computer and network security. Electronic form of espionage is easy to commit and hard to detect or prosecute for that matter. Even when the victim is aware that the sensitive information was disclosed, it is hard to pinpoint the perpetrator due to problems of attribution on cyberspace as discussed elsewhere. Parties committing such a crime on cyberspace can easily escape undetected due to the very nature of the cyberspace that promotes, as well as enables anonymity. Worse, the information owner may not even be aware that its trade secrets have been stolen. Due to the degree of sophistication in hacker tools, especially used by more orchestrated sources like electronic espionage committed by a group capabilities of which can be categorized as an advanced persistence threat, losing information on cyberspace may not always be obvious. Thanks to sophistication in methodology and resilience, an espionage act can take place without detection and the victim may not even know anything about it.

Not surprisingly, more and more governments around the globe are engaged in cyberspace activities nowadays that range from filtering network traffic, especially the Internet, to espionage, to actively interfering in other nations' affairs and networks with a DoS type of attacks. Governments have realized the potential of cyberspace for using it as a weapon for political pressures and economic gains. They see the ease of manipulating cyberspace to spy on their own citizens and others. Given these unprecedented potentials, more and more governments join the efforts and continue to exploit additional features. They find it strategically important to manipulate networks, explore technological breakthroughs, and tweak other workarounds with those technology tools yet to unleash even more potentials in this regard. The increasingly sophisticated cyber attacks involving government sources have led to the use of the term 'information warfare'. While it is now clear that governments already not only spy on each other but also attack one another, it seems likely that at some point in the near future there will be more serious and aggressive forms of such attacks, as well as defensive measures that could result in what one could aptly refer to as the 'information world war'.

Furthermore, a GAO's report to Congress has raised additional concerns about offshoring IT related works such as software development in general[165]. The main concern is that developing software in offshore locations, especially when the work is done on behalf of a U.S. government agency; such as, DoD could pose a threat to national security and critical infrastructure. Critical IT-based military systems using Commercial off-the Shelf (COTS) products could become dependent on developer who could be directly or indirectly associated with a foreign hostile nation or terrorist. Nothing could prevent a developer with an illicit intent from sharing government information it accesses with foreign hostile governments. The concern also is that COTS products developed in a foreign location by either foreign contractor or an offshoring U.S. investor abroad could include malicious code that can be embedded in the application system by a malicious programmer. Once used on government systems or

---

[165] See GAO, supra note 55, at 36.

networks, such an embedded code ('hidden features'[166]) in a piece of software or application system could be triggered anytime during its life-cycle to perform unintended actions. Concealed code can compromise classified or unclassified data, and take further actions to manipulate functionality and security of other systems that come in contact with the application or even trigger functionality failure in critical assets; such as, vital military weapons. The concern with the security of software development is heightened as computers nowadays perform far more critical tasks. When the security of system design and programming for a given application system is improperly monitored or overlooked, the integration of the application system with other critical systems leads to undesirable consequences. Depending on the type of critical systems, attacks carried out this way can have multiple consequences. An attack against critical infrastructure potentially goes beyond a mere system downtime and can cripple civilian infrastructure like transportation, medical facilities, and vital financial systems with the potential to cause damage ranging from financial turmoil, accidents, to in extreme cases loss of human life. There is the potential for an offshoring business setting to be an easy target for these attacks since not just government systems but applications developed for use in the private sector can be vulnerable to these attacks. To mitigate this, government and private sector users alike need to consider developing application systems in-house, especially when those applications will support core business processes, rather than outsourcing the building effort particularly to a foreign country based contractor. It seems

---

[166] See Jean Camp et al., Offshoring: Risks And Exposures, In the Globalization and Offshoring of Software, A Report of the Association for Computing Machinery (ACM) Job Migration Task Force, ACM 0001-0782/06/0200, at 6-21 (2006).

also prudent despite cost considerations that these users refrain from acquiring commercial off-the-shelf (COTS) products (COTS products can be less expensive than those built in-house) from abroad, especially from vendors in unfriendly nations. Bottom-line, malware can be embedded in application systems by government or private sources for economic benefits or political reasons and consequence can be severe. But in many cases the victim itself can be at fault due to improper oversight during application development or acquisition.

c) Disruption of Service Attacks

The speed of computing and processing capabilities continues to evolve, where timely access to information and processes becomes paramount. The demand for higher bandwidth and faster data transmission continues to grow as well because timely delivery or access to information is very important for some business processes than others while technology that meets this demand also continues to evolve. However, independent from technological capabilities that allow much faster access and processing speed, various incidents can cause disruption in these technological resources. To sustain continuity in their business processes, almost all stakeholders rely on uninterrupted support from their computing resources. Therefore, it is critical that user communities or clients (in a client-server architecture) have a timely and reliable access to information and information system or its processes. The property of these resources being accessed reliably and in a timely fashion, as well as useable format is known as availability. Availability is an important aspect of the security objectives in information security as defined by NIST, the notion of which has been modified by a security best practice recently[167]. The most current approach interprets the availability of information assets to include the utility of accessible information. Meaning, any information asset when available should be in useable format and the availability objective, therefore, should cover the utility aspect of the protected information[168]. Otherwise the availability or accessibility of the information asset alone is not sufficient for the user, and, thus, it is not sufficient to contend with accessible information in corrupt manner when addressing availability issues. Availability of certain kinds of information can be critical and so is an uninterrupted use of or access to an information system that processes or stores such critical information.

Availability is not immune from cyber attacks since any cyber attack for the most part impacts one or more aspects of information security objectives (confidentiality, integrity, and/or availability). Although many cases of the impact on information assets' availability can involve accidents (e.g. transmission cable getting cut by an earth quack, and so on), the focus here is on active and man-made malicious acts against continued service. In the past few years most of cyber security's focus has been on confidentiality and integrity, but the security community is catching up in terms of understanding the issue of availability and how to address disruption, or rather to avoid one.

The most common method of attacks targeting the availability of information resources is Denial of Services (DoS) attack. DoS; however, can be caused by either a deliberate attempt to disable and crash a particular targeted system or by spread of malware – worms, viruses, etc. that overwhelm

---

[167] Id. at 13.

[168] Id. at 13.

networks and servers[169]. A deliberate DoS attack usually takes place using computer network resources. In a typical DoS attack, an attacker, for instance, uses a specialized code to send a flood of data packets to the targeted computer with the aim of overwhelming its computing capabilities. Once the attack is successful and the system is overloaded with repeated fake requests, the system can no longer handle legitimate requests.

For cross-border transactions involving multiple networks on cyberspace, a hybrid of the simple DoS, known as Distributed Denial of Service (DDoS), becomes even a more potent source of service disruption. DDoS exploits the immensely distributed nature of the Internet, through which it can, for instance, easily cripple the availability of information resources on an offshoring site network. DDoS is a network based attack that can be launched after an attacker gains illegal administrative access to as many computers on the Internet as possible, in many cases through a command and control mechanism using a network of multiple infected computers known as BotNet[170]. The attacker uses these multiple computers to send a flood of data packets (e.g. ping of death, a simple but effective attack when multiple sources are involved[171]) to the target computer.

---

[169] See Chandler, supra note 121, at 236.

[170] This was the case with a malicious code called Coreflood according to a Department of Justice civil complaint and criminal warrants filed in 2011. Corflood attackers infected thousands of computers and allowed those to be remotely controlled by the attackers for purposes of stealing personal and financial data; see a press release from the Office of Public Affairs, The United States Attorney's Office, Department of Justice takes Action to disable International BotNet, April 13, 2011, also available at: http://www.justice.gov/usao/ct/Press2011/20110413-1.html, (last visited Jun. 22, 2011).

So in the case of an offshoring facility which more likely relies on network resources for external communications, not just a computer or server within the enclave, but the entire network can be brought to a still stand since network appliances; such as, routers can also be overwhelmed with such traffic. The attacker loads DDoS enabling software, often by planting a Trojan horse[172], on various distributed machines turning them to zombies[173], which then later be used to propagate the attack. There are many tools; such as, scripts and mobile codes, available today, some of which can be used in combination, for example to build a BotNet capability and enable launching of a compounded DDoS.

In a sample attack scenario, an attacker surreptitiously forwards a bot malware (a program agent which acts automatically on behalf of their parent program) to several computers. Why do these computers cooperate and participate in this process? Well, to begin with these computers have some security vulnerabilities which will make them potential candidates to become zombies. The zombies themselves are victimized for the most part due to lack of protection on their part. So, for instance, if a computer is inadequately patched, i.e. not kept up-to-date with proper security software; such as, an antivirus, antispyware, or hosts malicious pieces of software like Trojan, chances are it easily becomes a target of a DDoS attack thereby itself becoming an attacker as a zombie.

The bot exploits security holes in these computers and infects them by making configuration changes that allows it to prepare for further exploitation and control. The malware then

---

[171] See PFLEEGER ET AL., SECURITY IN COMPUTING 415 (3rd Ed., 2003).

[172] See id. at 419.

[173] See Chandler, supra note 121, at 236.

opens a backdoor on the infected computers for the attacker to browse or modify files. The attacker remotely installs additional malware, often a Trojan horse to turn these computers into zombies so that they perform more directed actions including sending concerted messages, emails, etc to the actual DDoS target.

Alternatively or in addition, the attacker can also remotely install malicious software on vulnerable computers and establish a BotNet. The BotNet allows the attacker to centrally command and control the infected computers, and steal credentials, credit card data or other sensitive information. Typically, the original DDoS attacker is not only able to control the zombies often disguising their identity to orchestrate the entire attack process, but dig even deeper into these zombies to steal their sensitive data. The attacker is hard to identify in many cases as the attacker can spoof a source IP address to impersonate a legitimate user thereby falsely representing an entity on the one end of the network. And this can be accomplished through a session hijacking or man-in-the-middle attack[174].

Once zombies are established and start launching an attack, they typically inundate the target network/computer by forcing the target to use up computation resources in response to a simultaneous flood of requests, among other things.

With respect to distributed cyber attacks as in other ways of malicious cyber incidents, the questions become: is there a legal recourse for victims and how can these can be proven or is it possible to attribute actions to a source with some legal certainty? These questions are particularly relevant with regard to liabilities in DDoS attacks. More importantly, both the source of

---

[174] See PFLEEGER ET AL., SECURITY IN COMPUTING 407 (3rd Ed., 2003).

DDoS and participating zombies entail implications for legal liabilities. However, a possible lawsuit as a result of a DDoS attack can also involve a third party, software developers. Developers are on the hook for flaws, if proven that their products did not do what they are supposed to do, i.e. fending off possible intrusion by hackers. But this can only be possible if a given product is expected to guard against such attacks in addition to its other ordinary functionalities. If a software product was supposed to help with DDoS attacks in particular and yet did not do its job to prevent such attacks, then its developer maybe subjected to legal liabilities. On the same note, if a computer of an unsuspecting user that uses a certain software product to avoid being high-jacked as a zombie or being targeted by malware attacks including Trojan horse and yet unwillingly becomes a zombie, then there is a remote possibility to subject the developer of this malware protection software to liability.

Meanwhile, the fact that zombie owners may not have been aware of the DDoS attack per se, cannot be a successful means of defense in a lawsuit. However, an unsuspecting owner possibly becoming a perpetrator himself/herself as their computer turned zombies may not necessarily be held responsible for the act and damages thereof. The duty of care requirements established for the two-stage test developed in *Cooper v. Hobart*[175] may not be successfully established for the owner. Thus, zombie owners themselves may not be held liable for damages sustained by a DDoS victim. Even a gross negligence on the part of the owner may not suffice to justify foreseeability and to hold the owner accountable for all DDoS susceptible computers in the world.

On the other hand, computer owners and software

---

[175] Cooper v. Hobart, 2001 SCC 79, a Canadian Supreme Court case; also see Chandler, supra note 121, at 256.

purchasers who may become DDoS victims themselves or end up being zombie owners are required to exercise due diligence as well. They need to keep up with software updates provided by vendors (software developers) and apply appropriate patches. That will help them exculpate liability suits by DDoS victims and any counterclaims by software vendors who are eventually held liable for software flaws that resulted in a DDoS. So for zombie owners and DDoS victims what this means is that at least in lawsuits against developers, there is a likelihood that all victims could be subject to liability for contributory negligence. But a contributory negligence can only be accepted when a duty of care is present on the side of the DDoS victims who purchased and used the flawed software in question, regardless of whether the software was supposed to help against becoming zombie or ultimately to fend off the DDoS itself. Establishing a duty of care in turn for software purchasers using the two-stage test as has been applied in *Cooper v. Hobart*[176] may not be straight forward. But an argument can be crafted to an extent possible that when the software users neither apply critical patches nor periodically scan their system environments, they negligently disregard the duty of care reasonably expected of any computer system owner and user.

In sum, disruption of services on cyberspace by means of attacks like DDoS have become an everyday occurrence. The above scenario evidences the fact that there is a possibility that not only a DDoS attacker, if identified, but under circumstance software vendors can be held liable for DDoS damages. The victims too could end up sharing the liability as vendors can exculpate part of their liability by suing the victims for contributory negligence.

---

[176] See Chandler, supra note 121, at 256.

d) Cyber Attacks Targeting Personal Privacy

Personal data of millions of people are widely available over cyberspace, thereby also being exposed to individuals who would make an illicit use of such information. Due to its tendency to frequently utilize international communication networks and the Internet for a cost effective data transfer, IT service offshoring in particular may expose sensitive data in similar ways making data incursion a possibility. Vulnerable data from an offshoring business process perspective includes PII belonging to employees and customers both at home and abroad.

Under a few legal regimes personal privacy maybe protected by law and its violation may result in prosecution of some sort. However, it is better to avoid privacy from becoming a legal issue in the first place. One way to do that is by protecting personal data; such as, PII not to be disclosed or accessed in an unauthorized manner. The majority of personal privacy issues arise due to inadequate or insecure handling of personal data by a custodian, a good example being the case with offshore investors themselves. Regrettably, individuals (employees or customers) have almost no control over their information maintained by the custodian. From the data custodian perspective, securing PII may be achieved by implementing appropriate security mechanisms; such as, access control enforcement and encryption tools on the systems or networks that deal with such data. But this depends on who controls what or which network and may get more complicated in cases where the custodian uses third party networks or distributed storage devices; such as, storage area networks (SANs) over which the custodian has no control.

The disclosure risks become even greater when increasingly distributed networks are used or when such use involves the latest outsourcing option known as cloud computing[177] that promotes leveraging shared resources. Greater flexibility for availability and the need for cost cutting drive the interest for many firms including those in offshoring business model to recourse to cloud services. There are clear opportunities and benefits for offshoring firms to take advantage of both the various deployment models of cloud (public, private, and hybrid) on the one hand, and the service models (infrastructure, software, and operating system based clouds) on the other[178] . One of the biggest concerns with cloud computing is that shared resources may expose company owned personal information to third parties without consent or accidentally[179]. The fact that the cloud

---

[177] Cloud computing by the way has nothing to do with bunch of computers floating in the sky/cloud. Rather cloud is the term adopted due to the use of an abstract cloud-shaped diagram to denote shared resources in such a computing environment. Cloud computing involves the use of computing resources (hardware and software) that are delivered as an on demand service over a network - typically the Internet. NIST Special Publication 800-145, The NIST Definition of Cloud Computing, 2 (September 2011), defines it as '...a model for enabling ubiquitous, convenient, on-demand network access to a shared pool of configurable computing resources (e.g., networks, servers, storage, applications, and services) that can be rapidly provisioned and released with minimal management effort or service provider interaction'.

[178] NIST Special Publication (SP) 800-144, Guideline on Security and Privacy in Cloud Computing (Draft), 3 (January 2011).

[179] This was the case, for instance, with one cloud computing provider, Dropbox, which had an authentication glitch in its storage web site on June 22, 2011. This incident allowed unprotected access to customer sensitive data by anyone accessing the site using any password. Although the incident was discovered and fixed a couple of hours later, the degree of scare was substantial, for details, see a news post on CNNmoney.com: Dropbox's password nightmare highlights cloud risks, available at:

software, infrastructure, or platform may involve a large pool of diverse users, by itself can put the individual users at a heightened risk for potential data leak. Faster dissemination of such data to everyone on the cloud, as well as beyond becomes more than likely if there is a weakness in the shared resource or, worse, if such a weakness is exploited by an intruder. Cloud services may be used by clients that do not limit the availability and use of social media, personal Webmail, and other publicly available sites or additional clouds. This can be a concern as attacks like those utilizing social engineering can compromise the security of the client with a possible spill-over effect on the underlying platform, and eventually on the cloud services accessed[180] by other customers. Generally, those using private cloud models have more control over their data, and, thus, lower risks compared to those using economies of scale type public cloud computing.

Aside from concerns associated with platforms being used for processing and storing PII, the perception for privacy vastly differs from country to country. The same is true when it comes to protection of personal privacy. For example, under some legal systems there is no clear distinction between privacy and personal data, though they are not necessarily the same. Hence both end up sometimes being used interchangeably. Conceptually; however, both can be independent from one other. For instance, breach of some personal data may not necessarily result in breach or invasion of privacy, and vice versa. Although both concepts have some overlaps, generally privacy can be broader compared

http://money.cnn.com/2011/06/22/technology/dropbox_passwords/index.htm?iid=H_T_News, (last visited June 16, 2011).

[180] NIST Special Publication (SP) 800-144, Guideline on Security and Privacy in Cloud Computing (Draft), vii (January 2011).

to personal data. Privacy has also long been recognized by states that do not even have data protection rules[181].

That being said, the definition of privacy or rights of personal privacy may not be the same around the world. This could be attributable to variances in ideological, cultural, and legal settings. Possible breach of privacy that can be considered illegal or even have punitive consequences in one legal system can be a minor ethical offence in another, and so on. Difference in legal regimes across the globe is nothing new but some countries have not only laws addressing personal privacy but they do so in much stricter terms. The EU and Canada have such strict data privacy laws that are comprehensive and far-reaching in some respects with possible negative repercussions on offshoring[182]. The reason for possible impacts of such laws on offshoring transactions is that at least in some cases offshoring business model is underpinned by personal data that needs to be processed, transmitted, and stored.

Stricter rules like the ones provided by the EU can overly restrict cross-border data transactions, in particular business processes dealing with personal data[183]. Because of such a strict stance on consumer privacy, EU's privacy law is said to be consumer friendly. It restricts business's right to use consumer data for marketing purposes. The U.S. privacy laws, on the contrary, essentially leave businesses free in this regard[184]

---

[181] See Christopher Kuner, An International Legal Framework for Data Protection: Issues and Prospects, 6 (2009).

[182] See Camp et al., supra note 160, at 6-12; See PFLEEGER ET AL., SECURITY IN COMPUTING 603 (3rd Ed., 2003).

[183] Jeff Collmann, Managing Information Privacy & Security in Healthcare European Union Privacy Directive Reconciling European and American Approaches to Privacy, Healthcare Information and Management Systems Society, 1 (January 2007).

thereby providing consumers with little protection. Consequently, consumer's private data tend to be readily available for businesses under the U.S. privacy regulation, while that is not the case under the data protection laws of the E.U. This means consumer's data is less likely to be accessed through network incursion and stolen by illicit users under the E.U. laws in comparison with the situation under the U.S. legal regime.

Meanwhile, attacks, especially cross-border intrusions against privacy and identity have been on the rise again due to the proliferation of the international ICT. This implies that there is much greater need for offshoring investors to implement more resilient information security mechanisms to protect PII and other customer data. Such precautionary measures benefit both compliance with strict data protection laws and help avoid legal liabilities for data breach caused by lax security measures.

Incursions against personal privacy and data result in not only identity theft that has come to be one of the most prevalent consequences of stolen PII, but some cases even involve loss of personal dignity or invasion of privacy in some other ways which have shameful consequences for the victim. More extreme cases involve incidents where fraud victims end up being falsely accused of a crime. A good example involved a victim who was falsely labeled as a fugitive[185].

In sum, while privacy is misunderstood, misinterpreted, or regulated with various levels of rigor under different legal regimes, loss of privacy may carry severe consequences for the

---

[184] Solveig Singleton, Privacy and Human Rights: Comparing the United States to Europe, Cato White Papers and Miscellaneous Reports, (December 1, 1999), available at: http://www.cato.org/pubs/wtpapers/991201paper.html, (last visited April 20, 2011).

[185] See Camp et al., supra note 160, at 6-16.

victim. The impact of loss of personal data is not limited to a mere stolen identity with some negative financial outcomes which could certainly be severe and incalculable at times, but invasion of privacy could further carry negative consequences for victims both legally and socially.

e)   Credit Card Fraud and Identity Theft

ICT has changed the landscape of the crime commission profoundly. It has provided the tools and platforms that the criminals can easily access and use. For instance, cybercriminals can now use fake websites in a hacking method called phishing.[186] Hackers build a website that looks almost identical to e.g. a local bank's website to lure unsuspecting bank customers and capture credit card information to eventually steal financial resources. These criminals would use spoofed emails or IP addresses to impersonate the originator. In the worst case scenario a perpetrator would install certain malware variants on a victim's computer that can manipulate maintenance backdoor on the victim's computer and make it more manageable for the hacker. The hacker then installs a Trojan horse or spyware[187] through the backdoor to perform much more harvesting on the computer including key logging without the victim's knowledge. A malware

---

[186] See Mohamed S. Abdel, Identity Theft in Cyberspace: Issues and Solutions, 15 (2006).

[187] An example of a family of malicious software defined as "Software that is secretly or surreptitiously installed into an information system to gather information on individuals or organizations without their knowledge", e.g., a key logger, see Committee on National Security Systems (CNSS), National Information Assurance (IA) Glossary, CNSS Instruction No. 4009, at 70 (April 26, 2010).

with the key logging ability is especially notorious because it is able to accurately capture everything the user types on the keyboard including log-in credentials for accessing bank accounts. Trojans of course appear to be pieces of useful software for the victim while in reality these types of malware intend to perform actions not described in their purpose. All of this can be initiated via a spam email directing the victim to do different things including a visit to the sham website so that the perpetrator behind the email in turn will intercept credentials and dig into more useful information of the unsuspecting victim.

Nowadays much of private information or PII is part of public records or even if that is not the case, a lot of custodians like credit bureaus make it much easier for potential intruders to harvest and use such personal information for illicit purposes. Technology contributes to this as well by providing the tools, but ultimately people or firms responsible for protecting their customers' data negligently or intentionally ease the access. One case in California illustrates this more precisely, where a woman (not even as an employee) was able to download credit information of hundreds of perspective tenants with a click of a button[188]. But it was the credit bureau that never checked whether the woman fulfilled at least a simple 'need to know' access test.

Even more concerning are cases involving internal threats, where employees with full access privileges to customer data turn their backs on their employer and device a plan to defraud customers. This situation is better exemplified in the case *R v Thompson*[189], where a criminal lawsuit was brought in England

---

[188] See Abdel, supra note 180, at 13.

[189] See R v. Thompson [1984] 1 WLR 962 at pp. 967-8, in C. REEDS, op. cit. p. 248; see also Abdel, supra note 180, at 19.

against a former bank employee, a computer programmer, in Kuwait for obtaining property by deception. Evidence proved that he utilized his programming skills to create a script that instructed the banking system to make money transfers from accounts belonging to the bank customers. Again this is another example of how rampant insider threat can be. It demonstrates how computer systems can be abused by unscrupulous power-users like a programmer or system administrator when no restrictions are built into the system. This is a good lesson for lacking security measures that should include auditing, limiting unauthorized escalation of privileges, and disallowing multitasking through segregation of duties where no one individual acts upon different transactions in a computer system.

Credit card fraud is another epidemic of global proportion which both individuals and financial institutions/businesses continue to fall victim to[190]. A study conducted by the Verizon Risk team revealed that the records from compromised payment cards (data in those cards) is the number one hacked data and data breach incidents (representing about 96% of all records stolen and 78% of all incidents).[191] This can be evidenced with the two largest

---

[190] Identity theft the number one incident for individuals (about 11.7 million individuals affected in 2008) caused by stolen credit card information as a statistical report by the United States Department of Justice Bureau of Justice Statistics showed, available at:
http://bjs.ojp.usdoj.gov/content/pub/pdf/vit08.pdf, (last visited June 6, 2011).

[191] See a study conducted by the Verizon risk team with cooperation from the U.S. Secret Service (USSS) and Dutch High Tech Crime Unit, 2011 Data Breach Investigations Report, 50 (2011), also available at:
http://securityblog.verizonbusiness.com/2011/04/19/2011-data-breach-investigations-report-released/, (last visited October 12, 2011). The cost of data breach skyrocket in 2011 – more than $130 billion for U.S. companies already as of July 2011, see The Cost of Cybercrime at CNNmoney.com:

incidents of data breach in the same year, 2011, which involved an unauthorized access and stealing of credit card information from two big companies[192]. It can be witnessed from these incidents that stealing records related to payment cards is the most lucrative criminal activity for hackers[193].

Hackers break into computer systems operated by businesses and steal credit card numbers of consumers by accessing databases and downloading information for later use often through impersonation, e.g. ID theft. These hackers even manufacture counterfeit cards based on the information they obtain via hacking to expand profitability of their fraud activities. They buy and sale counterfeit cards as well as stolen credit card information through channels established for this purposes known as *"carding forums"*[194]. Lacking computer security

---

http://money.cnn.com/galleries/2011/technology/1107/gallery.cyber_security_co sts/, (last visited July 20, 2011).

[192] Several firms were affected during 2011 but Sony and Citigroup are the two most prominent organizations falling victim to huge data compromise as of June in 2011. Citi announced on June 16, 2011 that hackers stole credit card information of its customers (over 360 thousand customer accounts); see CNN news available at:
http://money.cnn.com/2011/06/27/technology/citi_credit_card/index.htm?iid=H _T_News, (last visited June 16, 2011); see also a CNN report regarding the massive data breach on Sony, where tens of millions of credit card numbers were stolen from the three Sony gaming systems, available at
http://money.cnn.com/2011/05/10/technology/sony_hack_fallout/index.htm?iid= EL, (last visited May 22, 2011)

[193] Around $2.7 million just from Citigroup's data breach; see the report supra note 239, available at:
http://money.cnn.com/2011/06/27/technology/citi_credit_card/index.htm?iid=H _T_News, (last visited June 16, 2011); see also The Cost of Cybercrime at CNNmoney.com:
http://money.cnn.com/galleries/2011/technology/1107/gallery.cyber_security_co sts/, (last visited June 17, 2011).

safeguards have already exposed many businesses to such attacks where credit card information of millions of customers have been stolen causing unprecedented sums in financial loss, in most cases through identity theft[195].

The study by the Verizon team also indicated that in terms of attack methodology, hacking ranks number one followed by the automated malware functionality itself (e.g. spyware, key-logger, etc.), of which key-logger accounts for the majority of malware attacks[196]. The reason maybe that once released malware can automatically act, i.e. with or without further active involvement of hackers, and result in additional cyber security

---

[194] A hacker, for instance, pleaded guilty for credit card fraud and ID theft before a U.S. district judge in Virginia admitting to these crimes. Also law enforcement found over 675,000 credit card numbers and fraudulent transactions worth over $36 million in his possession; see Computer Crime & Intellectual Property Section on a United States Department of Justice website: http://www.cybercrime.gov/hackettPlea.pdf, (last visited June 3, 2011).

[195] Compared to traditional frauds committed against victims in a face to face contact, online frauds appear to be more lucrative in terms of magnitude of financial resources involved in a single attack/hack and the level of efforts needed by the fraudster as a number incidents have shown: Citibank lost $12 million from its customer accounts in a single attack see Abdel, supra note 180, at 6; more losses appear to occur at credit card payment processing centers, e.g., perhaps the largest number of cards, over 100 million, got stolen from one of such processors, Heartland Payment Systems Inc., in January 2009 as reported by Computerworld, Heartland Data Breach Sparks Security Concerns in Payment Industry, available at: http://www.computerworld.com/s/article/9126608/Heartland_data_breach_spark s_security_concerns_in_payment_industry, (last visited June 6, 2011); For various reported incidents, see Computer Crime & Intellectual Property Section on a United States Department of Justice website: http://www.cybercrime.gov, (last visited June 6, 2011).

[196] See the Verizon study, supra note 238, at 69; also available http://securityblog.verizonbusiness.com/2011/04/19/2011-data-breach-investigations-report-released/, (last visited July 20, 2011).

breaches. The fact that the majority of hacking also takes place through some manipulation of malware, demonstrates how malware remains to be the most preferred way of hacking. That is because a lot of times pieces of malware are placed in action to directly or indirectly exploit backdoors on computer systems left open for maintenance purposes. In many cases backdoors are utilized to install spyware, disable security controls, and send data back to external destinations[197]. The magnitude of these breaches and host of cases indicating lost assets witness how vulnerable data is at both big and small company data centers, and how sophisticated, as well as versatile attack methodologies can be.

Citigroup, one of the major firms which fell victim to the data breach mentioned above, later stated that its customers would lose nothing[198]. But in reality the hacked data carries the risk of further identity related issues for the customers affected at least in the long run. Such data ends up being bought and sold through carding and thus there won't be an end for the victims' loss of financial assets or privacy. Nor will there be an end anytime soon for possible liability lawsuits to the organizations losing customer data. The breaches that already took place may continue to haunt these organizations and customers alike for years to come. That is, once security breach incidents occur in this manner, there will not be an easy way out from the mess. In some

---

[197] See the Verizon study, supra note 239, at 69; also available
http://securityblog.verizonbusiness.com/2011/04/19/2011-data-breach-investigations-report-released/, (last visited July 20, 2011).

[198] Citigroup announced on June 16, 2011 that hackers stole credit card information of its customers (over 360,000 customer accounts); see CNN news available at:
http://money.cnn.com/2011/06/27/technology/citi_credit_card/index.htm?iid=H_T_News, (last visited June 16, 2011).

cases, it seems like companies and their customers end up cleaning this mess for years.

For those already affected by data breaches and others, this could be a good lesson forcing them to take a hard look into their security approaches. This could persuade many organizations to act instead of just a simple maneuver often using the press in an attempt to control damage. The situation will more likely force them to revisit and overhaul data security mechanisms they may have in place, and avoid further breaches through implementing compliant and resilient safeguards utilizing standards; such as, that of the Payment Card Industry Data Security Standard (PCI DSS).

Statistics compiled after data breaches on affected organizations showed some correlation between non-compliance with the PCI DSS and the level or frequency of data breaches[199]. As stated elsewhere, computer systems lacking recommended controls can easily be a target and misused by both external hackers and internal users alike, who strive to satisfy whatever criminal intentions they may have at a cost of both businesses and consumers. Strict application of separation of duties guard transactions against internal threats; such as, rogue employees particularly in financial systems while all other threats against financial systems containing credit card information may be mitigated with adherence to the PCI DSS, among others.

---

[199] See the Verizon study, supra note 238, at 63; also available http://securityblog.verizonbusiness.com/2011/04/19/2011-data-breach-investigations-report-released/, (last visited July 20, 2011). And the cost of data breach rose more than $130 billion in 2011 for U.S. companies, see The Cost of Cybercrime at CNNmoney.com: http://money.cnn.com/galleries/2011/technology/1107/gallery.cyber_security_co sts/, (last visited July 25, 2011).

i. *Personal Data as a Commodity*

As for the root cause of negligence in handling personal data, there seem to be two factors at play. There is security lax by data custodians, which contributes to data breaches and there is the legal framework that mends or breaks security requirements. Data security requirement backed by law can result in better safeguards while lack of such legal environment will contribute to poor handling of personal data or worse some laws create an environment where personal data may be bought and sold as commodity. Some legal systems treat private information or personal data like property. In those legal systems, e.g. the U.S., property rights extend to data, meaning data, under circumstances, can be bought and sold like property[200].

In the U.S. there is a data subject who may or may not own his/her data available on cyberspace or otherwise maintained by a custodian, e.g. an ISP, because such ownership can cease to exist through transfer of the ownership to the custodian. And there is a data owner, the ISP in the example, who, once gains ownership to personal data of a data subject, can sell the data to third parties. The third party can in turn resell the information or even misuse it in some other fashion. Since property is an alienable right, once data is owned by another party or sold, the subject's right to data is lost. In essence personal data becomes commodity that depending on demand and supply can be a great source of profit in the marketplace. Turns out extending property laws to data benefits businesses, but leaves the data subject in the dark in many respects.

---

[200] Aspray et al., supra note 9, at 195.

The fact that personal data can be turned to commodity leads to more dangerous situation. Since businesses own personal data, they quickly realize that they can make money with this commodity and it turns out money can be made in a big way if the data can be more refined, targeted, and organized in useful ways for marketing. Now the fact that intermediaries such ISPs are by default well positioned to be able to dig much deeper into customer information, gather all about the customer, get hacked, sell, or use that information for profit makes a lot of sense for both good and bad guys. And ISPs too realized this possibility where they actually use much more intrusive tools or algorithms more potent than cookies to collect data (both personal and business) of their customers. These algorithms help the data miner effectively track the customers' behavior in Internet usage, where the refined data in this manner becomes a powerful and valuable profit making information machine. Anything they collect along with the billing information they already have and own per the U.S. law becomes the best data mine for use on the market.

It does not surprise anyone that ISPs are said to use deep packet inspection mechanisms that allow them to not only record email addresses but even sift through email contents as well[201]. But even more concerning is that all of this makes such companies a target for data hackers on the one hand and marketers on the other. Hackers need this data for purposes of either personal use, i.e. to take advantage of it through ID theft and credit card fraud, or to provide it for sale. Marketing firms seek this data pretty much for the same goal as that of ISPs, making money. But once equipped with the sea of data about each customer, they will do the actual dirty trick that the ISPs won't necessarily do

---

[201] Richard M. Marsh, Jr., Legislation for Effective Self-Regulation: A New Approach to Protecting Personal Privacy on the Internet, 15 Mich. Telecomm. Tech. L. Rev. 543, at 547 (2009).

themselves, i.e. marketing firms perform the refining job by applying data mining tools. These tools analyze the data to determine customer likes and dislikes, as well as needs and wants to better customize advertising offers for products and services.

In all of these, the data subject may be left with very limited options to be able to salvage whatever can be done to control damage. Only when integrity is in question in the process of credit reporting, may these limited options become available for U.S. consumer through the Fair Credit Reporting Act of 1970[202]. For integrity issues, i.e. apparent errors in credit reporting, the Fair Credit Reporting Act affords the subject to limit damages through redress, access, and enforcement options. This law allows the data subject to view credit reports and if incorrect, to request correction, or utilize other possible enforcement tools to minimize further effects.

ii. _Possible Consequences of Credit Card Fraud_

With regard to harm resulting from stealing financial data, the impact is not limited to loss of financial assets. While loss of credit card information and ID theft as a possible consequence of that lead to a multitude of long and short term economic and financial consequences including tarnished credit, even loss of jobs, and so on, there is at least a remote chance for an additional damage not associated with property or personal injury. Fraudulent transactions involving credit card and identify theft may even lead in extreme situation to loss in commercial context unrelated to personal injury or property damage. One could, for example, imagine a loss unaccompanied by damages directly

---

[202] Aspray et al.., supra note 9, at 195.

associated with an ID theft. And this kind of remote but possible damage can also be covered under the contemporary law of tort, where the damage could be contested through tort claim. This seems to work wherever courts do not tend strictly apply the tradition of common law.

Loss not related to personal injury or property damage, also referred to as *'pure economic loss'*[203]is limited but normally accounted for hereunder. So the enduring question is whether such expansion of tort law should also be allowed for cyber born losses. Courts are generally reluctant to allow such claims even in non-cyber tort cases basically following the common law tradition. The common law approach does not seem to allow recovery of economic loss where a plaintiff suffers neither physical harm nor property damage. In the *Martel Building Ltd. v. Canada*[204] case, the court adopted some taxonomy of test steps in an attempt to ensure that its decision favoring the plaintiff did not create an unbridled wave of inappropriate lawsuits and indeterminacy of liability, inter alia[205]. This court, by recognizing the possible consequence of such expansion, disallowed compensation for pure economic loss.

A conclusion like the one in *Martel* is not necessarily without merit when it comes down to cyberspace. A different conclusion would have not set a standard for filtering legitimate claims. It court could have set a precedent for an unlimited number of liability seekers, as well as a quantum of damages, especially those caused by distributed chain reaction attacks like

---

[203] See Jennifer A. Chandler, Security in Cyberspace: Combating Distributed Denial of Service (DDoS) Attacks, University of Ottawa, 259 (2004).

[204] Martel Building v. Canada, 2000 SCC 60 at para. 36 , [2000] 2 S.C.R. 860.

[205] See Jennifer A. Chandler, Security in Cyberspace: Combating Distributed Denial of Service (DDoS) Attacks, University of Ottawa, 260 (2004).

DDoS. The point is that it is theoretically possible to consider recovery of cyber based damages based on the concept of the pure economic loss. However, in favor of legal certainty, cyber cases in particular should be limited in this regard. Or the common law concept should apply to cyberspace cases while a deviation should only be sparingly applied to remote damages cyber realm to prevent flood of tort cases that could result from a chain of events.

6. Cybercrime: Problems with Attribution and Prosecution

a) What Constitutes a Cybercrime?

Illicit cyber incidents, minor or major, abound in the information age. But whether and how to sanction these incidents with criminal penalties will depend on how a given society feels about or regards such incidents. That is because, on the one hand, not all incidents on cyberspace qualify as a criminal offence. Nor do they warrant investigation or allocating in many instances already overwhelmed law enforcement resources for prosecuting these incidents. On the other hand, whether to qualify any given cyber based incident as a crime will depend on a criminal system, and its legal norms to classify and define such offences. Regardless, a cyber attack which is considered non-criminal in one jurisdiction might very well be viewed otherwise in another.

Legal systems all over the world attempt to regulate cyber

born criminal activities one way or another, but there is no homogeneity in that regard. None of these legal systems follow any standard approach in passing laws that deter cyber offences through explicitly identifying and defining each specific offence or sanctioning these offences. Some create certain categories for cyber based offences, which include cyber trespass, cyber violence, and cyber obscenity[206] while others consider any motive aimed at conducting fraud, ID theft, and copyright infringement using computers as a criminal offence. While there is no a standard way of categorizing or defining offences on cyberspace, more important aspect of such offences has been the question of how offenders can be prosecuted by the state that represents the victim's interest and in which jurisdiction the perpetrator can be brought to justice.

In regards to terminology related to cyber offences, it must be noted that there is a frequent use of 'computer crime', 'cybercrime', and 'internet crime' synonymously, and sometimes imprecisely, although these terms do not necessarily mean the same thing. But for many, the important characteristic of cyber based crimes regardless of the term used is the fact that cyberspace (which includes the Internet) is used as a tool for crime commission. As a result, any criminal act that is possible because the actor exploits the capabilities available on the Internet and its technology in terms of speed, connectivity, anonymity, and absence of geographical boundary to elude a timely adjudication can qualify as a cybercrime. Based on this definition, the use of the term 'computer crime' may be a misnomer since even what the term 'computer' entails cannot be

---

[206] Konoorayar, supra note 90, at 422. For exhaustive list of criminal offenses on cyberspace, see GERALD R. FERRERA ET AL., CYBER LAW: TEXT AND CASES 300-307 (2000), where computer crime and cybercrime are synonymously used.

defined precisely. Using the term computer has often led to some confusion among law makers[207]. That is because computer technology is used in many things and computer technology as well as its usage evolves faster, thus, making it hard to limit the scope of its definition in legal terms. So trying to define computer born crimes under the label 'computer crime' is more confusing compared to use of the term 'cybercrime' as the latter denotes the relation of the act with cyberspace in more definite terms. Indeed, since the notion that crimes in the computing world that we are concerned with take place using digital networks, cyberspace, one way or another makes the above definition better suited for the term cybercrime not computer crime.

Meanwhile, an attempt to neatly define cyber offences often doesn't help solve cross-border criminal offences as long as there is diversity in criminal systems. Various legal systems not only classify such crimes differently, but interpret the same in a variety of ways. In fact, there are differences in treating criminal acts at state and federal levels, for example within the U.S. itself, which makes parallel prosecution for the same offence even in one nation inevitable. As stated earlier, some jurisdictions sanction cyber offences by category while others enumerate known criminal conducts as extensively as possible and impose different sanctions[208]. Part of the problem for such a wide ranging

---

[207] See PFLEEGER ET AL., SECURITY IN COMPUTING 591 (3rd Ed., 2003).

[208] Most legal regimes and some updated penal codes now include and criminalize certain conducts as cybercrime. These include ID theft, phishing, cyber espionage, spam, etc, whereas the Council of Europe Convention on Cyber-crime of 2001 categorizes cybercrimes into four, while leaving rooms for extension by signatories: (1) offences against the confidentiality, integrity and availability of computer data and systems; (2) computer-related offences, (3) content-related offences; (4)offences related to infringements of copyright and related rights; see http://conventions.coe.int/Treaty/en/Treaties/Html/185.htm, (last visited June 16, 2011).

difference in regulating cyber crimes has been the fact that cyber offences cannot always be neatly associated with physical assets like traditional offences. Overall this confusion leaves cybercrime to be misunderstood by law makers, who do not always have clarity about offences associated with the virtual world, and to be inadequately classified, as well as improperly defined in criminal codes.

One thing is clear, i.e. legislators around the world have realized that their existing criminal codes that were meant to deal with the concept of crime based on physical world have no match for offences emerging from the cyber world. This legal vacuum has forced many legal systems to revamp their existing laws. But many of these countries attempt to enact new legal norms by including each new type of offence as they go. That is, these legal regimes enact laws as new offences emerge from cyberspace and get noticed often based on the level of damage such acts have already inflicted.

Since technology and its interaction with society keep outpacing the regulatory process; however, the legal community has often a lot of catch-up to do. This situation often results in some hasty regulations where law makers do not have time for a thorough research in terms of accounting for precise definition and appropriate normative coverage for intended criminal sanctions. Hence, there is often emphasis on inclusion for identified individual offensive behaviors on cyberspace, rather than an attempt to precisely define these acts. So one can see that there have been attempts within a few criminal law regulations around the globe to cover cyber born offences as fast as possible, rather than worry about accuracy in delineating the scope of these crimes, let alone providing an unequivocal legal definition for each cybercrime.

b) Legal Problems of Attributing Cybercrime

One of the biggest problems in cyberspace is the issue with attribution, which involves the problem with effective investigation and identification of sources of cyber offences. It turns out attribution often becomes a legal hurdle during investigation and law enforcement efforts. The root cause for this challenge is that cyberspace has become more complex because of the Internet which is both ubiquitous and independent due to the inherently global nature of the Internet. Cyberspace as a whole is independent in part because the Internet is independent in a sense that the underlying infrastructure of the Internet is not wholly subjected to any single national legal system. Meaning, while the underlying infrastructure of the Internet may be managed by fragmented network enclaves, the Internet itself tends not to fall under a single legal system or control of a single network, or government regime. Rather, cyberspace as a whole is not necessarily limited by geographical boundaries to be subject to individual national governments, hence, apt to benefit from self-governance.

Self governance promotes cyberspace, so content some scholars, where the governance for cyberspace should at the same time involve diverse players in shaping models and adopting common principles for such governance[209]. Cyberspace also

---

[209] UN Framework Convention on Internet Governance created a mile stone by establishing the WGIG. WGIG report in June 2005 included: a working definition of "internet governance" as "the development and application by Governments, the private sector and civil society, in their respective roles, of shared principles, norms, rules, decision-making procedures, and programs that shape the evolution and use of the Internet." Also see Joanna Kulesza, Internet Governance and the Jurisdiction of States Justification of the Need for an International Regulation of Cyberspace, 17 (2003).

appears to benefit from self regulation as well via a self-regulatory body similar to the cross-border retail credit card networks like Visa and Master Card[210], which are largely governed by commercial laws but have certain provisions of their own. However, from the cybersecurity standpoint, cyberspace currently benefits more from the incomplete yet only available regulatory frameworks provided in varying normative coverage by Nation-states. The national regulatory environment at least for now seems to provide for better means of criminal prosecution and transparency in attribution for illicit cyber incidents. Until we have globally applicable legal norms for cybercrime, national laws remain to be the most potent resources providing more effective tools than a self-regulated environment.

Yet, since no national legislation can be expected to effectively solve issues in global cyberspace and that with an extended international application, an overarching international legal instrument is needed. Currently there is no universal legal authority or any other effective means that allows successful attribution, investigation, or prosecution of cybercrimes which often have an inherent cross-border effect. The only exception being the EU's Convention on Cybercrime[211] that only a handful countries ratified, no other multilateral treaty has been in effect as of yet. Universally applicable legal norms have to yet be crafted at the global stage that could, inter alia, define cybercrime,

---

[210] Jane K. Winn, Electronic Commerce Law: Direct Regulation, Co-Regulation and Self-Regulation, CRID 30th Anniversary Conference, Cahiers du CRID, 4 (September 2010).

[211] See the European Convention on Cybercrime (2001); also see Stein Schjolberg and Solange Ghernaouti-Helie, A Global Treaty on Cybersecurity and Cybercrime, at 2 (2011); also available at: http://conventions.coe.int/Treaty/en/Treaties/Html/185.htm, (last visited June 16, 2011).

facilitate attribution, promote international cooperation for prosecuting criminals, and universally characterize forms of cyber offences.

Since cybercrime introduces conceptual blurs, this leaves much to be desired with regard to helping legal community; hence, an unequivocal definition for each individual unlawful behavior on cyberspace is needed. Conceptual clarity will prevent perplexity among all parties involved in dealing with cybercrime. It will be helpful if there is a standard way of characterizing origins, actors, tools used, and destinations or potential victims. A clear characterization of criminal acts on cyberspace could shed more light on the definition blur of cybercrime that currently exists. Whether a given cyber attack constitutes an act of war is left to be debated as there is no agreement among scholars as to what criteria should be fulfilled for an act of war. Moreover, even if there is a consensus on cyber war being qualified as an act of war, whether the involvement of a government supported hacker alone or the severity of such government backed actions suffice to qualify a cybercrime as an act of (cyber) war is still a much debated subject[212]. Some normative clarification of that too is need under some international law. For example, a precise definition on criteria for an act of (cyber) war under an international legal norm would help one determine, among other things, whether an act originating from a government party but targeting another country or sovereignty of such is a cyber crime that constitutes an act of war.

Meanwhile, in terms of securing cyberspace, not even international legal norms alone can solve the security issues

---

[212] Reich et al., Cyber Warfare: A Review of Theories, Law, Policies, Actual Incidents - and the Dilemma of Anonymity, in European Journal of Law and Technology, Vol. 1, Issue 2, at 3 (2010).

underpinning the Internet and overall cyberspace. Rather, collaborative efforts among market forces, regulation, and private sectors (companies who own and operate networks and systems)[213] are needed to mitigate some of these issues. From the international law perspective, as mentioned earlier, no such normative system for cyberspace exists as of now (neither in the form of treaty nor as a statute) that might apply universally except recommendations or regional conventions[214]. So the question of what cybercrime or when cyber attack qualifies as a crime is, or how to resolve attribution related issues globally remains yet to be addressed.

But in the meantime, since self regulation does not seem to provide the tools necessary to support effective attribution and enforcement for offences on cyberspace, issues with cyberspace continue to be dealt with variously at national and regional levels. In short, since attempts to find plausible and universally applicable solutions for these questions have failed so far,

---

[213] Collaboration and cooperation should come from several dimensions because cyberspace is global – meaning it involves various actors in the global market place, its security is best addressed through shared responsibilities and cooperation among those actors; see Stein Schjolberg and Solange Ghernaouti-Helie, A Global Treaty on Cybersecurity and Cybercrime, at 17 (2011), also available at:
http://www.cybercrimelaw.net/documents/A_Global_Treaty_on_Cybersecurity_and_Cybercrime,_Second_edition_2011.pdf, (last visited December 10, 2011); also see The World Bank Group, supra note 33, at 2.

[214] E.g., the ITU's cyber security recommendation ITU-T X.1205, see International Telecommunication Union – Telecommunication Standardization Sector (ITU-T), Recommendation ITU-T X.1205, No. (2008); also see a recommendation by Schjolberg et al., supra note 204, at 2. For regional conventions, see the European Convention on Cybercrime (2001); see Schjolberg et al., id. at 2; also available at:
http://conventions.coe.int/Treaty/en/Treaties/Html/185.htm, (last visited June 16, 2011).

national sources of rules remain to be the best option currently for seeking help with transnational attribution and enforcement.

In sum, we find that legal authority available and possible at national levels is more effective to meeting the challenges of attribution at least for offences that can be attributed to and prosecuted within a given national boundary. Yet, practical observations have proven that no national legislation alone can effectively resolve issues in cyberspace, especially when such issues have transnational connection.

Simply put, since national laws cannot avoid conflicts when they have an extended international application, there is no way national rules alone can be relied upon for cyber offences that have cross-border effects. While international solution remains elusive in this regard, hope is that global community understands the urgency of cyber issues and reaches some consensus to provide normative solutions. Such solutions more likely involve overarching multilateral instruments that have binding effects on global cyber users and nation-states, and could shed some light in addressing, inter alia, the above questions. Legal conflicts and legal vacuum can be avoided with universally applicable legal norms. But these norms have to be negotiated by the international community making sure that they are capable of defining cybercrime, facilitating attribution, fostering international cooperation for prosecuting criminals, and universally characterizing cyber attacks.

c) Challenges in Litigating Cases from Cyberspace

Defining cybercrime may be hard as we saw in previous sections, but prosecuting such a crime or litigating a tort case involving computing tools is even harder for the following reasons. First, its very nature of being based on cyberspace makes cybercrime technically more challenging for law enforcement in terms of identifying and prosecuting its perpetrator as described in more detail in the next section. The challenge of prosecution stems from the fact that there is lack of physical evidence in many cyber born cases. Secondly, the complexity of rapidly changing technological tools used on computing machines and cyberspace makes it harder for courts, lawyers, and investigators to present the case and determine the truth of the matter. This complexity affects legal proceedings because all parties involved (jurors, judges, prosecutors, and defense) may not necessarily understand computers or the various tools used to commit crimes[215].

Lack of technical understanding will inevitably impact legal rulings as well by judges for both civil and criminal cyberspace cases. For example, it is quite possible for a judge to arrive at legally sound decision while making gross mistakes technically due to fundamental flaws in technical details obtained from erroneous expert testimonial and similarly unreliable sources. The reason is that in the era of information technology, judges face highly technical cases associated with computing that forces them to be at the mercy of computer experts. So, judges could base their rulings on technically flawed or insufficient accounts provided by expert witnesses and yet cannot make an educated guess due to their utter lack of technical understanding of computing.

The fact that lack of expertise in computing could sometimes lead to an unwanted outcome is best exemplified in the civil case of *TR Investors, LLC v. Genger*[216]. Genger involved a

---

[215] See PFLEEGER ET AL., SECURITY IN COMPUTING, 586 (3rd Ed., 2003).

[216] TR Investors, LLC v. Genger, No. 3994-VCS, 2009 WL 4696062 (Del. Ch.

dispute regarding spoliation of files from a disk, where the court ruled in favor of the plaintiff following the expert witness provided by plaintiff. In a nutshell, the defendant had deleted data after the court issued an order enjoining the parties from any changes in the status quo of the files. But the deleted data was not part of the original data. The original data could not be fully recovered with forensic tools in the first place as it was destroyed by the court's own explicit order. The intent of the order was to encrypt some files on the disc belonging to the defendant, but the encryption process created additional copies of files by rewriting everything in the unallocated space on the disc that was the center of the contention. The rewriting process due to encryption deleted the original, discoverable or forensically recoverable files and not the later deletion conducted by the defendant who was also acting in *bona fide*. The defendant deleted the files not to hide evidence by destroying the files willfully[217] unlike the witness account as provided by the plaintiff's experts, but the inadvertent court order itself led to encryption that reconfigured the disc space and in doing so made the original data unrecoverable. This crucial fact was not provided to the court as part of the expert witness which could have ultimately altered the course of the

---

Dec. 9, 2009); for details on the court error, see Garrie et al., Legally Correct But Technologically Off the Mark, North Western Journal of Technology and IP, Vol. 9, No. 1, at 2ff (October, 2010).

[217] While willful destruction of digital evidence is almost always easy to persuade courts to find spoliation, see Carlucci v. Piper Aircraft Corp., 102 F.R.D. 472, 483 (D.C.Fla. 1984), a number of other court rulings show that neither negligent nor companies' retention policy based destructions are not spared from courts' sanctions; see Lewy v. Remington Arms Co., 836 F.2d 1104 (8th Cir. 1988); For more court rulings involving divided approaches when it comes to spoliation, see http://cyber.law.harvard.edu/digitaldiscovery/library/spoliation/spoliationanalysi s.html, (last visited June 22, 2011).

judgment in favor of the defendant.

Technical challenges lawyers face are more pronounced in cases involving electronic discovery (e-discovery) in determining the integrity of digital evidence.[218] As numerous court cases show, this is especially the case with spoliation where potential electronic evidence is suspected of being tampered with or destroyed, willfully or unintentionally. Clearly lawyers rely on the expertise of computer forensics professionals for reproducing or recovery, retaining, and analyzing evidence (computer files, etc.). But the real problem is maintaining the integrity of the original evidence while recovering and reproducing the evidence in the forensic process since it is sometimes difficult, especially with files, to differentiate between original and copy, or to tell if a recovered copy truly represents the original. For example, when a lost original file is reproduced, there is no guarantee that a recovered file is tamper-proof, i.e. it is extremely hard to tell if the copy does not incorporate a few changes or it is entirely altered. The nature of such forensically recovered evidence whether good or bad could eventually dictate the litigation outcome, and alter the equitability of the whole judgment.

Finally, for cases involving cybercrime, it is not always possible to determine monetary value of computer or information system artifacts subject to such crimes. It is easy to determine the value of a blank disc, but if such a disc contains information; such as, PII, it is not easy to know what the value of privacy or confidentiality of the data on the disc is when the PII is compromised. Lack of specific information on real value or the

---

[218] Electronic discovery, or "e-discovery", refers to discovery in civil litigation which deals with information in digital (*electronic*) format, see http://www.transperfect.com/TLS/resources/resources_faq.html, (last visited June 22, 2011), while digital evidence refers to computer-generated data that is relevant to a case and obtained through the e-discovery

extent of damage might affect investigation and prosecution, i.e. the law enforcement's willingness to give attention to and prosecute it as well. By the same token, lack of ability by the court to determine the real monetary value of privacy will affect the outcome in civil judgments.

Similarly, even when prosecuting a given cybercrime is possible, if there is no cooperation on the victim's side to work with investigators, there won't be a successful prosecution. Unless the victim is willing to report the incident, provide enough information for investigation, and help bring the perpetrator to justice, nothing can happen. Lack of cooperation by the victim not only obscures access to cybercrimes by prosecution, but it also help conceal potentially destructive behaviors and criminal acts on cyberspace.

Some organizations, especially businesses which rely on customer relation may choose to keep silent even if they sustain significant damage to avoid negative publicity that could affect their reputation, public relations, and customer base[219].

Publicity of a computer attack can galvanize more attacks in similar ways (so-called copycat attack)[220] as well, which is why many entities unfortunately choose to remain silent thereby helping obscure criminal activities and letting criminals thrive with additional attacks on other victims. It is unfortunate for law enforcement and other victims that may become potential targets by hidden criminals, but not reporting cybercrime is a common problem. The fact that some organizations decide not to report cybercrime is not without some justification. While there is no question that criminal offences on cyberspace will inevitably cause more wreak-havoc on other unsuspecting victims if remain

---

[219] See PFLEEGER ET AL., SECURITY IN COMPUTING, 587 (3rd Ed., 2003).

[220] Id.

unreported, not reporting may benefit the original victim. By not disclosing the original attack, the victim avoids further damage by others that might use similar (copycat) methods to launch their own attacks. As a result, many computer crimes including those that inflict immeasurable damage continue to remain unprosecuted.

d) Technical Problems of Attribution: Capabilities & Concerns

For purposes of understanding the concept behind the term attribution , attribution as it relates to cybercrime can be defined as an attempt to figure out who is attacking whom and where the attack is originated from on cyberspace. The location where the attack is originated from may be physical (a geographical destination in a given jurisdiction) or logical (an IP address in a TCP/IP network). Attribution, thus, involves determining the identity of the actor as well as the physical origin of the act and the ability to respond appropriately against the actor, the actual perpetrator, who originated the attack[221]. But the originator's identity could be anything. It could be a user account on a system or IP address on the user's computer, but it could also be a sponsor, such as, a government agency which backs an attack. Or it could be a computer of an unsuspecting owner whose computer might have been hijacked to participate in a cyber attack.

But neither identifying the perpetrator nor pinpointing the location with some technical certainty is easy in cyberspace given the complexity of the Internet infrastructure and anonymity afforded by it.

The current Internet architecture allows anonymity with no

---

[221] See Ron Keys & Jim Ed Crouch, International Cyberspace Considerations, in CyberPro May, 2 (2010).

standard provisions for traceability. The following scenario illustrates the technical challenges faced today in achieving attribution. A denial of service attack disabled dozens of government and commercial web-sites[222]. But no one knew for sure whose action it was behind the attack. Some blamed government sources from two different countries while others suggested it could have come from any sources as the attack was unsophisticated. It was much later determined that the attack actually came from a town in England[223]. In spite of the ability to trace-back as far as the location in England, though, the investigators were not able to pinpoint the real perpetrator, an individual person or entity, behind the attack. This is partly due to the fact that the TCP/IP architecture which is the backbone of internetworking allows anonymity of nodes and users on the Internet.

The anonymity is accomplished through the fact that the TCP/IP layer uses packet-switching, where data is transported along the remaining layers and other hubs in chunks called packets. To make things worse, each of the other layers adds its own information piece to every packet and forwards the slightly changed/enhanced data to the next destination (remaining layers, various routers, and so on). Finally the packets coming from different paths, directions, and routers are reassembled into a meaningful format (text, graphics, executable program, virus, etc.) by the transport layer at destination and presented to the target. Theoretically, it is possible to determine footprints of packets on each hub other things being equal. However, that is not always a straightforward situation in IP routing. Because the source IP

---

[222] This scenario is originally described by Hollis, see Duncan B. Hollis, An e-SOS for Cyberspace, 22 (2010).

[223] Id.

address on these packets can also be modified by an attack called IP spoofing (explained below), any attempt to trace-back such packets and their real origin (the source IP address) encounters the challenge of going through each and every hub where the packets came through and got re-routed, thus, making the whole endeavor time consuming, not to mention further legal barriers. Such legal hurdles exist, for instance, if there is a need for physical searches and seizures, which may be relevant under circumstances, for system log review at those hubs or ISP data centers.

The matter of searches and seizures gets worse adding to the dilemma when the hubs involve cross-jurisdictional destinations or foreign unfriendly nations. And attackers know that and are constantly exploiting such routing problems[224]. TCP/IP is designed with simplicity, but not security in mind and to use IP addresses which can be traced if used in static state. Meaning tracing may be possible if the IP addresses are not dynamically provisioned to various modems, as often the case within ISPs. Of course, tracing IP addresses back to original device may be successful only if the log is available and accessible for investigation. Even then, locating the IP record won't be the end of the story since the IP address used to initiate the attack may not be attributed to its owner (real user of the machine or device) with certainty due to possible spoofing[225]. By spoofing the source

---

[224] Attribution has inherent problems including attribution delay, failed attribution, and misattribution; see David A. Wheeler, Techniques for Cyber Attack Attribution; Institute for Defense Analyses, 51 (02007); also see Keys et al., supra note 220, at 5.

[225] Is the process of faking the sending address of a transmission to gain illegal entry into a secure system, and the deliberate inducement of a user or resource to take an incorrect action. Impersonating, masquerading, piggybacking, and mimicking are forms of spoofing.

IP or impersonating someone else, the attacker is often able to evade true identification. The attacker can even place a false flag implicating an otherwise innocent individual or another source like a foreign government and leave investigators grapple with the unknown.

Moreover, many ISPs do not even keep system logs of IP and user specific activities for an extended time due to the sheer volume of often overwhelming daily information communication.[226] Whether ISPs are required to divulge information of their customers in investigations like this is another question, which was answered in the positive at least by one court in *Recording Industry Assoc. of America v. Verizon Internet Services*[227]. But regardless ISPs and similar intermediaries have become more valuable for law enforcement simply because it is more efficient to analyze user activity from these gateways, instead of looking for mostly dispersed nodes used by individual cyber criminals. Intermediaries provide centralized activity gateways that can be used to plan and implement cost effective investigatory and law enforcement mechanisms[228].

In any case, the preceding sample incident clearly demonstrates how difficult it is technically to attribute a given criminal responsibility online. The reality is that attackers with adequate technical skills can remain anonymous at will and continue to evade criminal prosecution or avoid responsibility in civil litigation.

---

[226] See Hollis, supra note 221, at 24.

[227] Recording Industry Assoc. of America v. Verizon Internet Services, 240 F.Supp.2d 24 (D.D.C. 2003), also available at: http://www.dcd.uscourts.gov/02-ms-323.pdf (last visited December 12, 2011).

[228] Joel R. Reidenberg, States and Internet Enforcement, University of Ottawa law & technology journal, at 224 (undated publication).

The question of how to solve the problem of attribution on cyberspace is a much debated topic, but whether to use much more intrusive techniques and tools to ease attribution has also become more controversial. Simply put, attribution maybe made easier using some combination of intrusive technology and cooperation, while on the flip side any technical breakthrough making attribution easier comes with a tradeoff for privacy advocates. Therefore, the enduring question is how much of attribution capability is too much? The answer to this question depends on who is being asked, and there are two extremes: those for total control of the cyber underworld by all means and the opponents who would like to see privacy on cyberspace not exploited by any means. For proponents, it is extremely important to ease law enforcement efforts in terms of cost and time. Law enforcement community would also be interested in ensuring collection of reliable evidence for effective prosecution by using all available technical attribution tools.

On the opposing side, some groups consider any method of attribution on the Net unacceptable. In countries like the U.S., many wary citizens could find it a violation of freedom of expression and privacy to see their net activities monitored by any party or tool. One group, the Electronic Frontier Foundation (EFF), in particular takes the quest for freedom of speech and privacy on cyberspace to a whole new level. The EFF attempts to enforce user rights on digital world through not only an active advocacy for the freedom of the Internet itself, among other things, but by doing so through litigations[229].

Besides, the fact that potentially more powerful identification and tracking tools can be placed at the hands of,

---

[229] See EFF's legal cases also available at: https://www.eff.org/cases, (last visited December 11, 2011). Also see Hollis, supra note 221, at 28.

especially tyrant governments around the world will put certain category of people, e.g. political dissidents, deserving some anonymity in danger. Making attribution tools non-intrusive ensures some anonymity for internationally persecuted political dissidents, among others, just to name a few benefits. Therefore, any technical fix for attribution challenges will most likely be in collision course with the needs of freedom seekers, as well as demands from freedom advocates around the world, and within the Internet community in particular.

In terms of the availability of tools and techniques, there are adequate sources that can equip both sides: law enforcement and privacy seekers. So in favor of those who fight for privacy, just like there are plenty of tools that attempt to block or filter the net traffic, or counter anonymity problems[230], there seems to be also no shortage in technical tools that can counteract attribution tools, anonymizers in particular. Certain anonymizing tools are powerful enough to enable anonymity and circumvention. They include proxy servers, some of which are even available on the open source for free[231]. The anonymity tools such as Tor[232] (a

---

[230] There are many tools and devices currently on the market that promise all kinds of functionalities including de-anonymizing, intercepting traffic, tracking user behavior, logging activities, etc. as could be observed from various presentations during an Intelligence Support Systems (ISS) conference in Dubai, UAE (2011), see http://www.issworldtraining.com/ISS_MEA/index.htm, (last visited December 6, 2011).

[231] They include proxying methods (e.g., http and CGI proxy), IP tunneling (e.g., VPN), re-routing tools, and distributed hosting. See, Hal Roberts et al., 2007 Circumvention Landscape Report: Methods, Uses, and Tools, The Berkman Center for Internet & Society at Harvard University, 22 (March 2009). The freely downloadable software from the Tor project is an example of this; see https://www.torproject.org/ (last visited April 20, 2011).

[232] See the Tor project: https://www.torproject.org/, Hal Roberts et al., 2007 Circumvention Landscape Report: Methods, Uses, and Tools, The Berkman

proxy service) takes advantage of the existing TCP/IP architecture to hide IP addresses of its users and, of course TCP/IP already has an inherent capability to work against a trace-back. But neither anonymizers (circumvention tools) nor filtering methods are absolute as any of these methods can be broken if sufficient amount of resources are invested.

Regardless, as some new techniques continue to emerge to get around anonymizers and other methods which try to counteract identification efforts by law enforcement, there are those which help conceal identity on the Net with brand new capabilities. In the end, the fight between these opposing methods seems to have been set off most likely for an unending battle. Therefore, the problem surrounding investigation and attribution of cyber attacks will not seem to be solved anytime soon. And this is especially true for an attempt to bring about a lasting solution for the problem with technical means alone.

e) The Need for International Cooperation in Investigating Cybercrime

Attribution is not just technically challenging but it demands enhanced international cooperation for taking actions against unauthorized behaviors during cross-border cyber transactions. Cross-border cyber issues have resulted in an international legal conundrum with respect to jurisdiction (both civil and criminal), investigation, and enforcement. As stated elsewhere, diversity in legal frameworks, differences in security standards, and only sporadic prosecution of cyber security breaches at various jurisdictions are already a challenge for protecting consumers in cross-border transactions. Proscriptions without the ability to

Center for Internet & Society at Harvard University, 278 (March 2009).

prosecute a perpetrator have no deterring effect[233].

Furthermore, there exist stark differences across legal regimes when it comes to securing cyberspace. The differing views in dealing with cyber security actually exacerbate the situation with lack of cooperation. This diversity will only help undermine international attempts to fight against all sorts of cyber corruption. Yet, despite all these differences, there is a growing consensus demanding international cooperation and collaboration to ensure successful identification and adjudication of criminals more realistically[234]. Countries have a predisposition to assume the responsibility of regulating and enforcing laws of all facets of life including those that could help ensure international cyber security in their territories. Because of this, some contend that there should be international norms that define such *"national responsibility for quelling cyber conflict that is originating from, or conducted via that nation's territory"*[235].

Improving attribution mechanisms along with the possibility to adjudicate cyber criminals will deter cyber attacks as attackers know that they are less likely to evade prosecution. Aside from technical capabilities, enhancing attribution capabilities will only be possible through cooperation in enforcement despite variances in underlying legal systems across national boundaries.

Some parts of the world have more robust domestic laws and enforcement mechanisms relevant to computer crimes that could be used to facilitate attribution endeavors. Yet there are other parts of the globe, which are only just beginning to try to catch up with technology born criminal aspects of their legal

---

[233] See Duncan B. Hollis, An e-SOS for Cyberspace, 17 (2010).

[234] See Keys et al., supra note 220, at 3.

[235] See Hollis, supra note 232, at 23.

systems, while there are still others that are in the dark with no functioning legal systems let alone anything meaningful is happening in the cyberspace front.

Meanwhile there is neither a common understanding nor standard approaches in regards to implementing cyber security controls that make such accountability possible. For example, the ability for after the fact auditing of security incidents relies on the capability of monitoring system and user activities, logging events, proper data storage, and information sharing, all of which should be in place following some standard. In fact ISPs that come in contact with much of the cyberspace traffic and have the ability to enable such security audit are not legally required to keep information on such traffic. Nor are countries required to abide by any international legal norm to maintain/store and protect cyber security relevant events to facilitate possible e-discovery or evidence seeking in the event there is a cyber attack. No universally binding international norm (hard law) requires or for that matter not even a soft law urges nations in specific terms to subject their citizens to cyberspace related investigation or attribution process.

The problem with attribution must; therefore, rely on voluntary cooperation. But since not all countries may be willing to cooperate in this regard, especially in situations with adversaries, the need for cooperation inevitably calls for regulatory mandates at the global scale. International initiative in this regard could go a little further and account for cyber security safeguards for citizens within member states. In light of improving international cooperation, for instance, multilateral legal norms can be crafted, which not only promote cooperation among states, but mandate government protection for citizens. Under such norms, citizens would have the right for privacy and their personal data as well as financial assets could be protected against external cyber attacks where, if an attack originates from non-national territory, the citizens (victims) could be able to ask their government to pursue civil or criminal actions against foreign individuals or entities. Among other things, victims could demand their national government to seek permission or authorization for physical search and seizure on personal computers of citizens in other nations for purposes of cyber forensic. To date; however, while such cooperation has been seen to be organized through a handful bilateral agreements[236], universally applicable cyber security related multilateral agreements have not come to light yet.

One notable exception of a multilateral instrument with regard to facilitating investigation is the cybercrime treaty signed by the U.S., Canada, Japan, and 22 European countries[237]. This treaty will allow investigation and prosecution of major cybercriminal activities within countries which are parties to the convention. Though this treaty constitutes a major step in the right direction at least in promoting cooperation and facilitating attribution, it won't suffice to cover the vast majority of the world cyber community. Since the majority of countries are not part of this convention, cyber criminal incidents originating from or traversing via those non-party countries potentially remain to be difficult to solve. Cyber criminals can exploit this situation and use

---

[236] Federal Trade Commission within the U.S. has concluded a range of such agreements entitled 'International Antitrust and Consumer Protection Cooperation Agreements' with various countries; see http://www.ftc.gov/oia/agreements.shtm, (last visited December 11, 2011).

[237] Signed in November 2001 by more 29 countries, entered into force in 2007 for the U.S.; also See PFLEEGER ET AL., SECURITY IN COMPUTING 589 (3rd Ed., 2003); For chronological timeline of the convention, see a Department of Justice website: http://www.cybercrime.gov/intl.html#Vb, (last visited June 11, 2011).

various routes and stepping stones around these countries to launch attacks. When such multiple nodes at multiple non-treaty jurisdictions are used, it becomes much harder to resolve identity and ultimately the crime in question.

EU's Data Retention Directive is another example of multinational legal efforts to enable attribution. This directive lays out requirements for communications network providers to retain traffic and location data for six months at a minimum to enable the investigation, detection, and prosecution of serious crimes. The directive has; however, encountered a stiff resistance from national sources even within member states due to both technical and legal hurdles in its implementation[238]. It can be noted that this legislation came into effect as a direct consequence of the aftermath of the series of terrorist attacks in the U.S. and Europe between 2001 and 2005. This implies the fact that the main goal of this legislation may not have been cybersecurity, rather it could have aimed the fight against generic terrorist activities, where individual planning terrorist attacks could easily be identified, tracked and apprehended using cyberspace technologies. The reason is that individuals with terrorist intentions tend to take advantage of cyberspace for their group mobilization and planning efforts which could leave footprints on cyberspace. The fact that these footprints can be captured and stored electronically under this directive makes it easier to audit and track activities of individuals suspected of planning any terrorist acts.

Meanwhile, this directive clearly shows a departure from the EU's protectionist approach for consumer with its more stringent Data Protection Directive of 2002. The Data Retention

---

[238] Lukas Feiler, The Legality of the Data Retention Directive in Light of the Fundamental Rights to Privacy and Data Protection, in the European Journal of Law and Technology, Vol 1, Issue 3, at 4 (2010).

Directive, while being a sort of 'blanket' data retention requirement as indicated in *S. and Marper v. United Kingdom*[239], reflects a contradictory stance in itself with regard to the EU's own position in data protection. Inevitably, the retention policy has become controversial due to a possibly severe interference with fundamental human rights. Nevertheless, it is a beginning of an acknowledgment for the need to facilitate transnational crime investigation for this is one and may be the only way of preserving electronic data from the EU's standpoint to enable cyber forensics and e-discovery.

f) Applicability of the State Responsibility Doctrine to Cybercrime

In the absence of new international universal legal norms for cyber security, it becomes necessary to answer questions as to (a) if the existing international treaties could assist in determining a state's obligation to cooperate in cybercrimes regardless of the state's own laws, and (b) whether duties and obligations of state under the public international law can apply to cyberspace related cases involving citizens of a given state.

To address these questions, first it is necessary to look into the rationale behind the basic principle of the state responsibility itself. A state is responsible for internationally wrongful actions that can be imputable to it one way or another.

State's responsibility is often accepted if an obligation can be established for the state. This is, meanwhile, a generally accepted principle, which has been adopted into the International

---

[239] The European Court of Human Rights stated that it was 'struck by the blanket and indiscriminate nature' of UK laws that allowed fingerprints as mandated by this directive; see Feiler, supra note 237, at 16.

Law Commission (ILC) draft code. Imputability under Chapter II of the ILC draft statute is often possible when state agents act on behalf of the state and this is consistently the case, especially in human rights abuses (murder, torture, etc)[240]. It is; however, unclear as to what constitutes an internationally wrongful act. ILC did not define wrongful acts, nor did it explain what should constitute state's obligation towards international community. These, according to Chapter I, Article 3 of the ILC draft code, are left for other international legal norms to deal with.

Furthermore, it is equally unclear if such a responsibility also exists with respect to wrongful actions by one state's citizens against another state or foreign citizens. If a stricter, more conservative interpretation of this responsibility were to be applied, then the state would only be responsible for acts it directly authorizes or should assume responsibility because an act was committed on its behalf[241].

Encountering similar conundrum, international tribunals including the International Court of Justice (ICJ) have generally adopted two competing standards called effective control and overall control[242] as a test mechanism to establish state's responsibility. Notwithstanding, with respect to cyber attacks,

---

[240] Maeve Dion, Keeping Cyberspace Professionals Informed, in CyberPro, 3 (December 2009).

[241] Some argue that based on ICL's draft Article 11 no act of individuals or groups should be considered as an act of state, apart from imputable actions. Also see MALCOLM SHAW, INTERNATIONAL LAW, 551 (4th Edition, 1997).

[242] Effective control exists where non-state actors perform their acts under complete dependence on the state as exemplified in Nicaragua v. United States, 1986, at 110, and overall control exists where the state has a role in organizing and coordinating the non-state actor's actions; for details see Scott J. Shackelford State Responsibility for Cyber Attacks: Competing Standards for a Growing Problem, at 5.

either or both of these standards may not work well. The effective control approach requires much higher standards of proof placing huge burden of proof on plaintiff. Indeed, the effective control approach may turn out to be extremely difficult to prove given the elusive nature of the Internet architecture which enables anonymity. Under the effective control approach; therefore, it is much easier for states to conceal the real perpetrator behind an act of information warfare and get away with their responsibility.

Unlike effective control, so argue some commentators, the overall control standard would ensure state attribution in cyber attacks even when complete control is lacking or cannot be proven[243]. They contend that holding states accountable for their citizens' actions based on overall control supported by existing obligation can be used analogously and extended to cyberspace cases. This is also consistent with another approach that will base the decision of state responsibility on the degree of due diligence or lack thereof exhibited by the State[244]. Accordingly, states may have to exercise due diligence to even prevent known and impending cyber attacks when technically possible or at least facilitate investigation and identification, as well as prosecution of a responsible party. So based on this premise, as long as it can be proven[245] that the state is or must have been aware of a serious

---

[243] Such an expanded approach of the overall control standard was used in the Iran hostage case decided by the ICJ (United States v. Iran, 1980, p. 29); for details, see Scott J. Shackelford, From Nuclear War to Net War: Analogizing Cyber Attacks in International Law, Berkeley Journal of International Law Vol. 27:1, at 6 (2008).

[244] See Sean Kanuck, Sovereign Discourse on Cyber Conflict Under International Law, Texas Law Review, Vol. 88:1571, at 1592 (2010).

[245] While the due diligence approach may seem plausible, it is rather difficult to prove that a state has not taken necessary measures to fail the due diligence test; see Kanuck, supra note 243, at 1592.

cybercrime, the state must be held accountable. Even if the state has not been aware, due to its potential to go after and identify an actor using tools and techniques at its disposal or ones belonging to ISPs in its territory, the state is better positioned in this regard than any other entity to account for crimes committed by citizens. As a result, if the state must have known illegal cyber activities by its citizens based on its ability to manage and control territorial ICT, then this establishes the obligation for the state to exercise due diligence. And there is the implication for the state to assume a responsibility under international law to control at least technically possible attacks and facilitate law enforcement. If the state yet fails to perform such duties, the state did not exercise the due diligence expected from it. The state would also fail the due diligence test, if it did not cooperate with investigation or did not enable attribution. Here not the action or inaction itself but the failure to perform due diligence by the state can be attributed to the State.

Meanwhile, international jurisprudence in general has recognized few exceptions that are attributable to states no matter what. Such exceptions include traditionally high-profile criminal cases (genocide, crime against humanity, etc) committed by individuals[246] yet considered as serious crimes, for which the respective state must be held accountable. Under such exceptions, state's responsibility can be drawn from its general obligation to meet certain requirements towards international community even if the state itself or its agents were not said to be acting. For instance, the question of state responsibility has been answered in the positive in cases calling for full cooperation of a

---

[246] See Hari Hara Das, PRINCIPLES OF INTERNATIONAL LAW AND ORGANIZATION, New Delhi, at 128 (1995).

sovereign territory in bringing an individual accused of genocide or crime against humanity to justice. On a similar note, some courts seem to recognize state responsibility based on the obligation to conduct due diligence even in cases not involving crimes against humanity. For example, the U.S. Supreme Court recognized duty of government with respect to preventing money laundering. The court stated in *United States vs. Arjona*[247] that the state needed to conduct due diligence to prevent a person in its territory from counterfeiting foreign currency. So the court's position, at least from the standpoint of the U.S. Supreme Court, suggests that not only especially gruesome crimes like mass murders but other serious offences too can qualify as a high profile crime to base state's obligation.

With regard to offences on cyberspace, the enduring question is whether cybercrime could also be a good candidate to qualify as a high profile crime to easily establish state's obligation. The next question is whether states can actually be held accountable for cybercrimes not committed by them or their agents under the exception rule. Whether state's obligation should cover cybercrimes committed by third parties, will depend on whether one has a liberty to categorize cyber attacks as a high profile crime in the traditionally recognized sense to justify state obligation under the exception rule.

It can be argued as follows to demonstrate that cybercrimes too could fall under the exception rule. This position in turn becomes a foundation to justify further arguments and establish state's obligation. First, one could infer from the consideration based on exceptions that nothing prevents any crime considered serious from being covered by the general obligation rule. Secondly, since cybercrime can be serious and in some cases even

---

[247] Id. at 128

have genocidal consequences, an application of the general obligation threshold should also be possible on cyber born crimes. To buttress this, several countries already consider at least severe cases of cyber-crime as a national security issue and treat the same as serious offences. Such an elevated treatment suggests that, for national security reasons, these countries consider cybercrime as something that needs special attention from the standpoint of prevention, deterrence, control, cooperation, and sanction. In many occasions nation-states seek support and rely on interventions from international community to prosecute and punish offenders in serious crimes. Since national jurisdictions cannot successfully prevent or prosecute cybercrimes on their own, the need for international intervention and cooperation becomes paramount and necessary as well. This is true in terms of deterrence, enforcement, and criminal sanctioning for these crimes the same way as it is for other egregious crimes like genocide, etc.

By the same token, at least some serious crimes recognized under the exception rules can be analogous to serious cybercrimes as well. For example, a cyber attack that results in a loss of or severe damage to a critical infrastructure could be compared to at least money laundering crime that draws similar societal attention due to gravity of its possible consequences. Loss or damage in a critical infrastructure can have severe consequences, effects that range from severe economic damages to loss of life. Given the recognition of state's general obligation for a money laundering crime, which is of equivalent nature in terms of gravity of the act and its cross-border effects, cybercrimes with similarly grave consequences across cyberspace too should be recognized as generally falling under state's obligation. Indeed, given the technological capabilities today, certain categories of cybercrimes can result in severe consequences ranging from crippling critical public infrastructure to loss of multiple human lives which could be equated under circumstances with even genocide. The gravity of certain cybercrime consequences could warrant a state responsibility, if proven that the crime has originated from a specific geographical territory regardless of the actor.

Cybercrime has inherent cross-border characteristics, prevention of which requires states' active involvement due to the ability by most states to control the ICT infrastructure in their territory, which enables cyber-activities. Arguably by providing ICT capabilities and thereby also enabling connections to outside world, nation states willingly participate in the global ICT and pave the way for their citizens to make or break rules on cyberspace. Through this participation, they establish an international obligation to ensure that their portion of the global ICT (cyberspace) is secure and not used covertly or overtly for illicit purposes including causing damage across borders[248]. It is; therefore, plausible to argue that states should assume responsibility not only for imputable actions but for non-attributable offences of illicit residents when their territories act as a safe sanctuary for criminals.

Cybercrime thus can be considered as an act, for which a state, under whose purview it could be committed, should be held accountable both under the traditional sense of state responsibility and the due diligence test.

Another factor to consider for justifying this conclusion is the fact that cyber criminals often use state territories as a safe heaven, usually since states intentionally or unbeknownst to them harbor and protect such criminals. Criminals tend to use such state

---

[248] See Sean Kanuck, Sovereign Discourse on Cyber Conflict Under International Law, Texas Law Review, Vol. 88:1571, at 1591 (2010).

territories as a safe sanctuary under the umbrella of sovereignty, where they cannot be located and prosecuted. The reason is that any intrusion to those territories without explicit permission from the state involved would constitute a violation of that state's sovereignty rights.

That said; however, the overall success of confronting cyber security challenges including attribution and enforcement still depends on cooperation and collaboration not just among states, but private sector, and international, as well as regional organizations[249]. The reason is that nation-states alone cannot make a difference in that respect. Nor do they possess technological capabilities paralleled with that of private sector to address cyber security issues with technical means within their geographical boundaries. To be clear, even if states can be responsible for cyber offences in their territories, this responsibility can be severely limited by technological factors. The technology becomes another part of the equation to effectively limit states' ability to control cyber activity in a given geographical territory. States build and manage ICT infrastructure with or without the help from private sectors, but that doesn't necessary means all nations are well equipped with all the capabilities to include well trained human resources, legal and policy measures, and technology to effectively control everything that can take place on cyberspace within their ICT purview. There is no question that many nations lack these capabilities. This hurdle leads to the question as to whether states' general obligation to account for cybercrimes in their territories could be seriously impacted. Can states be held responsible for cybercrimes committed by some

---

[249] Report of the Group of Governmental Experts on Developments in the Field of Information and Telecommunications in the Context of International Security to the UN General assembly 65th Session, at 7 (July 2010).

unknown party in their territories even when they cannot afford technological or other means either to identify and apprehend actual perpetrators or to prevent the crime itself from occurring in their territory in the first place?

Technology in the private sector continues to outpace the ability of governments in the public sector to keep the same pace. This is true in terms of human capital, which cannot catch up with the ever changing cyber technology and know-how with appropriate training. It is also true that most governments cannot afford funding highly advanced ICT equipment and applications, which makes them incapable of keeping up the pace with faster changing technological landscape[250]. For this reason, every effort to enforce in many cases already weak policy and legal measures by these governments, at least for those nations which have such measures, often remains to be of no avail. Therefore, it is unclear as to whether there is any justification in expecting states in general let alone those jurisdictions with much weaker ICT capabilities to assume responsibilities and be liable for threats posed by non-state actors, where they have neither political interests nor technological abilities.

In fact economically poor countries with weaker ICT can be targeted for the very reason that they are weak in defending themselves or their portion of the global ICT. That is, poor countries are more susceptible to attacks that manipulate technical defense capabilities. The potential consequence is that bad guys could exploit this weakness in these nations and use these territories to launch cyber attacks with the further potential that the same nations become legally liable under the general

---

[250] And this problem is said to be true of both developing and developed countries though there is a huge gap between both camps in terms ICT capabilities. See Sean Kanuck, Sovereign Discourse on Cyber Conflict Under International Law, Texas Law Review, Vol. 88:1571, at 1590 (2010).

rules of the state responsibility more often than countries that have adequate resources to defend their ICT.

It is possible that technologically weak nations cannot escape legal responsibility for a cyber offence whether it is of large or small scale due to their lack of resources and, thus, technical inability to curb any illicit cyber incident of any proportion from taking place. A major hacker who manipulates a weakness in the ICT or minor script kiddies who happen to play around with newer hacker tools yet end up setting off a major incident on cyberspace are a good example, for even a minor criminal activity on cyberspace is no match to the poor nation. So given this situation, expecting an economically poor nation, in particular, that has neither resources nor technical know-how to fight against these attacks on their own at first seems to lack any plausible justification. While such a conclusion inevitably amounts to a double standard, it seems reasonable to hold these states accountable only when they are prepared to or have the ability politically and technologically[251] to effectively counter cyber threats in their territories. However, there is no merit in suggesting that countries lacking sufficient resources should be left alone. Even poor states should not be allowed to exculpate themselves from this obligation only because they cannot implement efficient cyber defense for economic reasons. If their defense against the state responsibility principle is attributable to their pure political will, such a defense cannot hold water. Even if these countries lack technical resources to prevent cybercrime originating from their territories, they can be expected to fully cooperate with international community and law enforcement in terms of investigation and apprehension of suspected culprits. Their responsibility in this regard includes cooperation to

---

[251] See Kanuck, id, at 1591.

extradite suspects, who otherwise cannot be prosecuted in their physical location, for example, for lack of criminal sanction for their behavior. So the extent of state responsibility for these nations lies in their obligation to cooperate and facilitate investigation as well as prosecution in the event that their citizens or private entities are suspected of committing cybercrime.

In sum, there is no doubt that nation-states continue to be overwhelmed by challenges even though they attempt to pervasively exert their sovereign power to control both territorial and non-territorial cyberspace threats. No country as yet seems to have been successful in bringing cyber security threats in its geographical boundary under control. This limitation arguably weakens the notion of state responsibility argument at least with regard to nations which have little or no technical capabilities in supporting cyberspace. At a minimum the technological factor brings up the question of fairness in applying the state responsibility doctrine, especially with regard to the general obligation exception. If this question is given effect and determined unfair for the poor nation to implement expensive technology resources, this position at least partially defeats the previous arguments that state's responsibilities should be drawn from the due diligence doctrine and general obligation based on the graveness of the effect of a cybercrime. Yet it can still be argued that the state responsibility doctrine stands regardless while consideration must be had in enforcing the doctrine. This consideration becomes necessary if a country's defense against this doctrine rests in the technical inability, i.e. to be able to prevent cybercrime with technical means within its sovereignty, is in question. In the end, the doctrine must be expanded to cover the realm of cyberspace and nothing prevents it from getting to apply on cybercrimes even when the technology factor erodes state's responsibility and weakens the applicability of this doctrine across the board.

Chapter 3 Cyber Laws: Adequacy, Challenges, and Effects on Offshoring

A. *Cyber Security Regulations of Host Countries*

1. Availability and Efficacy of Cyber Security Regulations

a) The Need for Cyber Security Regulation in General

There is no question that cyberspace presents the new legal frontiers for many countries and legal communities all over the world. The way various countries approach cyberspace, whether they deal with cyber security using existing or new regulatory frameworks may eventually determine whether they succeed in controlling at least their portion of cyberspace. These regulatory frameworks also determine whether positive or negative effects their legal environments have on IT service investments in form of FDI. One must note that regulations including those directly aimed at cyberspace can all affect the landscape of cross-border transactions involving FDI in general or offshoring service FDI, in particular.

While we look at the effects of existing or newly enacted laws by host countries on IT enabled service FDI, the focus here is on those regulations directly related to cyberspace. In the past few years there have been attempts to regulate some aspects of cyberspace through national regulatory regimes. However, while even those regulated aspects have not been effective to fully account for cyber based transactions, other aspects remain to be addressed through national or international legal regimes to effectively deal with issues in cyberspace. Particularly, national regulations have not been able to catch up with the pace of technology to successfully cover cyberspace. This may in part be because no nation can control the Internet or has the right to do so assuming the Internet represents the majority of the space on cyber-world called cyberspace. The further assumption is that the Internet being a global network, when fully regulated, will cover the remaining portion, the non-national/non-territorial space of cyberspace.

Meanwhile any intent to control the Internet by any one particular government is a hotly debated issue. There are two major camps of fierce arguments: those that advocate free flow of information and exchange of ideas, and those who fight for some accountability through government control[252]. Those advocating for the freedom of the Internet contend that too much control would discourage technological advances in cyberspace, whereas those against the uncontrolled free flow of information are concerned about all the security issues cyberspace entails as has been discussed so far.

The arguments for and against government control tend to be lengthy because of the term 'control' while both have merits of

---

[252] See James Gannon, The Middle Lane on the Information Superhighway: A Review of Jack Goldsmith's and Tim Wu's 'Who Controls the Internet?' Illusions of a Borderless World, at 461 (2006).

their own. But one must first differentiate between 'government control' of the Internet per se and government's attempt to regulate behaviors on cyberspace at least within its territories, hence, its regulatory control of cyberspace within its jurisdiction. So, when it comes to the former, given the global characteristics of cyberspace, the Internet in particular, full control by a given state government of the entire network of networks may not be practical, let alone such a control is legally possible due to jurisdictional limits. It must be noted that even the historic but necessary indirect control by the U.S. government over the domain name registration through the Internet Corporation for Assigned Names and Numbers (ICANN) agency has been a thorn in the side of many. The ICANN, an NGO, has caused some tensions among governments and independent organizations around the globe[253].

Nonetheless, governments can and should be able to promulgate laws that govern cyberspace as it relates to their internal ICT in order to ensure national security and provide security frameworks for information exchange in their territories and beyond. Thus, the latter argument with respect to the necessity of government control in so far as regulating cyberspace for security reasons is concerned, is justified. But this is not to say

---

[253] Especially because administering even other sovereign states' domain names to the extent that these names should be authorized, registered, or even disallowed lies at the hands of ICANN, an American NGO; See Joanna Kulesza, Internet Governance and the Jurisdiction of States: Justification of the Need for an International Regulation of Cyberspace, 10 (December 2008).; This was inevitable also because the Internet was born in the U.S. through the ground-breaking ARPANET (the predecessor of the Internet) research efforts conducted by the U.S. Defense Department between 1969 and 1989 (see GERALD R. FERRERA ET AL., CYBER LAW: TEXT AND CASES 3 (2000), even if the Internet later might have been considered as being a 'global commons' as some may argue; see Sean Kanuck, Sovereign Discourse on Cyber Conflict Under International Law, Texas Law Review, Vol. 88:1571, at 1575 (2010).

information flow on cyberspace should be controlled through over-regulation or otherwise, so much so that cyberspace is not only monitored but all information is subjected to some level of scrutiny. If government control is not limited, this will lead to government's ability to censor information traffic at will. This has already led to some unscrupulous actions by some national governments which often operate under the umbrella of enforcing legal or policy regime. Some middle ground between too much control through too strict legal norms and too little control through too lax regulatory regimes or no regulation at all should be attained.

Regulating cyberspace at national level provides some level of assurance as far as consumer protection is concerned, and this is particularly true for not just cyber transactions within the national limits affected by such regulations, but cross-border flow of information. Cross border transactions have to rely in part on the regulatory and policy frameworks supporting the cybersecurity of other networks outside national boundaries. Furthermore, depending on other factors that influence technical capabilities and international cooperation, appropriate national regulations will also provide a supportive platform for international attribution of cybercrimes.

Indeed, today's complex cybersecurity challenges, the attempt to contain growing cyber born crimes and damages, which continue to prompt new regulations speak for themselves and underscore the need for regulatory intervention in many aspects of cyberspace. There is no convincing argument suggesting otherwise that cyberspace can successfully be made safe and secure without some control through regulations. Law makers everywhere, confronted with cyber security issues, have realized the need for regulatory intervention in cyberspace. They look into ways to regulate various aspects of cyberspace to provide cyber security frameworks.

As cyberspace grows in complexity, so is the need for examining existing laws to identify loopholes, the need for looking new issues, and eventually for ways to address new issues that must be accounted for with new regulation. For instance, there are multiple pending cyber security legislations in the U.S. not to mention the ones already in effect, all of which are necessary to govern various aspects of human conduct and business transactions associated with cyberspace. One such pending law (the Cyber Security Act of 2009), if finally enacted, will have a generic applicability over cyberspace. This legislation eyes improvement in global trading through cyber security norms[254]
.

b) Further Justification for National Cyber Regulation

As mentioned elsewhere, no reliable legal norms exist for cyberspace including the Internet as of yet that applies at multinational level, let alone universally, except a few regional cooperative arrangements. Globally there is a legal uncertainty as the result concerning applicable laws, evidence, and legal redress for cyberspace born incidents. This uncertainty is particularly underscored in cross-border transactions involving the Internet, e.g. e-commerce. Consumers, law enforcement, outsourcing clients, and offshoring service FDI alike grapple with legal questions related to applicability, jurisdiction, etc. of various fields of law, which include private, public, criminal, and tax laws.

---

[254] Bierce & Kenerson, P.C, Cyber Security Threat Management in Outsourcing: The Coming National Security Regulation of ITO, BPO and KPO, available at: see www.outsourcing-law.com, (last visited July 20, 2011).

Weak or non-existent cyber security regulation poses a broad potential risk to cyberspace in general. In the same regard, globalization adds substantial level of complexities and opportunities for exploiting the global ICT by bad guys. The risk of lack data protection on cyberspace caused by weaker regulation can be considerably exacerbated by the need to exchange sensitive data long distances across international boundaries. This is usually the case with IT offshoring where not only security weakness in a given geographical territory poses threats to investment data, but such data has to traverse multiple networks through various secure and insecure nodes, as well as gateways, which act as stepping stones. As a result, especially offshoring service FDI and/or its IT outsourcing service providers could be exposed to elevated level of security threats in the first place resulting from weaknesses in cyber security regulation across the globe.

Sufficient legal instruments could lay the foundation for the underlying cybersecurity measures. This legal foundation helps govern all aspects of cybersecurity and behavior of user community by mandating and establishing a variety of security requirements. Lack of such an underpinning normative support via legislation means that there are no legal instruments that could be invoked both in terms of substantive and procedural sources of law. Lack of legal frameworks further means there is no strong backing for enforcement in policy frameworks and security requirements. Legal and security policy instruments could be used as deterring means besides their application in the event cyber security breaches take place. This deterring effect will benefit stakeholders by providing some assurance in reducing potential internal and external threats.

Regulations in cyberspace could also help promote security awareness and back efforts to strengthen critical infrastructure through use of a sustainable ICT technology. Effective regulations could lead to overall improvements in ICT infrastructure, weaknesses of which could invite increased level of vulnerabilities within the communication network; such as, Internet backbones, in particular of a given national forum. ICT weaknesses will lead to a heightened level of risks for all cyberspace users including offshoring business. When there is no adequate protection for data and systems, offshoring projects in IT and IT-enabled services are less likely to take place. The negative impact in investment decisions will depend on the risk impact level as assessed by potential investors and awareness of such weaknesses by investors. But as it can be imagined, negative reaction by the investors who make risk based investment decisions is more than likely. The reason is that investors are much more likely to be financially impacted, among other things, by lack of security safeguards for their proprietary information such as digital intellectual properties. Lack of regulatory frameworks supporting cybersecurity eventually becomes a backlash on behalf of national efforts to attract digital investors via other incentives.

c) Regulatory Responses to Cybercrime

Regulations aiming at cyberspace security are just one aspect of the possible strategic measures available to law makers to ensure cybersecurity. But such regulations are in many ways very effective in addressing issues faced by cyberspace communities. As mentioned earlier, cyber legislations in general have more deterring effects on unacceptable user behavior in cyberspace. For less serious acts in cyberspace; such as, minor copyright infringements, civil actions can be pursued by victims. In the U.S., for example, individuals, business entities, or government agencies like the Federal Trade Commission in the U.S. can go after perpetrators often with intellectual property lawsuits that usually culminate in monetary fines or restitution.

But more potent methods of deterring criminal conducts on cyberspace are needed and those methods also need more potent sanctions and enforcement mechanisms. That is, the most effective regulation in terms of again deterrence and sanctioning illegal user actions cannot be the one that does not impose sanctions, nor is any provision that does not rely on some effective enforcement mechanism. That is to say, on the one hand, there is unacceptable behavior on cyberspace that needs to be sanctioned and dissuaded by appropriate legal provisions. On the other hand, there is a need to specifically define the unacceptable/illegal behavior and address some form of punishment for the behavior, and specify how the punishment should be enforced. When we look at all categories of law, public and private, only public law, namely, the criminal jurisprudence seems to be the best and appropriate tool to effectively dissuade criminal intents even on cyberspace. The reason is obvious, i.e. the state that enforces criminal provisions has the means and power to outlaw certain behaviors, punish those behaviors, and enforce the sanctions. As a result, criminal conducts on cyberspace can be enforced with the help of substantive and procedural laws in criminal jurisprudence; such as, penal codes. A criminal statute has the ability to not only define what is unlawful or a criminal act on cyberspace, but to also impose penalties for those defined criminal conducts. Criminal law embracing cyber offences; therefore, becomes the best legal instrument that can dissuade potential offenders because it can be invoked and enforced with punishments ranging from longer jail time to big fines, to other serious inconveniences and injunctions.

The important question becomes whether nations have criminal laws in the form of statutes or case laws that are sufficient and up-to-date to cover cyber offences. The answer in most cases is in the negative. Many nations find their criminal justice system is no match for crimes in cyberspace frontiers. So there is no question that these outdated criminal laws in many parts of the globe need to be updated in some ways. Confronted with an unprecedented degree of expansion and frequency of illicit incidents in cyberspace, many legal systems have done just that, i.e. they started work on some level of overhaul in their criminal jurisprudence. National law makers in many parts of the world have been constantly responding to threats on cyberspace with cyber security regulations[255]. Surveys indicated that the focus has been on more potent and deterring measures leading to response with criminal legislation[256]. Their regulatory efforts include making sure that certain conducts they deem unlawful in cyberspace are made punishable by imprisonment and serious fines.

In the U.S., Computer Fraud and Abuse Act of 1986 was the first federal legislation that recognized certain computer based acts as a crime[257]. Other laws followed soon after including those

---

[255] For a list of countries with laws in craft or under development, see news on cybercrime legislation around the world posted on: http://www.cybercrimelaw.net/Cybercrimelaw.html, (last visited June 11, 2011).

[256] About 70% of the countries responded to a survey in between 1999 and 2001 had cybercrime legislation already enacted or in process as early as those years; See David D. Elliott & Tonya L. Putnam, International Responses to Cyber Crime, 37 (2001). But this is a good indication for a possible trend between then and now that the number must have gone much higher, meaning more countries may have by now either enacted their own legislations or ratified the European Convention on Cybercrime

intended to protect children, financial assets, and intellectual properties, among others, whereas a range of states in the U.S. have also adopted in some fashion a number of statues to outlaw similar acts committed using computers and the Internet.

The majority of the developed countries so far have enacted laws to deal with cybercrimes while many developing countries have not done so due to the fact that developing countries have many other pressing priorities that they need to confront first. On the one hand, in addition to dealing with poverty, many developing countries have other traditional crimes that needed to be prioritized. On the other hand, it is not surprising to observe such a huge gap between developed and developing countries in terms of regulating cybercrime. Economically well off countries have not only ICT capabilities that allow cybercrime to thrive, but also technical capabilities to identify and prosecute perpetrators, while countries with primitive ICT infrastructure or no ICT[258] almost do not see relevance to cybercrime in their priority list. Yet there are some other developing countries including very few in the Sub-Saharan region[259] that have either already managed or in

---

[257] See GERALD R. FERRERA ET AL., CYBER LAW: TEXT AND CASES 308 (2000).

[258] Many countries in the developing world still lack fully functional ICT while such infrastructure in some other parts of the world, e.g., parts of Africa is still in a planning phase.

[259] E.g., Kenya and South Africa have already enacted such laws, while Botswana has a draft law; see Fawzia Cassim, Formulating Specialized Legislation to address the Growing Specter of Cybercrime: A Comparative Study, PER VOLUME 12 No 4, at 65 (2009); At least other African region meanwhile attempts to address cyber crime issues with central emergency response capabilities, e.g., East African states of Uganda, Kenya, Tanzania, Rwanda and Burundi were planning to set up Computer Emergency Response Teams (CERTs) to fight cybercrime; see http://news.idg.no/cw/art.cfm?id=CBB60BB2-1A64-6A71-

process to enact cyberspace related laws to counteract cybercrimes.

Meanwhile even if poor countries lack technical capabilities and intent to prioritize cybercrime, certain cybercrimes equally thrive in developing economies as well despite primitive ICT platforms. Some cyber criminals, at least those using simple social engineering methods over the Internet continue to lure unsuspecting Internet users across the globe into divulging personal and financial information. And these criminals do not necessarily need a broad-band based ICT for committing such crimes. They do so using mere dial up Internet access. All they need is some way of sending spam emails, establishing further contacts with unsuspecting responders who get lured to divulge more personal information, and continue communication even by phone until the victim gives in and provides access to financial resources. So there is a need even in countries with low level of Internet penetration, to provide some normative coverage for cybercrimes in their criminal jurisprudence even when this countries lack technical platforms and capabilities to support investigation and attribution.

d) New Frontiers in Criminal Legislation

Regulators have been more engaged in sanctioning cyberspace conducts that they deem to be criminal offenses through cybercrime legislation. While their efforts have been

---

CEB17DB32C209CD3, (last visited June 19, 2011). Still others in Africa, in particular either did not consider such legislations at all or fail to pass one, e.g., the Nigerian legislators just rejected a far reaching law against cybercrime in April 2011; see
http://www.theregister.co.uk/2011/04/01/nigeria_cybercrime_law_fail/, (last visited June 19, 2011).

more geared to sanctioning cybercrime than addressing other aspects of cyberspace with similar laws, they quickly realize that they are now dealing with new frontiers of criminal jurisprudence. For many criminal jurisdictions, this was entirely new experience, where they have realized that there is a need to embrace new normative approaches in their criminal laws that cover crimes dealing with intangible offences in virtual space. Not only is there the need to accommodate unlawful conducts on cyberspace, but to shift away from the traditional notion of legislation. That is, they now have to embrace the idea that their existing legal norms that outlaw corporal/physical environment based offenses also include new legal frontiers that should address crimes based on intangible offenses in virtual environment[260].

Others have found that their traditional criminal statutes that are grounded in the territoriality principles either did not apply at all or were insufficient to account for unlawful cyber conducts. Hence, they faced the options of either amending existing penal codes or promulgating new sets of criminal law provisions to deal with the new cyber born criminal frontiers[261]. While some have managed to promulgate cyber laws that tend to address both cybercrime and non cybercrime (e.g. e-commerce) aspects of cyber security,[262] others have faced normative

---

[260] See GERALD R. FERRERA ET AL., CYBER LAW: TEXT AND CASES 301 (2000).

[261] Enacting new laws in many cases actually turned out to be useful because of coverage, in the absence of which law makers would have to amend every other law to account for computer or cyberspace related actions; see Ferrera, supra note 22, at 308.

[262] For instance, "Indian cyber law is primarily designed to promote e-commerce, but it has also introduced key elements of cyber deterrence"; see Lan, et al, Global Cyber Deterrence: Views from China, the U.S., Russia, India, and Norway, 9 (April 2010).

challenges in enacting laws for cyber conducts. These challenges involve both trying to exhaustively cover cyber conducts that can be elevated to criminal offense in the fastest changing technological landscape and normatively characterizing those conducts in an unequivocal manner in order to prevent unpredictable outcomes.

Meanwhile, with regard to the notion of cybercrime, there are stark differences across legal systems. But in general, what must be considered a cybercrime can be determined in two ways[263] :

(1) As stated elsewhere, cybercrime can be defined based on how computers are used to commit the act. Since computers have to be used both as a tool and target by criminals to commit certain crimes, cybercrime can be classified based on an action itself, e.g. transmitting illegal materials on a network or use of hacker tools and techniques. An example of the latter is a BotNet[264] used to launch an attack by manipulating a pool of computers and controlling them. A BotNet manipulates a network of computers that a hacker establishes to compromise the security of target systems and cause financial damages, as well as steal important information, all by using the capabilities of computing technology[265]

---

[263] For details see GERALD R. FERRERA ET AL., CYBER LAW: TEXT AND CASES 302-303 (2000). For more extensive coverage of criminal conducts on cyberspace, see Marco Gercke, International Telecommunication Union – Understanding Cybercrime: A Guide for Developing Countries, Draft, 113-166 (2009).

[264] Maybe defined as a network of infected computers centrally controlled by hacker-tools to inflict further damages on information in those computers or users; for a sample attack, see the DOJ's April 13, 2011 news release, the United States Department of Justice Bureau of Justice Statistics report, available at: http://bjs.ojp.usdoj.gov/content/pub/pdf/vit08.pdf, (last visited June 6, 2011)..

(2) Criminal offenses in cyberspace can also be determined based on the protected target (e.g. people, businesses, government, tangible, and intangible properties), where crimes are committed against these targets while computers are used just to enable these crimes. Normally, these are traditional crimes that can be committed without computers but yet computing technology maybe used to either enhance the commission of the crime by increasing the chance of evading prosecution or computers are used as alternate tools. In other words, these crimes are made more sophisticated through the use or involvement of computer technology and the Internet[266].

Regardless of how national legislators attempt to define and sanction cybercrime via regulations, it does not take long for any law maker to realize that cyber security needs a concerted effort at the global stage. Protecting digital assets, deterring criminal behaviors, and prosecuting offenders on cyberspace turns out to be more than what a given nation-state could handle alone as most cybercrimes are inherently transnational[267]. While that is the

---

[265] Such crimes can rightfully be defined as computer crimes since computers are both the tools and targets.

[266] Some offenses need more complex understanding of computers, e.g., crimes against intangible property, e.g., hacking into a database, infecting a system with a malware, while others are less complex or do not need sophisticated knowledge of computers, e.g., spamming, hate crimes, harassment. More examples see GERALD R. FERRERA ET AL., CYBER LAW: TEXT AND CASES 304-307 (2000).

[267] The Internet and cyberspace have overcome the geographical boundaries defining nation-states, hence crimes committed on this virtual space transcend national territories thereby creating challenges for law enforcement and complicating jurisdiction; for challenges on cybercrime and the need for global cooperation, see Gercke, supra note 262, at 63. "Cybercrimes are global crimes", see Schjolberg & Hubbard, International Telecommunication Union ,

case, there are also wide ranging differences among nations in susceptibility to potential vulnerability[268] as much as the gaps in what is considered a criminalized conduct and protected subject, as well as object. As a result, what may be protected or considered a criminal offence in one country may not be treated as such in another. For instance, privacy is highly regarded and protected by law in many Western societies, whereas the same may not be true in certain other parts of the world.

This discrepancy can cause problems in the intergovernmental efforts that may now be underway or take place in the future to harmonize cybercrime laws.[269]

These challenges coupled with the two most difficult problems for law enforcement in cyberspace: identification and jurisdiction[270] have made collaboration and cooperation both at

---

Harmonizing National Legal Approaches on Cybercrime WSIS Thematic Meeting on Cybersecurity, Geneva, 5 (June 28 – July 1, 2005).

[268] Some countries may be more vulnerable to cyberspace terrorism based on political or other predispositions, whereas others may be targeted for other reasons. Also some countries may be less vulnerable due to the degree of use of cyberspace based on complexities in their technology and ICT. Hence, "not surprisingly, the least computerized societies have been the slowest in passing national legislation"; see Elliott, et al., International Responses to Cyber Crime, at 51 (2001).

[269] Harmony in not only recognizing common cyberspace offences but defining those conducts is needed to better enforce laws across national boundaries. See also Gercke, supra note 262, at 79. Acceding or ratifying the Council of Europe Convention on Cybercrime is one way of overcoming these differences but enforcement may still pose a challenge; states should also create some harmony in their substantive laws by recognizing offences that are common to cyberspace; for more, see Schjolberg & Hubbard, Supra, note 313, at 10. Consensus is also need in procedural laws to enable attribution and evidence handling, as well as enforcement; for details, see Elliott, et al., International Responses to Cyber Crime, at 51 (2001).

[270] Attributing an offense to a perpetrator in cyberspace is more difficult due to

supra-national and international levels an essential part of combating cybercrimes. Cybercrimes not only continue to thrive spreading across national boundaries very easily utilizing the coalition of networks, the Internet, but the attack methodologies continue to evolve as well. The global characteristics of cybercrime along with the evolving attack landscape continue to make attribution and apprehension of perpetrators more and more elusive, especially for national law enforcement.

Many types of cyber attacks are now automated or use open and anonymously shared software products designed to make development and global spread of viruses much easier[271]. This potential prompted some to call for regional and international cooperative efforts which resulted in a few tangible multinational initiatives. Such initiatives include at least one multilateral agreement, the most notable in this regard to date being the Council of Europe's Convention on Cybercrime[272]. This agreement, albeit not adequate to fully accommodate the needs of law enforcement worldwide, serves as a milestone for being a major step towards a cybercrime convention at a global scale. This convention may serve as both a model for similar attempts at international and national levels, and as a major tool in combating cybercrime for the nations that ratify and adhere to its scope, as

---

the anonymity created by the TCP/IP building blocks and establishing personal jurisdiction over the offender is another hurdle prosecution has to overcome in pursuing cyber criminals; GERALD R. FERRERA ET AL., CYBER LAW: TEXT AND CASES 302 (2000).

[271] See Marco Gercke, International Telecommunication Union – Understanding Cybercrime: A Guide for Developing Countries, Draft, 113-166, at 83 (2009).

[272] For this and other regional conventions, see Schjolberg et al., supra note 204, at 2; The convention text is also available at: http://conventions.coe.int/Treaty/en/Treaties/Html/185.htm, (last visited June 11, 2011).

well as willing to cooperate with others.

In the context of a digital investment in an FDI setting, it must be acknowledged that there is no doubt cybercrime legislation at all levels will have some effects on investment decisions. Countering criminal offences with more potent cybercrime legislation has more deterring effects on criminals than other cyber security regulations. Therefore, investors dealing with sensitive data belonging to both customers and employees, and their own intellectual property rights will definitely see cybercrime law as more encouraging and lack of it as a threat since potential perpetrators won't be discouraged without effective criminal sanctions. Deterring cyber threats with legal means will boost investors' confidence, which in turn positively affects investment decisions, i.e. to determine whether or not to do business in a certain region or forum. Thus, other things being equal, the existence of cyber security frameworks based on deterring legal norms will have correlative effects on a country's ability to attract IT enabled FDI.

2. U.S. and EU Cyber Laws: Anti-Offshoring Implications

a) Cybersecurity Regulations in General (U.S. and EU)

The world community has a long way to go in terms of regulating cyberspace in an exhaustive manner. Yet a number of countries, especially in Western Europe and North America have promulgated various IT security related laws far more than any other part of the globe. In particular, the EU and USA appear to have dealt with cyber security related regulations more than others in an attempt to curb cyber threats increasingly targeting these regions. In the U.S., both state and federal legislators have been engaged in addressing multiple aspects of cyber security. Several U.S. states have laws dealing with cyberspace at a varying degree. Though there are variations in the level of detail and focus areas, many states have their own privacy, health information, and data security laws. States like Nevada, Oregon, and Massachusetts have laws that regulate information security at a granular level.[273]

The federal government for its part has an array of similar statutes[274], which can be divided into two broad sets; namely, those covering government data and information systems while being in some respects also applicable to private sector, and those that deal with private sector information security. In regards to government information security, there are quite a few statutes: The Computer Fraud and Abuse Act of 1986, U.S. Economic Espionage Act, Electronic Communications Privacy Act, Federal Information Security Management Act (FISMA) of 2002, Privacy Act of 1974, and so on. U.S. Electronic Funds Transfer Act, Federal Computer Fraud and Abuse Act (CFAA), Sarbanes-Oxley (SOX), Gramm-Leach-Bliley Act (GLBA), Health Insurance Portability and Accountability Act (HIPAA), and Copyright Act, just to name a few, are special regulations mostly applicable to private sector. All of these laws require cyber security compliance one way or another. But whether or not they suffice to address current and future threats in a comprehensive manner can be debated. The answer

---

[273] Randy V. Sabett , The Evolving Legal Duty to Securely Maintain Data, The (ISSA) Journal, at 14 (January 2011).

[274] See PFLEEGER ET AL., SECURITY IN COMPUTING 588 (3rd Ed., 2003) for a few more examples along with short descriptions.

may most likely be in the negative because, given the fact that these laws (both sets mentioned above) in some respects do not require private sector to adhere to certain cyber security standards[275], other than general mandates, they are not adequate to account for every aspect of security threats.

EU on its part has enacted directives[276] in the areas of data protection and electronic communication intended to be used as a model by member countries. Although there are most likely variations in terms of coverage and depth of cyber security issues, each individual country within EU also as its own sets of regulation in this regard.

b) Regulatory Protection for Personal Data and Privacy

One notable area of cyber security regulation has been personal data and privacy within the EU countries and the USA. Security for personal data and privacy in light of the digital age has seen more attention, and as such has been a subject of hotly debated regulatory agenda within both the EU and U.S. The U.S. for its part has enacted the GLBA and HIPAA largely targeting the private sector, i.e. to address personal privacy issues within the healthcare and financial institutions.

GLBA covers protection of customer data used by financial firms. Perhaps the most important aspect of this regulation is that it requires development of information security program and periodic assessment of risks to account for the protection of customer data. HIPPA, on the other hand, will protect medical

---

[275] Bierce & Kenerson, P.C, Cyber Security Threat Management in Outsourcing: The Coming National Security Regulation of ITO, BPO and KPO, available at: see www.outsourcing-law.com, (last visited July 20, 2011).

[276] Including Directives for Data Protection, ePrivacy, and Data Retention

records of patients. It is more stringent than GLBA in that it not only requires the implementation of medical data protection mechanisms based on security best practices, but it also requires similar protection by organizations, which share patient information.

One of the most visible legislations on the EU side is the Data Protection Directive that, in the meantime, has been vetted through and implemented by all 27 member countries[277]. This legislation has historic roots in Germany where Europe's first data protection law was enacted by the German federal state of Hessen in 1970s[278], which was later redefined by the German constitutional court[279]. The refined version as interpreted by the German court was later adopted throughout Europe including the enactment of the data protection directive by the EU[280]. Meanwhile, the EU's model act has emerged as more stringent in terms of personal data protection requirements reflecting EU's more protectionist approach compared to the more business friendly privacy laws of the U.S.

Only HIPAA on the U.S. side comes a bit close to the EU's data protection laws in terms of protection requirements against the use of customer/patient data by third party. HIPAA requires protection of patient data by organizations, which share patient's medical records. However, it does not require patient's express/implied permission of data sharing with business associates (doctors, laboratories, etc) as long as such sharing is for

---

[277] See Kuner, supra note 175, at 5.

[278] See Kuner, supra note 175, at 4.

[279] Federal constitutional court of Germany (Bundesverfassungsgericht), Judgment dated December 15, 1983, 65 BVerfGE 1.

[280] See Kuner, supra note 175, at 5.

treatment, billing, and/or operations. HIPAA does seem to allow such limited sharing regardless of the location patient data is shared or used. This means, unlike the data privacy law of the EU, HIPAA doesn't impose restrictions on sensitive data like patient record not to be shared with external or foreign entities when certain conditions are not met. As long as these sharing entities adhere to more liberal privacy rules, or implement standard data protection mechanisms, HIPPA doesn't prevent sharing. In other words, unlike the E.U. law which requires express consent from data subject, HIPAA doesn't make the requirements more stringent by imposing such an additional requirement for an express consent by the patient.

The EU's stringent stance has not; however, escaped criticism. The directive has been criticized for being non-conforming with the information age technology, among other things, where it tends to almost freeze in time the technological advances of the information age, which aims to make conveyance of data faster, easier, and cheaper[281]. This directive cannot fully address the question of how 'express consent' should take place in transactions involving the Internet, email, telephone, where messages containing protectable data may hub from node to node in some cases including nodes (servers, networks, etc) outside the EU purview. It is nearly impossible to control Internet based data transfer from being relayed through uncontrolled territory or without involving "privacy invading"[282] technology tools/features at every step of the information highway. Of course

---

[281] See Solveig Singleton, Privacy and Human Rights: Comparing the United States to Europe, Cato White Papers and Miscellaneous Reports, (December 1, 1999), available at: http://www.cato.org/pubs/wtpapers/991201paper.html, (last visited April 20, 2011).

[282] Id. available at: http://www.cato.org/pubs/wtpapers/991201paper.html, (last visited April 16, 2011).

EU governments conveniently made exceptions for themselves under these restrictions. So too are some other non-profit, churches, etc exempt from this law as these organizations are allowed to keep information of their members[283] without members' express consents.

Since governments and other exempted organizations are allowed to accumulate personal data and that continuously, there is no bullet proof protection even under this directive. Meaning personal data can still be exposed to external threats from even locations of these entities depending on how such data is stored or protected. And privacy is still subject to intrusions through EU government powers regardless since nothing, not even this regulation stops government control and abuse of privacy.

Meanwhile, the protectionist nature of the EU's directive is reflected in the fact that it actually requires non-EU countries to provide equivalent protection when protected data is transferred from an EU country to non-EU destinations. There seems to be a clear implication here, i.e. too consumer friendly norms cannot at the same time be business friendly. Consequently, consumers will benefit at the cost of business/investment promotion while this legislation surely has a disincentive effect on foreign investors, especially on organizations dealing with active cross-border transactions between Europe and elsewhere.

The impact is two-folds. First, offshoring companies from countries with better data protection laws will suffer less but have to abide by added, scrutinized processes/steps for obtaining express customer permission. So countries like the USA have sought to alleviate this burden for the benefit of their corporate

---

[283] Id. available at: http://www.cato.org/pubs/wtpapers/991201paper.html, (last visited April 20, 2011).

citizens with some harmonizing measures like the 'Safe Harbor' provisions, a data safety framework. The Federal Trade Commission and the European Union, as well as Switzerland have agreed upon provisions to bridge the differences among the privacy and data protection laws[284], in which eligible U.S. companies register and self-certify.

Secondly, there are those potential offshoring companies, which are most likely marginalized as they may be automatically excluded because they are out of luck or cannot rely on such equivalent protection provided by their country of origin. Not every country has such regulation or any type of enforceable policy (though highly unlikely without regulatory backing) in place.

In addition, there is inevitably a wide-ranging gab in definitions and conceptual understanding of privacy as well in privacy laws even within those that implement E.U. regulations. The same is true at the level of both sides of the Atlantic (EU and U.S.) resulting in far reaching implications for business undertakings and sometimes inevitably lengthy, more often costly litigations.

Besides, EU has enacted another directive in the area of data protection as well. This directive, also known as the Data Retention Directive, has been in effect since 2005 with the aim to help counter terrorism. It requires electronic data retention for a period of time to enable electronic discovery whenever a criminal investigation becomes necessary.

The need for coordinated investigative efforts of

---

[284] The U.S.-EU & U.S.-Swiss Safe Harbor Frameworks: http://www.export.gov/safeharbor/, (last visited June 11, 2011); Bierce & Kenerson, P.C., Privacy, Data Protection and Outsourcing in the United States: http://www.outsourcing-law.com/jurisdictions/countries/united-states-of-america/privacy-data-protection-and-outsourcing-in-the-united-states/, (last visited July 20, 2011).

international crimes including cybercrime and cyber terrorism had led to this directive. The wave of perceived terrorist threats on cyberspace, among others, often necessitates restrictions on basic human rights. Such restrictions are also justified by the so called 'escape clauses' under international human rights' treaties, where states are basically allowed to restrict fundamental human rights if circumstances warrant such an action[285]. Nevertheless, there is a tension between fundamental human rights under the more generous privacy protection norms of Art 8 European Convention on Human Rights (ECHR) on the one hand, and the new data retention directive on the other. The main challenge is the ability to strike a balance between the need to limit data retention and access to the retained data in the interest of basic human rights, specifically privacy, and investigative cooperation. For this reason, member states are urged to incorporate the proportionality principle at a minimum when implementing this directive and enforcing it[286].

All in all, the advent of this directive for EU implies a departure from the EU's own position of privacy protectionism established under its more consumer friendly Data Protection Directive of 2002.

It is not a surprise; however, that the new data retention directive has encountered some protests in its implementation. It has seen a fierce resistance from sources of human rights - as expected, and national courts. Multiple court rulings in cases involving email and telephone communications pretty much held that many aspects of electronic and telephone communications constitute privacy and are protected under the ECHR, article 8, thereby implying that the directive may violate the fundamental

---

[285] Rob van den Hoven van Gendere, Trading Privacy for Security, 96 (2007).

[286] See Hirschheim et al., supra note 57, at 13.

rights of privacy[287]. Furthermore, the implementation of this directive turned out to face more scrutiny by national constitutional courts as both the legality and implementation scheme of the directive come under courts' review. Meanwhile the German Federal Court in particular has struck down an act intended to transpose the directive as unconstitutional. The court found that the transposition law would violate the privacy of communication provided by the German basic law (*Grundgesetz*)[288].

3. Challenges of Global Cyberspace and Internet Governance

a) The Regulatory Dilemma: Ubiquitous Presence of Cyberspace Across Fragmented Jurisdictions

A recent United Nations report on the information and telecommunication recognized cybersecurity as one of the most serious challenges in the 21st century[289]. According to this report, cyber security could undermine both national and international security. The nature of cyberspace is both global and national at the same time. It is global in a sense that it is ubiquitous and available everywhere with no geographical limits because it rides on global network of ICTs. As such, it cannot be fully contained within national borders in order for national law makers to be

---

[287] Lukas Feiler, The Legality of the Data Retention Directive in Light of the Fundamental Rights to Privacy and Data Protection, in the European Journal of Law and Technology, Vol 1, Issue 3, at 8 (2010).

[288] Also known as Verfassung (constitution); for more, see Feiler, supra note 286, at 4.

[289] UN Report, 65th Session, July 2010, supra note 248, at 6.

able to successfully and reasonably regulate it. Yet, it also has national characteristics since its risk management falls for the most part under the responsibility of organizations both from private and public sectors within each country. The Nation-States also control the physical infrastructure of ICT within their borders thereby being responsible for not only the make or break of such infrastructure, but for regulating it.

The global ICT is susceptible to disruption by all sorts of actors, who have a variety of motives. For instance, there are credible indications that states are using ICTs as instruments of warfare and intelligence[290]. And although a UN report denounced such an influx of terrorist attempts as of July 2010, ICTs remain a viable target for terrorist attacks[291] as well. There is no question that given the versatility of motives and technical tools, there is always the potential for all kinds of cyber attacks at various complexity levels and scales on cyberspace.

Cyberspace, if not adequately regulated from both national and international ends, will continue to be a breeding ground for criminals, who will flourish and wreak havoc on the peaceful usage of cyberspace by legit users (both organizational and individual users).

Thus as stated earlier, on the one hand, there is a need to identify and prosecute cyber criminals internationally with whatever legal norm applicable across borders, while, on the other hand, there is a need for individual nations to contain and control criminal activities within their borders with appropriate regulations.

However, it is fair to say that while national legal regimes have the responsibility to account for pervasive cyber activities

---

[290] Id. at 7.

[291] Id. at 7.

that are part of the realm of cyberspace but taking place within their national territory, such a regulatory containment maybe nearly impossible under circumstances.

National regulations could mandate the design of security measures that are more effective to deter and control cyber security breaches at least within the national jurisdiction. Many jurisdictions have attempted to just do that, albeit with some striking difference in scope and context. But it turned out cyberspace is not an easy task for national regulators as the realm of cyberspace goes beyond national borders. As stated above, all interactions with global cyberspace in a given jurisdiction cannot be fully covered normatively by national regulations. This is due not only to the fact that technology changes much more rapidly than a keep up with regulation, but parts of such interactions with cyberspace becomes none-national almost requiring new legal regime and may not be governed by national laws. And even if regulations attempt to keep up with the need to normatively cover ever changing technological advances, their enforceability becomes questionable too due to the cross-border nature of cyberspace and lack of international cooperation.

The global nature of cyberspace allowed the Internet not to be based on or controlled by any single legal system. The lack of Internet governance coupled with the global nature of cyberspace thus led to challenges with attribution for cyber attacks, as well as an influx of jurisdictional questions for cases emanating from cyberspace. Therefore, no single national legal system alone is currently capable of addressing many issues involving the Internet[292] and cyberspace. Neither is any other source, regional or

---

[292] Christoph Engel, The Role of Law in the Governance of the Internet Preprints aus der Max-Planck-Projektgruppe: Recht der Gemeinschaftsgüter (The Law of Public Properties), Bonn, at 8 (2002).

international legal regime, currently in a position to provide a self-contained and adequate legal regime to solve cyber security issues.

b) Lack of Regulatory Standards for Cybersecurity

Existing legal frameworks affecting cyberspace generally dictate the nature of cyber security policies and standards. Simply put, security standards tend to reflect applicable policies just as policies reflect governing regulatory landscape. However, the global diversity in regulations can easily be a good source of stark variances in policy frameworks, which in turn affect the development and content of cyber security standards. It is generally true that security policies can impact standards as policies proscribe security compliance norms and user behaviors that tend to specify scope in standards. But new policies can also take advantage of more established standards to specify better and more effective policy statements. Security standards can be inherited from security best practices while such best practices may be influenced by other sources. These sources are often based on more established nations and intra- or international organizations, all of which are subject to different regulatory and policy schemes. However, such inheritance will, in turn, hinge on existing legal and policy statements, in which case the policies and legal provisions may or may not allow such inheritance.

Governments often prefer to come up with their own standards, rather than importing one from another country[293] and it is not totally unusual that some jurisdictions may disallow all or

---

[293] See Charlie Kaufman et al., Network Security; Private Communication in a Public World, 34 (2002).

parts of even commonly used standards. So if for whatever reason no adoption of external standards is allowed (rare but can happen) or no legal or policy based cyber security regime exists, then, the only option for organizations in this legal system is establishing an ad hoc but non-binding standard internally, i.e. at an organization level. But with no legal or policy mandate, essentially there won't be enforceable provisions for both government and non-government entities. Hence, there is much weaker adherence to cybersecurity standards and; therefore, weak or total lack of protection for sensitive information in this particular scenario. Consequently, even if there are proactive organizations that may shop for commonly applied standards and best practices outside and implement those within their organization, not everyone will be doing the same because there is no mandate to do so. This leads to the situation, where those who are not willing to do more for the security posture of their systems or network enclaves, or unaware of the need to do so will remain to be the weakest link in the scheme of things. This weakness will eventually cross the national boundary and spill over to the realm of cyberspace thereby affecting more participants on the global cyberspace.

Furthermore, not every legislator has similar concerns or priorities when it comes to cyberspace. Indeed, not every legal regime is on the same page when it comes to understanding the notion of cybersecurity. They lack the urgency for safeguarding their ICT and either misunderstand or are ignorant of concepts behind what needs to be protected from whom, and how or why. For instance, privacy could mean just about anything within different socio-cultural settings. At a minimum, it could mean either personal privacy, data privacy, or both depending on how it is understood or interpreted in a given forum. This kind of understanding may be influenced by social, cultural, and religious pre-disposition, as well as ideological orientation of a society. Personal privacy may not be given as much weight as some other information subjects and objects in one culture and vice versa in another. Or for that matter the need for cybersecurity may not be as important for one society as it is for another, and so on.

A UN report on the status of ICT has indicated that the "varying degrees of ICT capacity and security among different States increases the vulnerability of the global network"[294]. The same report confirmed the fact that variations in national laws and security practices may hamper efforts that may be underway to achieve a secure and resilient cyberspace. Recognizing such possible setbacks, few international organizations have been attempting to boost cybersecurity awareness among nations with appropriate standards and common practices, as well as to help harmonize disparities in cybersecurity measures. For instance, the International Telecommunication Union – Telecommunication Standardization Sector (ITU-T) has put together cyber security recommendations/standards that can be adhered to or implemented by member nations[295]. However, many countries have remained uninterested in these standards either because of the weakness in their ICT level of complexity or because they are behind in crafting legal and policy frameworks addressing cybersecurity. The technology factor is true for developing economies, but as far as the lag in implementing workable legal frameworks is concerned, another factor maybe at play. The slow pace in adherence to more established standards can also be attributed to lack of political will by governments. Or these

---

[294] UN Report, 65th Session, July 2010, supra note 248, at 7.

[295] International Telecommunication Union – Telecommunication Standardization Sector (ITU-T), Recommendation ITU-T X.1205, 4/2008.

countries may still have outdated legal practices, where their overall legal systems desperately needing an overhaul of some sort and level. Especially when the underlying legal system needs some systemic changes in every aspect to include courts, legislative processes, and enforcement, then there will be little or no room for a cyber law in particular when this law will have to comprehensively address use and governance aspects in their ICT. Even if this kind of law is slated to or even managed to be enacted in some fashion, with the underlying weakness in legal practices, the new law will surely remain on paper. In the end cyberspace remains less secure and unreliable thanks to this discrepancy in legal standards, among other things.

Clearly, some legal systems become far behind in catching up with technology born legal concerns to be able to regulate unwanted cyberspace phenomena while others are ahead but not quite in the best position to account for events taking place beyond their territories. These discrepancies eventually create uncertainty for businesses and may even pave the way for restrictions in global economic activities[296]. Ultimately, all these factors contribute to non-standard approaches in legal and policy frameworks.

Finally, just as there are uncertainty and disparity in terms of developing, applying, or adhering to certain industry standards to help establish a resilient cybersecurity across national boundaries, there is uncertainty among businesses to engage in investment activities at offshore locations. Clearly, lack of forum

---

[296] Nonexistence of data protection mechanisms or requirements mandating such protection could be unsettling for cross-border investors that deal with sensitive data about individuals, which is protected by home country laws (e.g., EU's data protection laws). Thus, non-protection may dissuade potential businesses from investment engagements. For details, see Kuner, supra note 175, at 4.

legal and policy frameworks that are supposed to foster acceptable cybersecurity practices by mandating adherence to established minimum standards are the reason why we see disparity in implementing acceptable security practices. There is little doubt that weakness in adherence to security best practices can prevent IT firms from taking IT outsources tasks. For example, a potential client who wants to outsource IT tasks abroad to an IT firm could be scared away if the firm has this weakness. Similarly, weaker regulatory frameworks that do not take into account global market demands for IT offshoring have discouraging effects on IT related FDI. So do ineffective policy provisions that do not embrace global standards. These policies too overlook important factors for creating competitive macro-economic conditions in a given investment destination, and, hence have negative effects on offshore IT investments.

B. *Adverse Effects of Policy and Legal Frameworks on IT Offshoring*

1. Governmental Control over Offshoring and Consequences

a) Conflict Between Host Cyber Security Laws and Investment Incentives

i. *Sarbanes-Oxley Regulation in the U.S.*

Some regulations that are supposed to address certain business conducts of the corporate world sometimes end up producing unwanted results with regard to the same entities that are subject to such laws. In a few other cases, the same legal provisions may result in negative spillover effects on other unintended business entities. The Sarbanes Oxley Act of 2002 (SOX) appears to be one such law at least with regard to direct effects on corporate entities, but with unexpected outcomes.

Notably, the SOX law was enacted with the intention that it fixes the internal control flaws causing inaccurate corporate financial reporting. Internal control flaws would allow corporations to produce overstated or understated financial data. This can be done with the aim to either overstate profits thereby causing a bubble in company shares or understate profits to increase non-taxable net earnings. So, the SOX act is intended to prevent corporations from cooking the books. The lessons learned from corporate scandals in the past few years[297] have led to this regulation, and the law primarily targets the protection of share holders.

Illegal accounting practices by some corporate entities as has been observed over the years harm investors more than any other stakeholders in those firms. The reason is that inaccurate financial reporting with sometimes false or exaggerated earnings galvanize more investments (more sales in stocks), which, when the stock bubble bursts, in turn more than likely leads to loss in investment assets for investors. Once the deficiency is detected and disclosed, shareholders begin to panic, which more often results in a stock sell-off. An inevitable outcome would be a market crash, i.e. stocks of the affected firm plunge with the consequence that stock holders lose all or most of their investment stakes.

But before delving into the analysis of the perceived impact

---

[297] The financial scandals that led to the debacle of Enron and Worldcom, which resulted in the need to toughen oversight of corporate accounting and financial reporting, are a good example.

of Sections 404 and 302 of the Act on FDI, it is important to look into its effects on non-FDI investments that have been discussed by many in the legal as well as business literature[298]. It must be noted that FDI, particularly offshoring service FDI, as defined elsewhere in this discourse, ordinarily occurs when an entity from one country goes offshore to do business in the form of capital investment and provide services with its physical presence in another country. Typically, such an engagement involves an active management of the FDI business process in the foreign destination. Active involvement in the management structure of the business distinguishes FDI from an indirect foreign investment, notably portfolio investment.

The latter is still mistakenly categorized as FDI as well, when a multinational corporation (MNC) buys over 10% shares of an enterprise in a foreign country[299]. However, a share ownership like this alone should not constitute an FDI unless there is a significant shift in management structure as well for the benefit of the MNC. That is the MNC must control the enterprise's management to consider its 10% or more share itself as an FDI. This distinction is necessary here with respect to the categories of affected firms by the SOX legislation from the U.S. point of view. The rationale is that, even though this regulation may have had adverse effects on both business undertakings by national firms

---

[298] Trends in the foreign corporate listings on the U.S. exchange markets before and after the SOX regulation have been a subject of a variety of discussions in recent literary sources; see studies conducted including some statistics by Joseph D. Piotroski & Suraj Srinivasan, Regulation and Bonding: The Sarbanes-Oxley Act and the Flow of International Listings, (January 2008); and Peter Iliev, The Effect of SOX Section 404: Costs, Earnings Quality and Stock Prices (2008).

[299] Leon Trakman, Foreign Direct Investment- An Australian Perspective, 34 (January 23, 2010). UNSW Law Research Paper No. 2010-4, available at: SSRN: http://ssrn.com/abstract=1540289, (last visited December 10, 2011).

and portfolio/FDI engagements by foreign firms in the U.S., the nature of the impact on both categories is different.

Meanwhile, with regard to current studies related to SOX, neither FDI nor portfolio investment related findings could be relied upon compared to an overwhelming study sources related to the U.S. stock market listings by foreign firms. That is, when it comes to potential impact of section 404 on foreign investors, a majority of available study findings are rather more geared to stock market listings of foreign firms, rather than FDI oriented undertakings per se in the U.S. In other words, studies assessing SOX impact as it relates to exchange market listings are widely available compared to similar studies associated with SOX impact on FDI engagements in the U.S.

However, these sources and their findings can equally be indicative of the overall corporate reactions occurred after this legislation came into effect, which could also be analogized with respect to FDI elasticity.

Observations in those non-FDI studies suggest that SOX rules have been seen to negatively impact U.S. portfolio listings by foreign firms. In particular, studies targeting corporate behavior associated with the U.S. exchange market pre- and post SOX regulation indicated that this Act increased costs associated with the expected reporting and potential legal, as well as regulatory compliances of portfolio listings by publicly traded companies[300]. An exception to this tendency was evidenced in the fact that some 'quality' corporations actually preferred credibility despite subjecting themselves to stricter forum rules to countries with weaker legal frameworks. These so-called quality firms continue to list or did so anew after such stricter rules of SOX came to exist[301]

---

[300] Joseph D. Piotroski & Suraj Srinivasan, Regulation and Bonding: The Sarbanes-Oxley Act and the Flow of International Listings, 2 (January 2008).

. While few quality firms sought reliable legal platforms and chose the U.S. exchange market even compared to competing forums but based on net benefit, it has been observed that the U.S. listing after the Act has declined overtime. This finding suggests that the SOX Act has nonetheless an overall negative impact on the U.S. exchange listing (indirect investments) by foreign firms.

The same conclusion can be drawn with regard to foreign publicly traded firms having FDI presence in the U.S., where these firms too may have been equally impacted with regulatory compliance effects of the SOX Act. In reality there is nothing that prevents the same stricter compliance requirements and cost generating factors stemming from this legislation from being imposed on FDI. While FDI presence may be associated with incentives that could allow firms to offset the SOX impact, nothing prevents SOX rules from having similarly adverse effects on FDI in the U.S. The possible explanation for this argument can be drawn based on the applicability of SOX itself. Sections 302 and 404 generally apply to all publicly traded corporations within the U.S. which are subject to SEC reporting requirements[302] with the exception of a few non-publicly traded entities like the United States Postal Service, which chose to be subject to SOX. So there is the possibility that publicly traded firms include those that have FDI presence in the U.S., and all of these firms are equally subjected to the requirements under this law.

As far as the real effects of SOX are concerned, two major requirements drive the compliance efforts for public corporations with FDI presence. The main components of SOX requirements are disclosure controls under sections 302 and 404, and assessment, as well as disclosure of internal controls over

---

[301] Id. at 3.

[302] Id. at 8.

financial statements.

As anticipated, SOX increases the level of audit scrutiny in corporate financial practices, and the essence of such audits is the question of compliance with SOX itself. From the auditing point of view, SOX has changed the landscape of audit assertion and reporting in two ways thereby helping drive audit cost high[303].

First, SOX requires that the reporting firm's management certifies its financial report thereby assuming the responsibility for the validity and effectiveness of the internal controls in place to support the accounting records and financial reports. This aspect of the regulation actually added another scare for corporate CEOs or CFOs, or both. The reason is that they now can be held accountable for any financial misstatements caused by deficiencies in internal controls which they certify based on their assertion (also known as *'in control statements'*[304]) that they have evaluated the effectiveness of those controls. This requirement may increase the potential for legal liability of corporate leaders, and as such could be another impediment factor for foreign Companies.

Secondly, section 404 requires an auditor of the financial report to express an opinion on the management's evaluation of the effectiveness of the internal controls. The central compliance factor of section 404 requirement is the certification of the effectiveness of the internal controls. Both management and auditors need to make sure internal controls are not only in place but effective, i.e. working as they are supposed to in order to

---

[303] Hollis Ashbaugh-Skaife et al., The Effect of SOX Internal Control Deficiencies on Firm Risk and Cost of Equity, 9 (June 10, 2008).

[304] In control means that the organization has a well functioning internal control system that can be reline upon for accurate financial reporting, see Christine Bruinsma & Peter Wemmenhove, Tone at the Top is Vita! A Delphy Study, in the ISACA Journal, Volume 3, 40 (2009).

mitigate or eliminate financial reporting frauds.

Internal controls involve both computer and non-computer based safeguards. Information assurance plays a major role with respect to computer based controls and that is where IT security controls and their audit come in. Security controls if correctly implemented in a financial system ensure, among others, that there is accountability through traceability and a separation of duties, which is often an issue with financial transactions. These controls also ensure that financial data at rest or in transit is secure. While audit controls make sure that user actions and transactions on financial systems are traceable, IT security audits under SOX look into the existence and effectiveness of all security controls within systems that are involved in maintaining financial records and reporting.

The SOX provisions are mostly concerned with financial systems, that directly or indirectly process, store, and transmit financial data[305]. For this reason, SOX auditors spend lots of time to understand business process, identify system components, as well as controls in place or stated as implemented. Controls are identified, reviewed, verified, and tested for effectiveness. The outcome of such scrutiny is what the auditors will sign off on and also what the CEO and CFO may rely on to avoid legal liability. And such an audit report is also what the corporate leadership relies on to comply with the essence of the SOX regulation despite the elevated cost factor of audit exercises. The same report can be relied on for making further financial and marketing decisions by shareholders to assess financial situation of the firm and its internal control strength or weakness.

---

[305] Subject to additional controls scrutiny like FISCAM based general and application level controls audit, for instance, within the U.S. government agencies.

As stated earlier, both sections 302 and 404 requirements apply to public companies; such as, multinationals, which have a U.S. presence also in the form of an IT service FDI. They are equally subjected to the internal control evaluation and disclosure of material weaknesses, among others, under this regulation. The cost of compliance with the Internal Control Disclosure (ICD) procedure under section 404, in particular, is high for large offshoring service FDI firms in the U.S. as well. Therefore, the overall implication and possible conclusion that can be drawn from this scenario is that a foreign direct investor in the U.S. too may be discouraged by the SOX regulation as the cost of compliance weighs more than the benefit of investing and doing business.

That being said; however, unlike non FDI multinationals in the U.S., which are only involved in stock market listings, foreign FDI counterparts may offset SOX impacts with other benefits. That means even though ICD requirements are said to have negative impacts in terms of cost of compliance, foreign direct investors in the U.S. have other advantages over their counterparts which are just stock-market listed. These advantages could turn out to set those with FDI presence in the U.S. apart from non FDI multinationals in terms of net benefits.

One of such benefits as some have argued would come from the linkage between trade and investment. This linkage results in an increase in positive trade balance for foreign multinationals due to potentially high affiliate sales in the U.S. market[306]. Generally, foreign multinational direct investors utilize the foreign affiliates as a platform for sales of service products locally and in the form of exports, but these service products may come from

---

[306] See Catherine L. Mann, Offshore Outsourcing and the Globalization of U.S. Services: Why Now, How Important, and What Policy Implications? - In the United States and World Economy, at 291 (undated).

either local production facility (e.g. software programming center in the forum) or from their home or other international subsidiary locations. It is suggested that depending on market forces (potentials) and benefits, foreign parent companies may use the U.S. market more for tapping into domestic market while cutting back on export options[307]. In other words, they would use the host market for selling both locally produced and imported service products or intermediate imports.

The host market access would allow the parent investor to enable and promote affiliate sales locally more so than looking into options for exporting service products from the host location. Multinationals generally tend to take advantage of host market and increase sales if the market is attractive enough and profitable. In doing so, for the U.S. forum, multinationals increase their net benefits thereby offsetting costs caused by regulatory requirements like SOX and other overhead cost-factors.

Besides, foreign multinational direct investors in the U.S. are said to add less value in terms of FDI value as they have a high share of affiliate sales and intra-firm trade in the U.S. compared to their U.S. counterparts elsewhere[308]. Hence, such an increased use of investment platforms solely for purposes of domestic sales has an added side effect from the macro-economic standpoint. By way of an intra-firm trade between a parent and an affiliate, the parent eludes an export oriented FDI presence, which of course many developing countries hope for and expect from FDIs in their territories in an attempt to often stabilize trade deficits.

In the case of the U.S. too, thus, such an FDI ends up contributing little or none to export market with ultimate negative implications for the balance of trade, and consequently

---

[307] Id. at 292.

[308] Id.

for the overall U.S. macro-economy as well.

In sum, while there is a negative overall impact of SOX on all publicly traded firms with foreign origin, some foreign FDI investors on the U.S. soil tend to offset the cost of the SOX compliance with the potentially huge benefit of tapping into domestic market. This is possible as these firms can strategically align their U.S. engagement with a market oriented FDI business process. Overall; however, evidence suggests that the cost of compliance with SOX can more likely scares away firms, both FDI and non-FDI based investors, which do not have net cost benefits in doing business in the U.S.

ii.   *Privacy Regulations and Cost of Compliance (U.S. vs. EU)*

In addition to wide-ranging gaps in conceptual understanding of privacy, both EU and U.S. have rules that appear to favor either consumer or businesses. The personal data protection rules as enacted reflect the EU's consumer friendly stance, but not so for businesses compared to the privacy laws of the U.S. Not surprisingly the EU's data protection model law has been criticized for being too stringent when it comes to cross-border personal data processing by transnational entities.

As mentioned earlier, only HIPPA, on the U.S. side, appears to approach consumer protection in a little more strict manner, but not as strict as the EU's directives. Other U.S. privacy regulations are said to be more business friendly while these regulations tend to leave consumers to some extent in a limbo. There are essentially more wiggling rooms left for businesses in the U.S. when it comes to processing and transferring of personal data including PII. Hence online behavioral advertisers and most recently even phone companies have started to vacuum up consumers' sensitive information with no restriction and sell this data for huge profits[309].

The U.S. privacy laws also seem to have left courts struggle with the problem of determining harm when privacy breach is claimed. Several court rulings[310] support this tendency suggesting that businesses can own personal information belonging to data subjects and transfer or sell the same to third parties, and yet could not be held accountable as long as there is no visible damage, harm, or humiliation. In *Smith v. Chase Manhattan Bank*[311] , where the bank was sued in a class action for selling customer data to third parties, for instance, the court was looking for actual damage in the person of the claimant, instead of the security

---

[309] See Solveig Singleton, Privacy and Human Rights: Comparing the United States to Europe, Cato White Papers and Miscellaneous Reports, (December 1, 1999), available at: http://www.cato.org/pubs/wtpapers/991201paper.html, (last visited April 20, 2011). For details regarding the dilemma faced by the internet users on behavior based data mining and advertising, see Richard M. Marsh, Jr., Legislation for Effective Self-Regulation: A New Approach to Protecting Personal Privacy on the Internet, 15 Mich. Telecomm. Tech. L. Rev. 543, at 550 (2009). Phone companies in U.S. have started cashing in on their customer data and there seems to be no regulation to stop them from doing that. The type of information they have and can collect about each customer allows pinpointing customer's likes and dislikes based on web browsing habit, whereabouts, and even exact location at a given point in time. This allows efficiency in targeted advertisement. Hence it is a lucrative marketing strategy for both data collectors and buyers like small businesses. Verizon even changed its privacy policy more recently to benefit from such marketing; See David Goldman, Your phone company is selling your personal data, available at: http://money.cnn.com/2011/11/01/technology/verizon_att_sprint_tmobile_priva cy/index.htm?iid=HP_River, (last visited November 11, 2011).

[310] Daniel J. Solove, "I've Got Nothing to Hide" and Other Misunderstandings of Privacy, 769 (2007).

[311] See Smith v. Chase Manhattan Bank, 741 N.Y.S.2d 100 (N.Y. App. Div. 2002); see Solove, id. at 770.

breach itself or security interest of the plaintiffs. The court stated that such disclosure only affected confidentiality or breach of such. And confidentiality does not necessarily involve any emotional distress. Instead, according to the court, such a disclosure could only result in loss of trust. As a result, the court rejected the claim since the plaintiffs could not prove actual damages or personal injuries in any one of the class action members.

Some scholars believe that such court conclusions may have been the result of non-regulatory course of action by the judiciary, for example, due to setting a precedent by recognizing personal data as private property in court rulings[312]. Courts' own position to treat personal data as a commodity where third parties are allowed to own this data could have caused this confusion by eventually contributing to strikingly inadequate protection of consumer privacy by the same courts. One way such a derailment of the possibility for legitimate injunction could be prevented is through regulatory restriction of buying and selling personal data without subjects' consent. This could allow a victim of personal data breach to seek remedy through civil action or tort.

The U.S. stance on personal data, except with respect to medical records, is strikingly lenient when it comes to protecting consumers or data subjects. In the end, unfortunately, the U.S. legal system in its current format, like that of many other

---

[312] Richard M. Marsh, Jr., Legislation for Effective Self-Regulation: A New Approach to Protecting Personal Privacy on the Internet, 15 Mich. Telecomm. Tech. L. Rev. 543, at 550 (2009). The opposite argument is that privatizing privacy, which is a fundamental human right, makes it easier to legitimize data collection and exploitation as individuals may negotiate and usually allow such data treatment; see Richard M. Marsh, Jr., Legislation for Effective Self-Regulation: A New Approach to Protecting Personal Privacy on the Internet, 15 Mich. Telecomm. Tech. L. Rev. 543, at 551 (2009).

countries, is not adequate to protect personal data and privacy.

The EU's data directive, on the other hand, provides consumers with more ammunition while arguably hurting business community. From the compliance point of view, this has far reaching implications, especially for business entities dealing with active cross-border transactions.

In particular, the data protection directive imposes restrictions on data processing and transfer thereby granting data subjects more protection at the cost of, especially business to business transactions[313].

The processing restriction has two implications at a minimum.

First offshoring companies are not free in handling their customer personal data, i.e. they are required to perform extra precaution including obtaining explicit permissions from the subject before doing anything with the customer data.

Secondly, transfer to any other destination outside the EU will depend on the destination's adherence to the EU's strict protection standards and, thus these destinations will undergo further scrutiny or could entirely be excluded. This measure will result in some offshoring firms being automatically excluded *ipso facto* as they may not have equivalent regulations within their home countries. Even when home countries have some privacy laws, many firms cannot fully comply with the directive since their home country laws cannot meet certain aspects of the EU requirements, hence these firms cannot fully rely on anything to prove that the data they want to process/transfer will be safe at destination.

---

[313] Jeff Collmann, Managing Information Privacy & Security in Healthcare European Union Privacy Directive Reconciling European and American Approaches to Privacy, Healthcare Information and Management Systems Society, 1 (January 2007).

Many view this directive as a threat to business transactions since firms regularly transfer personal data around the globe in the normal course of their business transactions and such transfer often in the areas of trade, clinical research, and routine human resource management is inevitable[314]. These routine business dealings are underpinned by the exchange of personal information. Therefore, the inability to use such information will arguably severely undermine offshore transactions. All of this can be a challenge for offshore businesses in terms of time and resources when attempting to process and transfer customer data to a destination outside the EU.

Most importantly, the fact that businesses are subject to such stringent scrutiny with respect to the requirements to follow added steps for data transfer leads to more transactional costs. The overall implication is that offshoring entities have less of an incentive to do business under such regulation, especially when doing so would otherwise affect their bottom line, their profit. Global market place demands competitive advantages and companies grappling with such stringent requirements could easily see their competitiveness being eroded. Thus, this directive remains to be one of the EU's regulations that tend to deter offshoring rather than promote doing business in Europe.

To alleviate the burden of restrictions and costs, U.S. business community has resorted to another approach, which is essentially applying an additional step and voluntarily undergoing a certification process to achieve 'adequacy' status for data transfer. This process as mentioned before has come to be known

---

[314] "A finding of inadequacy jeopardizes all these transactions when personal data must flow from the EU to the United States", see Jeff Collmann, Managing Information Privacy & Security in Healthcare European Union Privacy Directive Reconciling European and American Approaches to Privacy, Healthcare Information and Management Systems Society, 4 (January 2007).

as 'Safe Harbor certification'. It is designed to facilitate the transfer of personal information to the U.S. [315], while providing some assurance to an extent possible to European parties or consumers involved.

The U.S. side too is not free from cost of regulatory compliance when it comes to privacy in business undertakings involving private data. The U.S. regulatory frameworks maybe lenient in terms of guarding personal data and privacy against the market place, but the fact that there are multiple layers of rules and regulations may have led under circumstances to 'over compliance'. The over-compliance comes from the fear to overlook one or more of the multiple layers of regulations in the United States, which leads to over investment in security mechanisms, as some have argued[316]. This could be true particularly in the healthcare field and could also be the case in privacy sphere in general within other business sectors.

As stated earlier, both states and federal government have enacted privacy laws to address various aspects of personal privacy in general and health information, in particular.

Many healthcare providers have sought to protect themselves from lawsuits by requiring permissions from patients

---

[315] Became effective in 2000 after years of negotiations and was developed by the U.S. Department of Commerce in consultation with the European Commission, see Collmann, supra note 314, at 5; also see The U.S.-EU & U.S.-Swiss Safe Harbor Frameworks: http://www.export.gov/safeharbor/, (last visited July 2, 2011); also Bierce & Kenerson, P.C., Privacy, Data Protection and Outsourcing in the United States, available: http://www.outsourcing-law.com/jurisdictions/countries/united-states-of-america/privacy-data-protection-and-outsourcing-in-the-united-states/, (last visited April 27, 2011).

[316] Daniel J. Gilman and James C. Cooper, There Is a Time to Keep Silent and a Time to Speak, the Hard Part is Knowing Which is Which: Striking the Balance Between Privacy Protection and the Flow of Health Care Information, 16 Mich. Telecomm. Tech. L. Rev. 279, at 331 (2010).

for every aspect of treatments. For instance, they require patients to explicitly allow disclosure of personal health information for treatment, billing, and health care operations. Such a consent requirement has been generally seen as an attempt to manage risks posed by possible lawsuits for not abiding by any of those clear and ambiguous laws that may apply to them one way or another. This can drive administrative cost for healthcare providers high and ultimately increase their overhead cost.

The cost factor could also play a role for other business sectors such as banks. Banking sector has to also comply with privacy laws at multiple levels, some of which are vague but could trigger unexpected liability or fines for non-compliance[317]. The Graham-Leach-Bliley Act of 1999 is the latest privacy regulation within the U.S. which imposes requirements on business entities dealing with personal and credit data of individuals. It requires, among other things, that each financial institution complies with the following three privacy rules while transacting with customers: namely, a) notification of customers about its privacy policy, b) full disclosure of circumstances under which customer data will be shared with third parties, and c) providing customers with an option to allow or not to allow such disclosure and sharing of data, so-called opt-in/out notification. This regulation gives the Federal Trade Commission (FTC) the authority to police and enforce this law. However, when it comes to privacy breaches or claims thereof by individual consumer, FTC can only get involved if

---

[317] That for example is the case with ambiguous state laws that under circumstances could trigger breach notification. But since it is unclear as to what exactly should take place for such notifications organizations may end over notifying their customers or patients. See Daniel J. Gilman and James C. Cooper, There Is a Time to Keep Silent and a Time to Speak, the Hard Part is Knowing Which is Which: Striking the Balance Between Privacy Protection and the Flow of Health Care Information, 16 Mich. Telecomm. Tech. L. Rev. 279, at 332 (2010).

the consumer files a valid complaint. Oftentimes consumers do not bother going that route. Notice that this law does not prevent a financial institution from sharing consumer data with their close affiliates, which could be all other banks and business entities that the institution does business with. Of course, the opt in/out option often goes unnoticed by customers even when they are asked to respond to notices because a lot of customers do not respond, in which case banks simply assume customers' permission and proceed with sharing customer data anyway.

Banks and other financial institutions that need to comply with these privacy and personal financial data rules under the Graham-Leach-Bliley Act may fear consequences of non-compliance with these, as well as any other unknown yet applicable provisions. The pressure to avoid sanctions leads to the need to invest in costly resources that must meet stringent compliance processes by these institutions. That is, these multifaceted rules will make them overly cautious, where these organizations could end up spending more money in information assurance programs, among others.

The compliance requirements in this regard could carry consequences for foreign investors in U.S. as well. Efforts to comply with privacy rules could drive the cost of doing business in the U.S. for those involved. Seen from a different angle, an offshore investor; such as, a foreign healthcare service provider wanting to do business in the U.S. would have to think twice before engaging in any business undertaking due to the added cost and may even be scared away. If potential investors are discouraged due to cost of legal compliance, as well as fear of liabilities derived from these rules, it means that these regulations are actually harming in some ways both home country businesses and foreign investors in the U.S.

b) Extraterritorial Implications of National Cyber Laws

i. *Extraterritorial Reach of National Laws in General*

Legal practice has proven that some national laws may find extraterritorial *de jure* or *de facto* application either by default or choice. This is especially true in the digital age where cyberspace allows actors and victims, as well as actions and consequences to be spread around the globe. Laws enacted to regulate certain conducts or aspects of transactions on cyberspace nationally can have global implications. The same is true with enforcing judgments in so far as a foreign subject/defendant is concerned, i.e. judicial judgments entered nationally but seeking international recognition and enforcement can have transnational consequences as well. Therefore, extraterritorial implication of law can be observed in terms of enacted legal norms applicable to non-residents and non-national entities, and judicial jurisdiction, where judicial judgments tend to contain *res judicata* effects across-borders.

Some legal norms while intended to regulate personal and corporate conducts inside a given national border may have an impact outside national borders, and vice versa. Some laws have the objective to directly address conducts by a foreign person (juridical or natural persons). The United States and other countries have laws with similar effects. With respect to the U.S., specifically, there are not only laws intended for domestic subjects yet have extraterritorial effects, but laws enacted with foreign subjects in mind entirely and so directly applicable to non U.S. residents. In fact, with regard to many cyberspace events, the U.S. is said to unilaterally approach issues by imposing hegemonic sanctions across cyberspace[318]. Other U.S. laws, which may or may not have impacts on cyberspace, but directly impact foreign entities/individuals include the Foreign Corrupt Practices Act, Alien Tort Claims Act, the Export Administration Act, and the International Trade in Arms Regulations. All of these implied or purely extraterritorial laws have relevance in terms of applicability overseas to offshoring service FDI of U.S. origin.

These and other not purely extraterritorial laws are more inclined to expand U.S. courts' extraterritorial jurisdiction with a lasting implication for parties involved in cross-border legal disputes including investors. The U.S. is generally known for its extraterritorial reach with legislation, but the fact that courts also tend to extend their jurisdiction through judicial precedent beyond the U.S. territory in turn appears to inundate their dockets with potential cases coming from around the globe.

The Supreme Court case in *Morrison v. National Australia Bank* [319] related to Section 10(b) of the 1934 Securities and Exchange Act exemplifies this. The U.S. Federal Circuit Court had

---

[318] See Christoph Engel, The Role of Law in the Governance of the Internet, Preprints aus der Max-Planck-Projektgruppe: Recht der Gemeinschaftsgüter, 13 (Bonn 2002).

[319] Morrison v. National Australia Bank, where the plaintiffs had purchased shares of National Australia Bank (NAB) in Australian securities markets, but sued NAB in federal court in New York under Section 10(b) alleging, inter alia, that NAB had misrepresented to shareholders its exposure to bad mortgages in a Florida subsidiary. See Wulf A. Kaal & Richard W. Painter, Extraterritorial Application of U.S. Securities Law – Will the U.S. become the Default Jurisdiction for European Securities Litigation? 6 (August 24, 2010). Also available at SSRN: http://ssrn.com/abstract=1664809, (last visited January 12, 2012).

adopted one of the most frequently used approaches known as 'conducts and effects' test. This test has not only been inconsistently applied, but also provided wrong impressions as far as the extent of jurisdiction (*in personam* and subject matter) is concerned. Section 10(b) applies to the question of jurisdiction with regard to cases from around the world. The conducts and effects test may have given a false impression to the Australian plaintiffs as well in the above Supreme Court case involving all Australian parties. Part of the motivation on the plaintiffs' side of the case like this could be attributed to lack of class action laws for securities in non-U.S. jurisdictions. While this case exhibits some similarity to the so called 'foreign cubed'[320] cases, perhaps there is an element of forum shopping as well since plaintiffs' motive may have been higher judgments or more lucrative settlements.

Morrison v. National Australia Bank involved an allegation for fraudulent securities transactions that took place in Australia, pretty much with no connection whatsoever with the U.S. forum jurisdiction other than the alleged U.S. participant, the Florida subsidiary of the Australian defendant. However, the subsidiary's participation did not pass the conducts and effects test because of the fact that buying and selling of the securities took place outside the U.S. When the history of this act was later analyzed, it was determined that the entire case fell outside the scope of the Act.

A group of lawyers and legal scholars later did an *amicus curiae*[321] intervention requesting the Supreme Court to narrowly interpret the conducts and effects test. The court ended up looking at the case and eventually struck down the entire case. The argument for dismissing this case and preventing the court

---

[320] Id.

[321] Id. at 3.

system from being flooded by cases from around the world was based on the historical analysis of the intent of the legislation itself by the Congress, which arguably never wanted to expand the applicability of this law[322]. The point is there are laws that have extraterritorial effects regardless of whether such provisions are originally intended to have these effects.

Clearly, the intended or unintended foreign reach of national laws can carry unwanted implications with respect to transnational business entities and foreign legal systems. The question of expanding legal applicability with regard to the impact on offshore investment can better be addressed by looking at specific legislations. Generally laws governing cyberspace tend to be exported to other jurisdictions for practical reasons. That is to say, if a protection is afforded by national law but the same is lacking elsewhere, and the security breach to a home investor takes place elsewhere, there is a question as to whether protecting home country legal norms need to come to the victim's rescue. While such a need based extraterritorial expansion may be necessary, it will almost always result in a jurisdictional and/or diplomatic collusion. But the expansion in this case can only be reasonable if there are no legal and jurisdictional conflicts, and neither any other legal recourse nor protection mechanisms exist.

From both the U.S. and EU perspectives, there are cyberspace laws not necessarily geared towards just extraterritorial entities, but towards both residents and non-residents, thereby being good candidates for export and application abroad by default. These laws appear to be resorted to regardless of the potential for tension between national (U.S. or EU) and foreign laws[323] applicable to cyberspace.

---

[322] Id.

[323] Such tension exists usually due to legislative jurisdictions also known as

A good example is the EU's data protection law that not only requires implementation of similar data protection mechanisms for EU subjects pretty much anywhere around the world, but also ends up indirectly being applied extraterritorially absent equally strong legal protection[324].

Another important legal environment affecting the digital world across cyberspace is the intellectual property right, copyright law in particular, which is 'strictly'[325] territorial in nature but yet may very well have extraterritorial effects. In the digital world, though copyright laws regulate protected digital assets within national boundaries, this protection still transcends geographical boundaries due to the nature of cyberspace per se.

Extraterritorial application and interpretation of national copyrights laws, any other laws for that matter, may vary by country. While this will depend on normative variations of national legislations, there is also the possibility that more markedly contrasting approaches are followed by judiciary of various countries. An almost classical case of cyberspace based copyrights infringement exemplifies this variance a bit more precisely. The issue involved peer to peer (P2P) file sharing products, court rulings of which resulted in two extremes with respect to determining liability by at least two court systems: the new inducement doctrine within the U.S. judiciary and an

---

jurisdiction to prescribe; see Denis T. Rice, Jurisdiction and e-Commerce Disputes in the U.S. and EU, Presentation at the Annual Meeting of the California Bar, at 2 (2002).

[324] In fact, the EU's data law will apply anytime personal data of EU citizens is processed and that is almost always the case where the Internet is involved. See Kuner, supra note 175, at 4.

[325] Graeme W. Austin, Importing Kazaa - Exporting Grokster, Arizona Legal Studies Discussion Paper No. 06-08, at 586 (April 2006).

elaborate use of 'authorization' concept by the Australian court[326]. Both approaches have been discussed in cases, *MGM vs. Grokster*[327] (U.S. Supreme Court) and, *Universal Music Australia Pty. Ltd. v. Shaman License Holdings Ltd.*, (P2P provider) by Federal Court of Australia)[328], among others. Although it seems more plausible and fair for enablers like Internet Service Providers (ISPs) to monitor authorization, Australian courts closely examine the 'authorization' concept similar to what is specifically laid out by the Australian legislator, yet often come to a different conclusion as the court did in the above case. Such conclusions obviously won't make P2P providers happy as they would find this approach harsh. Despite technical difficulties for P2P providers, the courts often find that P2P providers should be able to monitor file-sharing, lack of which could automatically be considered an authorization for infringement[329]. The authorization test itself could be interpreted broadly, whereby defendants could be unfairly treated as it was the case in *University of New South Wales v. Moorhouse*. Moorhouse involved a case where the Australian Federal court stated that authorization did not need to be express or actively pursued[330].

---

[326] Id. at 581.

[327] Metro-Goldwyn-Mayer Studios, Inc. v. Grokster Ltd., 125 S. Ct. 2764 (2005); see also Austin, id. at 577.

[328] See Austin, supra note 325, at 578.

[329] It is technically possible for P2P providers like Kazza to discriminate between licensed/un-licensed and copyrighted materials that could be shared by their users. And ignoring this capability is actively enabling copyright infringement given also the availability of tool to filter copyrighted materials which could be implemented by P2Ps.

[330] Decisions of the High Court of Australia: University of New South Wales v. Moorhouse [1976] R.P.C. 1141 (Austl.); See Austin, supra note 325, at 583.

The inducement theory, on the other hand, has been invariably applied by U.S. courts and allows parties to go after even foreign offenders with liability judgments as determined under U.S. laws. In its application to copyright infringements, this approach would almost always negate the strict territoriality principle, just like cyberspace itself. And in doing so, it almost seems to be more suited for IP disputes based on the fluid nature of cyberspace. The inducement liability as used in Grokster and beyond would allow extraterritorial *de jure* and *de facto* application of the U.S. copyright law thereby giving the innovators more freedom to create and distribute copyrighted materials across borders. There is a general tendency in the case law to apply the same approach developed by the U.S. courts on copyright infringement claims across international borders.

The problem is that, while the inducement theory has immensely eased the transnational application of the U.S. intellectual property laws, this approach never created any easy way to facilitate enforcement. It did not answer the question as to how claimants can actually enforce their IP rights abroad. Consequently, copyright owners find the inducement approach more beneficial since the approach conveniently lets the owners rely on and apply their home country law until they soon realize how difficult it is to enforce liabilities based on this indirect liability theory. Enforcing liabilities under this approach is especially beset with hurdles when the infringement occurs not only in one forum abroad, but in multiple foreign jurisdictions.

ii.   *Application of National Laws Abroad – Impact on Offshoring*

The extraterritorial reach of national laws could have

negative effects on cross-border digital investments in offshore locations as well, and these effects could be felt in at least two ways.

First, national legislations; such as, copyright, data protection, and SOX Acts can follow the home country investor abroad, and proscribe certain conducts or limit business activities abroad, whereby this extraterritorial reach could negatively impact the investor's business process. As in the *University of New South Wales v. Moorhouse*[331], for instance, if the P2P (Kazza) had a foreign subsidiary that has an FDI presence in another country, the court's judgment granting liability based on the home country's copyright law would follow the subsidiary. Kazza affiliates around the world could be directly impacted by this liability judgment as well. The effects do not end there. As it can be imagined, sustainable business continuity might have been questionable for Kazza, i.e. Kazza may have faced the option of going out of business considering the far-reaching consequences of the Australian copyright law, which applies pretty much anywhere, where the copyrighted work is 'communicated'[332]. The Kazza effects could force the foreign subsidiary to pay substantial restitution, where the imposed payment could affect the subsidiary in its profit margin. The subsidiary could even be deprived of business continuity the same way as it might well be the case with Kazza.

Similarly, the U.S. SOX legislation can be considered another example of national regulation with extraterritorial effects as its

---

[331] An Australian high court case; see supra note 371.

[332] Graeme W. Austin, Importing Kazaa - Exporting Grokster, Arizona Legal Studies Discussion Paper No. 06-08, at 571 (April 2006); also see Australian Copyright Amendment (Digital Agenda) Act, 2000, Act No. 110 of 2000 (Austl.), inserting § 31(1)(a)(vi) and 31(1)(b)(iii).

provisions could follow U.S. companies overseas. Specifically, SOX too can have the same effects on foreign cross-listed U.S. offshoring firms abroad as it does at home. U.S. multinationals with subsidiary in a foreign country in an FDI setting could be subjected to SOX requirements at home. Such an extended reach of SOX, may affect investment decisions, though not often decisively because investment decisions in many instances again hinge on the net cost benefits from such engagements depending on investment climate within a given host.

Secondly, extended application of home country legislation or court jurisdiction could have implications for legal conflicts resulting in adverse consequences for home country investors abroad. For instance, a home country law with certain requirement that applies to all home country firms regardless of their place of business, and a host country with its own legal norms applicable to FDI that contradicts the home country rules could end up generating conflicts in compliance for the foreign investor, FDI in particular. That can be the case with respect to the effects on companies subjecting to both U.S. SOX and EU's data protection directives. European companies listed or cross-listed in the U.S. stock markets, thereby voluntarily subjecting themselves to U.S. laws including SOX, could be in a dilemma of contradicting compliance requirements.

These companies face the problem of information disclosure requirements under the SOX Act in the States, while disclosure of some information may partially or entirely be prohibited under their home country legislations. That is true for European multinationals with FDI presence in the U.S. or otherwise doing business with U.S. affiliates, especially when these companies are dealing with sensitive customer data from both EU and U.S. This data may fall under the strict disclosure protection and express consent requirements of the EU on the one hand, and slightly liberal rules of the U.S. on the other, where these firms at same time attempt to compete against U.S. counterparts. In fact beyond the generally more liberal stance on personal data handling under the U.S. data protection laws, SOX actually entails disclosure requirements for all companies that are subject to its provisions albeit these disclosure requirements may or may not involve restricted data that the EU's directives attempt to protect. But there is the potential that SOX's disclosure requirements could collide with that of EU's directives. On the flip side, U.S. offshoring companies with place of business in any of the EU member states too will face similar issues with legal conflicts. But U.S. based offshoring FDI investors in Europe may take advantage of the 'safe harbor' provisions brokered by both EU and U.S. authorities to alleviate such conflicts.[333]

Again the real impact of the extraterritorial reach by certain regulations within the EU or U.S. is that these laws will undermine the flexibility of cross-border business transactions by imposing direct or indirect restrictions. The conflict resulting from opposing restrictions will not only impair business undertakings but the compliance process will delay projects and add cost for firms attempting to do business on either side. Companies on both sides feeling that their home country laws, in particular, significantly impair their business undertakings abroad would back out of their proposal or even discontinue existing investment activities including FDI projects.

---

[333] Bierce & Kenerson, P.C., Privacy, Data Protection and Outsourcing in the United States: http://www.outsourcing-law.com/jurisdictions/countries/united-states-of-america/privacy-data-protection-and-outsourcing-in-the-united-states/, (last visited July 20, 2011).

c) Cyberspace vs. National Public Policy and Security

i.   *Host Public Policy in General*

Under the international law, it is no longer disputed that nations generally have the right to defend themselves. This right has its roots in one of the oldest customary international legal principles afforded states – the right for individual or collective self-defense[334]. This principle, while somewhat weakened by the fact that it may not be enforced against powerful nations considered aggressor hence also described as *'bully dilemma'*[335], could provide bases for every country to protect its national security interests.

The question as to whether this principle applies to similarly aggressive conducts on cyberspace is highly debated. But it is also equally unclear as to if the self defense response to a cyber attack can occur through use of physical (armed) force[336]. These security interests are often stipulated in treaties and adopted in national security policy documents. A number of countries have additionally developed overarching national security policies. Some even include implementation plans in the form of national security plan. However, almost all of these policies exhibit

---

[334] As it has also been recognized by the UN in the UN Charter, Article 51.

[335] The situation is often noticed in the UN Security Council when sanctions are invoked against such bully states with a permanent membership on the UN Security Council, see Graham H. Todd, Armed Attack In Cyberspace: Deterring Asymmetric Warfare with an Asymmetric Definition, in The Law Review, 64 A.F. L. REV. (66), at 71 (2009).

[336] There is neither clarity in the definition of 'armed attack' in the UN charter per se nor does international legal practice sheds some light in this regard; see Todd, id. at 72.

variations in scope as can be anticipated, but their goal appears to be the same, i.e. curbing security threats no matter what the source is. There are differences, for instance, in the choice of terminology and contextual details. These variations could have an overarching impact on FDI policies as well since they could subject the underlying investment policies (e.g. USA and France[337]) or even investment undertakings directly to some scrutiny in the interest of national security.

National security interests often find recognition through provisions under various international instruments including bilateral investment treaties[338] and multilateral agreements, (e.g. World Trade Organization (WTO) incorporating Article XIV of the General Agreement on Tarrifs and Trade (GATT), Chapter XXI, North American Free Trade Agreement (NAFTA), and EU treaty[339], etc).

Provisions under these and more specifically investment treaties lay out certain conditions for either exceptions or exclusions for contracting parties. Although the language used to recognize the need to protect essential security interests in the investment treaties often lacks coherence[340], state parties could

---

[337] Such scrutiny is the case with the U.S. and France, where such plans state the importance of reviewing investment policy in the interest of national security protection. See OECD, Guidelines for Recipient Country Investment Policies Relating to National Security, Recommendation Adopted by the OECD Council, 12 (May 2009).

[338] Model BITs with such national security stipulations include those from the USA (Article 18, 2004 model treaty), Canada (Article 10, 2004 model BIT), and BIT between China and Philippines (Article 4, Sep. 1995). For a complete list of similar BITs, see OECD, id. at 32.

[339] OECD, supra note 337, at 17; see also OECD, International Investment Perspectives: Freedom of Investment in a Changing World, 97 (2007).

[340] Terms used include ordre public (French = public order), public policy,

be excepted from the requirements to implement all or part of the treaty if doing so would be contrary to their *ordre public* or threaten their national security.

Meanwhile, not only does the use of various terms in these treaties cause confusion, but the conceptual understanding of some of these terms (e.g. *ordre public,* public order, public security, or ~ policy) vary across various legal systems. Civil law countries' use of the term *ordre public* differs conceptually from that of the common law tradition because it is broader in meaning under the civil law regime. Under the civil law tradition, *ordre public* means public interest, which has broader implications than the contextual meaning for national security[341]. Hence, the European Court of Justice (ECJ) may have sought to resolve this confusion and may have been forced to differentiate between public policy and public security as its direction in its recent jurisprudence indicates[342].

The common law context of public policy too varies across common law countries. Under the U.S. legal system, public order does not have the same conceptual meaning as it is used in European legal systems or elsewhere. Instead, the U.S. legal system has a longstanding common law rule under the term 'public policy' that is somewhat equivalent conceptually to *ordre public* but equally susceptible to broad interpretation[343].

---

essential security interests, national security, though their meaning, in some cases, could overlap. Also see OECD, supra note 337, at 6.

[341] OECD, supra note 337, at 7.

[342] Id. at 8.

[343] For instance, the concept of public policy is part of the test in determining validity of a contract, especially when an agreement is suspected of being an illegal bargain due to restrain trade, unconscionability, tortuous conduct, etc.; See RICHARD A. MANN, SMITH AND ROBERSON'S BUSINESS LAW, 240 (11th

However, many legal systems seem to adhere to the same or similar conceptual interpretation for the term 'national security'. Regardless, despite the homogenous approach in the interpretation and understanding of the generic need for preserving national security interests, there are variations in implementing it. Hence, what is implied to be considered as national security, public policy, or public security/order deserving exception or protection in a given national forum depends on what the country considers critical for the safety and security of that nation. No matter how national security is defined, its implementation will affect an FDI directly or indirectly.

Both home and host states may use the public policy in broader context as an excuse for violating obligations based on a treaty or other investment regulations. ECJ in a number of its decisions recognized the need to interpret public order and security narrowly to counteract these concepts' being used as an escape goat. According to ECJ, reliance on *ordre public* is only accepted 'if there is genuine and sufficiently serious threat to fundamental interests of a society'[344]. ECJ does not seem to tolerate any derogation by member states from its restrictive views in this regard though member states are said to be free to specify the scope of public security as it relates to their own national interests[345].

Apart from the ECJ's limitation on public policy, the international customary law[346] under the 'necessity' clause test as

---

Edition, 2000).

[344] OECD, Security-Related Terms in International Investment Law and in National Security Strategies, 8 (May 2009).

[345] Id.

[346] International Court of Justice recognizes state obligation and exceptions thereto as a customary law: see OECD, supra note 337, at 100.

recognized by the draft ILC allows such excuses from state obligations[347]. Necessity under the draft Article 25 ILC could be invoked by states as a ground to exclude their obligations stemming from treaties or any other international provisions. The necessity provision acts as another source of exception on which a state could rely to avoid contractual or treaty obligations. The state can support its claims when it no longer honors its contractual or treaty based obligations with the claim that performing such obligations would otherwise threaten its national security. However, such exculpation is only allowed, where the wrongful action itself that a state seeks an exception for is not already disallowed under its agreement with the investor or under any other binding provisions that the state can be subjected to. Furthermore, the necessity invocation is limited to the extent that this claim is the only way remaining to address the national security concerns the state raises. The draft Article 25 ILC stipulates additional limitations (contributory negligence and impairment test regarding other states) on necessity claims, which are all generally even more restrictive than the ECJ's interpretation on *ordre public*.

In the end, there is a strong case for the need to balance both putting in place and adjusting/restricting national security provisions in the interests of the host national economy, in particular. National security measures are relevant for an investor, as well as investment promotion efforts from both home country and host country perspectives. Too restrictive national security measures will impair positive outcomes from investment incentives while at the same time drastically reduce investment portfolio. Therefore, whether it is a treaty or national security policy that dictates the normative stipulations essential to protect

[347] OECD, supra note 337, at 99.

critical national interests of the investor's home and host countries, it is vital that these norms seek some balance in order to both promote investment and protect security interests.

ii.   *Effects of Host Public Policy on IT-Enabled Service FDI*

As stated in preceding section, home or host national policies are not without negative consequences on foreign digital investments. Turns out national security policies can have wide-ranging effects, where in some cases their effects can be felt even by investors' home states. That is true regardless of intended targets by such policies. In addition, countries could also target one or more of other hostile nations with policy instruments, which becomes an issue when investors from those target countries engage in business in those aggressive nations. Or even if a given host country does not necessarily have specific targets in mind, its policy may irritate other nations.

Simply put, regardless of a given country's intentions to actively target other nations, this country could have policies in place which threatens national security of other countries. This kind of threat can originate from both host and home nations with respect to an offshore investor and target either of those nations.

Moreover, with regard to digital investment, countries could manipulate investment channels to target each other with cyber attacks. Hostile nations could actively or passively pursue cyber warfare against other targets. For example, if an investor home country becomes a target of a hostile nation-state that is a potential destination for a home investor, then the hostile host becomes highly concerning for the security of data belonging to the potential investor from the target (home) state. For example, the investor could become a target of a cyber espionage by state-sponsored actors in the host, which can be interested in this data for purposes of economic or military use. It is equally questionable and scary for investors from other nations who are passive targets by the unfriendly host state. For these reasons, many FDI decisions take into consideration the possible lasting conflicts of interest in their home country's national security interests and vice versa. International investment practice indicates that these kinds of conflicts have been said to heighten risk elements[348]. And in fact the elevated risk related to the conflict in national security interests of both host and home countries plays a major role in determining investment decisions even in private sector.

However, not every firm takes a note of national security issue before embarking on investment journey abroad. The reason for lack of consideration in this regard could be that many firms are more interested in profit potential and marketplace than the underlying national security consequence.

Some investors may not always be aware of national security consequences for their home states, but they will become aware sooner or later also based on their home state policies against all offshoring targets, and make adverse decisions.

But investors need not be surprised by unexpected realization of existing inconvenient policies. It is important that they seriously consider reviewing and understanding ahead the existence and applicability of national security provided under treaties and/or national regulations. Besides, they need to be clear from the outset about potential impacts on their digital assets and additional repercussions on national security interests of their home country. This will save them time, cost, and all other

---

[348] See Camp et al., supra note 160, at 190.

efforts from unwanted consequences from applicable host's national security norms with respect to not only conceptual understanding of these norms as interpreted in the prevailing host's jurisprudence, but the potential spillover effects of the norms' hidden agenda.

The logical question is what needs to be done to alleviate adverse reactions by both investors and home states against pervasive host public policies? The answer to this question is paramount in particular for countries which do not necessarily pursue aggressive policy agenda, but just simply want to compete against others to attract IT service FDI. That is because FDI incentives should consider adjusting restrictive national security policies. Competing nations will have to do due diligence not to discourage offshoring with too broad or restrictive security requirements. Similarly, home countries should not impose wide-reaching and unnecessary restrictions on their multinationals as otherwise their actions end up punishing both potential target nations and investors for fear of national security repercussion.

In sum, there are host and home country policy measures that are crafted in the name of national security but may have transnational effects. And there could also be policies that pursue non-national security rationale and become very intrusive especially for business undertakings under the umbrella of national interests. These polices end up creating diplomatic tensions and economic repercussions for both nations and corporate citizens. It is highly unlikely that offshore digital investors will be encouraged to do business in national forums with restrictive or intrusive security policy measures regardless of the policy measures having national security rationale. Investors could also stay away from forums, with which their home country is not in good terms or if the destination state poses risks for data breach due to the forum's active cyber warfare, digital intelligence, censorship, or economic espionage activities.

iii.   *Effects of Cyberspace on Host National Security; Implications for IT Service FDI*

When it comes to nations' voluntary or involuntary engagement to deal with cyberspace issues, in particular, the interaction and conflicts between cyberspace and national security become obvious. While this leads to the realization that threats from cyberspace have repercussions on national security, efforts to secure cyberspace will also have negative or positive implications to national security. Both the USA and Russia have emphasized that cyberspace based conflicts could significantly impact national security[349]. There is no wonder that nowadays more and more nations are cognizant of the threat posed by cyberspace to their national security while others show willingness to embrace cyber conflict as international issue or as a matter of international security[350]. Many of the major players on cyberspace: U.S., China, Russia, and France, among others, have

---

[349] Sean Kanuck, Sovereign Discourse on Cyber Conflict Under International Law, Texas Law Review, Vol. 88:1571, at 1586 (2010). Cyberspace has been described by security experts as the new frontiers of national security, see Kelly A. Gable, Cyber Apocalpyse Now: Securing the Internet Against Cyber Terrorism and Using Universal Jurisdiction as a Deterrent, at 17 (August 14, 2009), also available at: SSRN: http://ssrn.com/abstract=1452803, (last visited Dec. 25, 2011).

[350] Such was the case with the current U.S. government which along with the British government initially declined an international treaty restricting military use of ICT but later (in 2009) resumed dialogue regarding an international approach to resolve cyber security issues, see Kanuck, supra note 348, at 1588.

engaged in information warfare both in terms of offensive and defensive strategies for cyber attacks[351]. That is because they have recognized that information warfare poses impending sources of threat for any country that possesses ICT capabilities. More and more countries have the ability or at least the potential to equip themselves with such capabilities and attack each other. For example, an advanced persistent threat capability can easily be built based on the ICT capability and other resources that rich countries already have at their disposal. The question for any of these nations seems not if but when a given nation can launch a more potent and especially effective attack against any given adversary. There seems to be a fierce race currently among these nations to equip themselves with best resources in terms of human and technological capabilities that sets them apart from the rest in terms of defense and offense on cyberspace. And no country with available resources wants to be left out in this race.

Meanwhile cyber threats are not confined to government actors. National security could be affected due to cyber security risks caused by individuals, organized crime syndicates, and government sponsored actors. These threats can also be based on active or passive engagements by sources like foreign government agents acting on behalf of a government sponsor and those that pursue some other independent, organizational, or personal goals. Active engagements from government sources, often in the form of APT, may include use of electronic tools by one country to penetrate and collect intelligence relevant data from another

---

[351] China, France, and Russia have even acknowledged establishing programs to deal with cyber warfare in terms of both offensive and defensive capabilities, while about 33 other countries have capabilities to conduct electronic intelligence or cyber espionage; See Christopher Joyner & Catherine Lotrionate, Information Warfare as International Coercion: Elements of Legal Framework, 831 (2001).

hostile country, and so forth.

In regards to threats posed by offshore investors within recipient countries, both private foreign investors and foreign government controlled investors - so called Sovereign Wealth Funds (SWFs) play major roles. In fact, FDI in general is considered by many as a threat to national security of a host as the host government may cede control over certain resources.[352] SWFs, in particular, may pursue hidden political or other agenda while purporting to strictly engage in commercial activities contrary to what is ordinarily specified in pertinent investment agreements[353]
.

Host states cognizant of these risks could do whatever it takes to curb such threats. In addition to concluding treaties mentioned above, they counter such threats, inter alia, by implementing strict national policies, which should mandate monitoring and controlling of use, as well as access to national critical information and communication infrastructure. Countries like the U.S. have national security policy plans (also known as security strategies)[354] that impose monitoring or review

---

[352] In the U.S. for instance, one survey showed in 2006 that about 53% of the people surveyed exhibited negative sentiments towards foreign investors in the USA, maybe caused by the recent terrorist incidents; see Jason Cox, Regulation of Foreign Direct Investment After the Dubai Ports Controversy: Has the U.S. Government Finally Figured Out How to Balance Foreign Threats to National Security Without Alienating Foreign Companies? 295 (2009).

[353] Such SWF agreement among U.S., Singapore, and Abu Dhabi, for instance, explicitly defines the investment objectives in an attempt to mitigate the distrust any such engagement may cause. See OECD, Foreign Government-Controlled Investors and Recipient Country Investment Policies: A Scoping Paper, 7 (January 2009).

[354] As stated, for instance, in the United States (National Infrastructure Protection Plan, 2003); see OECD, supra note 352, at 43.

mechanisms over foreign investment activities at home to ensure that such activities do not overstep the bounds of public policy and national security interests. So, for example, host countries could have FDI monitoring policies that go beyond contract reviews, where they may even implement tools that monitor cyber activities on their ICT or electronic data traffic at national gateways in the name of national security. Some wary nations may end up taking extreme measures which can be stringent enough to subject ICT users including foreign investors to more scrutiny, exclusion, or to ultimately even discourage such users altogether. Some nations could even subject users including digital investors to willingly or unwillingly divulge sensitive data. These actions ultimately hurt the hosts' bid to win more digital investment by creating unfriendly atmosphere for this type of business model in particular.

iv. *Government Control on Cyberspace & Implications for Net Freedom*

More and more governments are actively engaged in cyberspace in an attempt to control and regulate activities on it regardless of the reason behind their attempts, i.e. whether this control is backed by the justification for fear of national security or not. The question, thus, is what, if any, would be the impact of such control attempts that may go far beyond the real national security interests on regular user? What if such pervasive government policies shield themselves behind the perceived fear of cyber security threats having national security implications, among others, but such policy measures being used as a mandate to go against citizens as well as businesses including IT investors? When does such scrutiny become a censorship and why is censoring net activities of individuals and businesses by government agents a major concern?

These are among the many questions raised by the cyber community, net freedom activists in particular. No matter how loud some advocates of Net (Internet) freedom voice their positions and intent for openness, it turns out the Internet is not so free after all or at least *"not exactly a safe-haven for activists"*[355] in particular. Thanks to all sorts of technological enablers, technical tools available today[356], the Internet traffic can, for the most part, be filtered, monitored, controlled, and blocked at will not only by tyrant governments, but private parties as well. Although some of these activities are legit, where data is collected, analyzed, and reported for national security and crime prevention purposes, some are not. Some countries have been observed to intensely censoring Internet traffic. Despite the sheer volume of this traffic, they are not shy of heavily canvassing through every IP packet coming and going across their boundaries using some battle-necks or checkpoints under the umbrella of national security. These checkpoints serve the purpose of tracking inbound and outbound traffic or worse totally blocking such traffic both ways termed as 'infoblockade'[357] if necessary.

---

[355] Both tools for censorship and circumvention, basically competing against each other have been actively marketed and distributed. See, Roberts et al., supra note 231, at 2.

[356] Although some filtered destinations use social and political methods as well, the most pervasive and last means would be the use of technical tools that can be placed in either at server, client side, or in between (network) since the Web is usually implemented based on client-server architecture. Such tools include usually router based IP block, DNS block, key word block, and stateful traffic analyses (firewall or router based). See Roberts et al., supra note 231, at 10.

[357] Christopher Joyner & Catherine Lotrionate, Information Warfare as International Coercion: Elements of Legal Framework, 838 (2001).

Traffic censorship has been the main reason over the past few years with countries like Saudi Arabia and China, just to name a few, that their citizens can be prevented from accessing certain sites that the regimes deem not acceptable for whatever reasons. Saudi Arabia is said to use an array of proxy servers to filter and block thousands of websites that do not fit the Kingdom's content profiling based on religious grounds[358] or political stigma. China too has been accused of tampering with cyber traffic and Net freedom. Its actions against political dissidents using the cyberspace as a weapon have often been criticized. China has allegedly implemented complex mechanisms for filtering foreign based websites and pervasively censoring outgoing content by engaging Chinese Internet Services Providers (ISPs)[359].

Various other countries, which have created such checkpoints for intercepting and analyzing Internet traffic often using Intelligence Support Systems (ISS), may have a variety of motives including silencing human rights activists or political oppositions, or even to use for ideological purposes. The recent political upheaval in the Middle East (as has been observed since

---

[358] Jonathan Zittrain & Benjamin Edelman, Documentation of Internet Filtering in Saudi Arabia, Berkman Center for Internet & Society Harvard Law School, available at: http://cyber.law.harvard.edu/filtering/saudiarabia/, (last visited June 13, 2011).

[359] China's position and intent may have been evidenced in its proposal to the U.N. group of governmental experts in January 2010, where China stated countries should "have the responsibilities and rights to take necessary management measures to keep their domestic cyberspace and related infrastructure free from threats, disturbance, attack and sabotage," see Kanuck, supra note 348, at 1591. Chinese Internet companies filter content published within the nation according to a report available at:

http://www.rsf.org/article.php3?id_article=23924; http://en.rsf.org/internet-enemie-china,39741.html, (last visited June 13, 2011). Also see Roberts et al., supra note 231, at 3.

the Spring of 2011), for instance, pushed some Arab countries to the limits that led them to do whatever they could to silence the uprisings. That may have prompted many of Arab countries to look into all possible and available defensive tools in IT solutions. Among other things, they have been said to engage Western IT contractors which provide various tools to deface opposition websites, capture, spy on, or track user activities on cyberspace[360].

But on the flip side, many countries may have legitimate intentions to do so. Arguably there are also justifiable concerns when it comes to imposing such control for impending legitimate national security threats if performed against specific actors based, for instance, on reliable intelligence sources. That is, monitoring cyber traffic can be justified to the extent that whatever solutions or tools these governments implement help them in this regard to mitigate cyber threats posed against their own critical assets or human life. In addition, the fact that not everything on the Internet is harmless, can be a point of argument to justify some non-pervasive protective measures. That is, it is also important to block contents that otherwise could be harmful to especially younger generation.

The argument as to what is good or bad on cyberspace can sometimes be difficult to delineate because it all depends on whose interest is at stake. So, some content that is profitable or in the best interest of a group supporting the content may turn out

---

[360] The recent Intelligence Support Systems (ISS) conference in Dubai, UAE, underscores just how insatiable the demand for such control in the Arab world currently has become. The tool and devices that are supposed to meet these needs are dubbed by some providers 'lawful' law enforcement supporting tools, so named in an attempt to obscure their real functionalities. See the conference agenda and IT solutions discussed: http://www.issworldtraining.com/ISS_MEA/index.htm, (last visited June 21, 2011).

to be bad for some of those consuming the content, and vice-versa. But at least there are cyberspace based contents that tend to justify, promote, or disseminate hate, genocide, terrorist activities, or other criminal activities generally condemned by the international community to pose international security threat. Some of these incidents are also considered international crimes, where nations have no choice but do whatever they can to bring perpetrators to justice. In other words, since nation states are bound under the international law to prevent or help prosecute these crimes, they have some leeway in applying available tools in investigating the sources of these crimes and monitoring suspects. And that could justify such censorship in almost every case.

v.   *Effects of Government Net Scrutiny on Digital Investor*

As stated earlier, some government attempts to scrutinize traffic on cyberspace may be justified given the fact that global cyberspace is considered a breeding ground for major cyber threats including cyber terrorism that could result in catastrophic real life events. Nevertheless, no matter what the motive is for such an interference with the normal flow of information over cyberspace, this could negatively impact some business activities more than others. For example, offshoring businesses relying on electronic data transfer can be adversely affected by such elevated, but unwarranted scrutiny.

The data security concerns resulted from China's censorship scare against some multinationals recently (the case of Google specifically) [361] exemplifies this to some extent. Chinese actions

---

[361] See Google on its official blog stated that Chinese hackers accessed Google email accounts of human rights advocates and Chinese dissidents also suggesting that the attack targeted 20 other big companies as well; see

may very well be government sponsored, where its national security policy may have been used as a source of the mandate. Meanwhile, China with no doubt is currently considered one of the most favored destinations for FDI in general due to its market size[362] and, thus, it seems that this type of scare may not always adversely affect every potential digital offshore investor's decision to do business in China. But the fact remains to be such that Chinese actions on cyberspace can in the end push many foreign IT investors to stay away from the country.

China's policy measure implies at least three disincentives for potential offshore investors in IT and IT enabled business process. First, the Internet checkpoints or hacking mechanisms built into the scrutiny process may act as a battle-neck for the Net traffic thereby slowing down Internet access or causing service availability issues.

The consequence is that companies cease to deal with this kind of obstruction. Even worse targeting big companies means not only scaring this companies away but also antagonizing relationships with those multinationals, as well as their home countries. In fact, China's stance in this regard could actually galvanize adverse home country actions against doing business in

---

http://www.sec.gov/Archives/edgar/data/1288776/000119312510005667/dex99 1.htm, (last visited May 11, 2011); also see Beth Bacheldor, What Google vs. China Says About Security and Offshore Outsourcing: Available at http://advice.cio.com/beth_bacheldor/what_google_vs_china_says_about_securi ty_and_offshore_outsourcing , (last visited May 3, 2011).

[362] Market size maybe very influential for FDI decisions, but it is said not to change investor's reluctance with regard to other discouraging factors like IP protection. See Michael W. Nicholson, Intellectual Property Rights, Internalization and Technology Transfer; Federal Trade Commission, at 2 (2001); This may hold true with regard to invading privacy or filtering network traffic too since informed investors are looking for not just local market advantages, but other equally decisive factors.

China. Home countries could react with restrictions of their own thereby suppressing any intentions many other companies may have to do business in China. Most importantly, this can catch IT investors entirely off-guard, whose business model involves intensive cross-border electronic traffic (e.g. B2B e-commerce) that highly leverages the Internet and relies on the availability of adequate bandwidth.

Secondly, the Government may engage force through hacking/filtering methods or try to work with an investor to access investor's sensitive data. But the investor will more likely be wary of sharing potentially sensitive information belonging to its customers and employees with the government willingly. The investor will also have no choice but try to fend off this access by all means including ceasing to do business with China. Otherwise, forced disclosure will affect customer trust and relations thereby negatively impacting the customer base of the companies affected.

Finally, Chinese actions systematically favor Chinese companies over foreign firms, thereby even acting as a "trade barrier"[363], since foreign investors won't have access to outgoing information related to business environment; such as, the nature of cyber security, investment climate, potential for profitability of products and services, etc. due to content blocking or filtering applied to outgoing information from Chinese side. At least internally, Chinese firms will have more competitive edges compared to foreign investor firms since they have access to wealth of information, understand business culture, language, as

---

[363] China actually controls/monitors the web at its borders by means of intermediary (ISPs) control; see Joel R. Reidenberg, States and Internet Enforcement, University of Ottawa law & technology journal, at 230 (undated); also *see* a report on the Web censorship: *A Trade Barrier?* Available at: http://en.rsf.org/internet-enemie-china,39741.html, (last visited May 13, 2011).

well as customer behavior (likes and dislikes). Foreign firms will have hard time sharing information with Chinese Internet companies who implement Internet traffic filtering/blocking/analyses mechanisms mandated by the Chinese government, whereas Chinese companies have nothing to lose since they have nothing to hide.

Censorship invades sensitive digital data belonging to investors, while infoblockade discourages potential new investors who may be less likely to get business relevant information from inland or may fear being disrupted in the normal course of business due to such battle-necks. All things considered, there is no doubt that Chinese actions will inevitably aggravate situations with respect to the total freedom of the Net that digital investment demands. This situation becomes a prime example of negative effects that government interference has on free enterprise, information flow, and digital investment.

2. Jurisdiction in Cyberspace: Effects on Digital Investment

a) Jurisdiction and Cyberspace: What Makes Jurisdiction in Cyberspace Unique?

Whether a transaction is cyberspace related or associated with any other commercial activity, disputes arising from cross-border transactions and use of cyberspace often lead to fundamental legal questions as to: (1) which country's courts should control the trial and enjoin parties' conducts (issues with choice of forum and jurisdiction), (2) whose laws should govern the case (choice of law), and (3) how should any judgment issued by a tribunal or court be recognized and enforced. Potential disputes whether civil or criminal, but emanating from cyberspace involve more than just those questions.

Indeed, dealing with cases from cyberspace will generate more questions than answers. Those additional questions emanate from issues ranging from the authority of courts and law enforcement to identify and subject parties to adjudication to those related to applying a particular law to the disputed matter on cyberspace.

These issues are more or less associated with how courts should treat cyber cases. Thus, while jurisdiction in general will be discussed in this and the following sections, the focus will be more on issues with adjudicative jurisdiction. Before delving into the various questions of jurisdiction associated with cyberspace as it relates to offshoring service FDI; however, it seems appropriate to analyze the context under which cyberspace or use of it involves jurisdictional problems.

Under public international law, jurisdiction is defined as the state's right to regulate conduct in matters not exclusively of domestic concern[364], which is a bit vague when the term 'regulate' is literally translated. Therefore, in more specific terms jurisdiction involves state's rights to not only regulate conducts, but to adjudicate cases and enforce domestic laws. While exercising these rights, since states sometimes end up dealing with matters not exclusive to their national boundary or domestic concern, such states often run into some conflict or competition with other states which claim similar rights and responsibilities to

---

[364] See Kuner, supra note 175, at 5. State's jurisdictional power is generally understood as including power to regulate, adjudicate, and enforce - for more on this see Henrick W. Kaspersen, Cybercrime and Internet Jurisdiction, 4 (March 2009).

do the same. This means under circumstances more nations may simultaneously have the same rights to assert similar jurisdiction based on equally justifiable concerns.

An attempt to regulate domestic affairs that have international consequences and subject non-residents to national tribunals or enforce domestic law internationally can result in jurisdictional competition. While an extraterritorial exercise of state power will encounter resistance eventually from other sovereign powers, under circumstances such an attempt could also constitute interference in the internal affairs of other nations.

Jurisdictional conflicts are more evident in cases and business dealings that have effects on matters across a national boundary, beyond the geographical limits on which a state exerts its sovereignty.

Thus, more often jurisdiction becomes a point of controversy in legal disputes arising out of cross-border transactions more than any other issues. Worse yet, due to the very reason that cyberspace and more specifically the Internet are involved, the question of jurisdiction, whether it is for subject matter, *in rem*, or *in personam* has been seen to become a center of controversy and increasingly more difficult to address. Jurisdiction is as much of a concern in civil/commercial matters as it is in criminal issues on cyberspace albeit it is possible for parties to mitigate such disputes at least on civil matters with choice of forum and applicable laws provisions. Selection of forum along with applicable law can be specified through choice of law clauses. Similar clauses are often included online on e-commerce transactions, which, if considered valid[365], could resolve the potential question of jurisdiction both over the parties and

---

[365] Validity might defeat its applicability just like any other contract, and its validity is tested using the same standards applicable to a contract.

subject matter[366]. Absent such choice of law clauses, any of the existing doctrines of jurisdiction will have to kick in and be applied as appropriate.

Jurisdictional doctrines for both civil and criminal matters are developed traditionally based on physical world and geographical boundaries. Common law tradition for example considers all crimes to be local that should be tried by the jurisdiction where it was committed[367]. But in the realm of cyberspace, the location or jurisdiction of crime commission and the victim can be different majority of the time, which essentially makes this common law position obsolete at least as far as cyberspace is concerned. That is because, for instance, the jurisdiction where a criminal act takes place or originates (e.g. a hacker from Russia launched a DoS attack on a U.S. based network) may not be interested to pursue the criminal since the case may not have any impact on national interests or is not economically worth it to allocate resources for the Russian jurisdiction. Of course the outcome would be different if the same crime is outlawed and subject to criminal prosecution in the Russian jurisdiction regardless of the location of the effect.

As stated earlier, the Internet as part of cyberspace[368] is by

---

[366] Such a contractual choice of law provision is possible for instance in e-commerce transactions, whereby the choice of law clause and the underlying agreement provided in the e-commerce site are subject to the same validity requirements as any other contract. But in terms of format, due to the fact that the agreement is stipulated only by one party and the other party (usually a consumer) has no options to change of adjust the language, agreements on e-commerce are subject to more scrutiny; see Denis T. Rice, Jurisdiction and e-Commerce Disputes in the U.S. and EU, Presentation at the Annual Meeting of the California Bar, at 44 (2002).

[367] Konoorayar, supra note 90, at 420.

its virtue borderless and fluid in nature with no apparent geographical limitation. This holds true as long as an opposing argument can be refuted. The opposing position states that it is technically feasible to segregate the Internet into geographical limits with the help of the IP address itself[369]. This approach assumes that IP address is provisioned statically or its origin as well as the actor behind the source node or machine the IP assigned to can easily be identified. In reality, such segregation is not entirely possible or meaningful as of yet since not only can IP address be spoofed, but the virtual space and its content including incidents are ubiquitous and available at all geographical locations simultaneously. Segregation does not make any sense at least from a cybercrime point of view since a phishing site can be accessed wherever there is Internet access. And the location of crime commission for the phishing site is not just the physical location of the perpetrator or the web hosting server, but the location of the server that enables such access could also be considered the location of the act.

This multiplicity of the location of act gave rise to the peculiar nature of the Internet, which has not only made part of the existing substantive legal norms obsolete, but it also did

---

[368] Cyberspace can be defined as a space of interconnected systems including the Internet and all other technologies and individual systems, as well as networks that make up such connections; however, some consider it as a component part of the Internet; See Konoorayar, supra note 90, at 423.

[369] This characteristic has not changed yet in part due to anonymity problems caused by e.g., spoofing/impersonating (see Konoorayar, supra note 90, at 415) even if some assert that there are "new geographic mapping technologies, by which visitors to a website can be identified through local-specific identifiers embedded in their IP addresses or browsers", see Jared H. Beck, A "Category-Specific" Legislative Approach to the Internet Personal Jurisdiction Problem in U.S. Law, at 4 (2004), for arguments supporting the existence of possibilities to geographically segregate the Internet.

complicate the problem of jurisdiction[370]. This also at the same time gave rise to the peculiarity of jurisdiction on cyberspace.

b) Jurisdictional Complexities in the Context of Offshoring

Since the scope of this discourse is limited to IT or IT-enabled offshore investment, where cyberspace plays a major role for cross-border transactions, jurisdiction on cyberspace becomes an important aspect of debates under cyber law. Jurisdiction in cyberspace warrants some analysis as it is often among the disputed legal elements in cases involving cross-border business transactions. With respect to an offshore investment project, one needs to address the following potential questions, among other things.

First, under what circumstances are issues related to an Internet jurisdiction relevant for such an FDI project? Secondly, what are possible solutions for such jurisdictional conflicts and confusions? And finally, what negative effects, if any, could cyberspace based jurisdictional issues have on the service FDI involving IT solutions?

While the last two questions will be addressed in the next few sections, the first question can be dealt with simply by revisiting the nature of such an offshore investment in a service FDI model per se. Looking into possibilities as to how offshoring activities might play out to cause cyberspace related legal disputes, which in turn could bring about jurisdictional questions, might help in this regard. As stated earlier under various topics above, an offshoring service FDI is apt to utilize computer, as well as networking technologies in cross-border settings. This inclination implies that such an FDI business model most likely

---

[370] Konooravar, supra note 90, at 417.

takes advantage of cyberspace, the Internet in particular in an extensive manner. And the fact that this FDI ends up using cyberspace to relay information, among other things, back and forth (e.g. between its foreign FDI facility and other locations inside or outside the host nation) or to provide other services using the Internet more likely brings the service FDI in contact with jurisdictional issues. These issues might result from potential cyberspace related disputes that the FDI may be part of.

Another reason an offshoring business process involves jurisdictional disputes may be that the offshoring service FDI maintains a Web site in support of its offshoring business process. For example, depending on the dichotomy of its website, i.e. whether it is commercial (e-commerce) or none e-commerce[371], the FDI will end up dealing with the question of personal jurisdiction, inter alia, in litigations resulting from its FDI business transactions. The majority of Internet related cross-border disputes involve questions with personal jurisdiction and that is due to the inclination of such transactions to involve e-commerce.

Meanwhile, a lot of e-commerce sites already include standard terms and conditions that consumers can read and accept/agree by clicking usually a radio button feature on the sites indicating assent, so called 'click-wrap'[372] agreements. These agreements usually include choice of law clauses specifying

---

[371] The distinction between commercial and non commercial websites is essential for asserting jurisdiction over out of state commercial websites in order to protect consumers, so argue the proponents of the new approach of jurisdiction known as category specific jurisdiction; see Jared H. Beck, A "Category-Specific" Legislative Approach to the Internet Personal Jurisdiction Problem in U.S. Law, at 12 (2004).

[372] Denis T. Rice, Jurisdiction and e-Commerce Disputes in the U.S. and EU, Presentation at the Annual Meeting of the California Bar, at 43 (2002).

applicable laws and forum as well, which are enforceable as long as they are valid. Click-wraps are subject to the same or more stringent validity requirements of law of contracts[373]. Enforceability of choice of law or forum can be resisted based on several validity requirements. Factors that can cause validity issues include generic contractual defects that are common on agreements (e.g. fraud, duress, etc), unreasonableness, and public policy[374].

Courts in the U.S. are; however, generally divided in terms of upholding or not recognizing choice of law clauses partly based on differences in state laws and partly based on the factors mentioned above. Public policy is a common reason cited for such denial, e.g. public policy being invoked in recognizing a consumer's lack of prior ability to negotiate such clauses on click-wrap contracts[375].

---

[373] So in addition to the standard contract validity requirement; such as, conscionableness, click-wrap has to show an option where the consumer has to explicitly accept and complete a purchase order, in a more stringent process implemented by the website called 'browse-wrap'; see Rice, supra note 372, at 365. Thus, mere presentation of a click-wrap site with a radio button option alone, that does not necessarily enforce the click-requirement, on the e-commerce does not suffice for a choice of law clause to be validated.

[374] See GARY B. BORN; INTERNATIONAL CIVIL LITIGATION IN U.S. COURTS: COMMENTARY AND MATERIALS, 170 (4th Ed. 2006).

[375] For instance, the California Court of Appeal invoking public policy denied the validity of a forum selection clause in America Online, Inc v. Superior Court, original case: America Online, Inc v. Booker, 781 So. 2d 423 (Fla. 2001 Ct. Appl.), while another U.S. federal court in Compuserve, Inc v. Patterson, 89 F. 3d 1257 (6th Cir. 1996) upheld a forum selection in a click-wrap agreement; see also Rice, supra note 372, at 44.

c) *In Rem* Jurisdiction and Domain Names

In rem jurisdiction too has gotten relevance in cyberspace. It has been quite consistently applied by U.S. courts in re domain name ownership disputes[376]. Domain name related *in-rem* disputes have become relevant in the context of the offshoring FDI as well. There is a potential for a digital investor to maintain a website as well as own a domain with a likelihood to get involved in an *in rem* dispute. Traditionally *in rem* jurisdiction entails physical location of the property in question and 'has long required that *res* (property) at issue has *situs*'[377] within the limits of a court that should exert its powers.

Despite the fact that the intangible nature of domain names contradicts the longstanding *in rem* jurisprudence, courts have held that there is an *in rem* jurisdiction as long as the domain name is *"within the control and dominion of an entity that is itself found within'*[378] the court's assigned administrative district. Such an entity is often not the domain owner but the registering

---

[376] This was exemplified and formulated in Porsche Cars N. Am., Inc. v. Porsch.Com, 51 F. Supp. 2d 707, 712-13 (E.D. Va. 1999) brought under the Trade Mark Dilution Act (Sec. 1655), where the court rejected the in rem stating this Act did not permit in rem proceedings. But most other courts including the U.S. Supreme Court later adopted the in rem applicability under this Act. Most of the domain name related disputes emanate from Cybersquatting, which means a "deliberate, bad faith registration as domain names of well-known and other trademarks in the hope of being able to sell the domain names to the owners of those marks; For details, see Thomas R. Lee, In Rem Jurisdiction in Cyberspace, Washington Law Review Association, available at: http://cyber.law.harvard.edu/property00/jurisdiction/lee.html, (last visited June 11, 2011); also see Rice, supra note 372, at 1.

[377] Id. at: http://cyber.law.harvard.edu/property00/jurisdiction/lee.html, (last visited June 11, 2011).

[378] Id.

organization. This position is also clearly indicated in the Anticybersquatting Consumer Protection Act (ACPA) 15 U.S.C. (§1125(d) (2) (c)). According to this Act, *in rem* proceedings can be commenced in a judicial district "*in which the domain name registrar, domain name registry, or other domain name authority that registered or assigned the domain name [at issue] is located.*"[379]

It is no surprise that, since registrars are often located in the U.S., such a holding has galvanized fierce opposition from non-U.S. jurisdictions. Simply put, this regulation and the supportive stance from the U.S. courts has inevitably resulted in some hostile reactions from other non U.S. fora as this would widen U.S. courts' jurisdiction over domain names. Apparently since an overwhelming majority of domains are registered in the U.S., courts in the States could inevitably entertain majority of domain cases. Opposition contends that this approach unilaterally expanded the U.S. adjudicative jurisdiction over domain names even if U.S. forums could have little or no direct connection to the dispute or domain name itself[380].

However, the protest against courts' position does not seem

_____

[379] And an entity here is a dealer (registrar) of the domain or authority who assigned the domain; for details on ACPA related cases see Martin Samson, The Anticybersquatting Consumer Protection Act: Key Information, Internet Library of Law and Court Decisions, available at:http://www.internetlibrary.com/publications/anticybsquattSamson9-05_art.cfm, (last visited June 8, 2011).

[380] This view further argues that such expansion would allow domain names to be unnecessarily segmented by physical locations though it is unclear from the contention as to what functional or technical consequence, if any, such segmentation would bring about to negatively affect domain names per se except jurisdictional shift to some degree; see R. Polk Wagner & Catherine T. Struve, Realspace Sovereigns in Cyberspace: Problems with the Anticybersquatting Consumer Protection Act (ACPA), Berkeley Technology Law Journal, Vol. 17, No. 1, at 41 (2002). Available at SSRN: http://ssrn.com/abstract=321901, (last visited January 12, 2012).

to have any merit as their argument disregards the importance of the hierarchical domain naming convention and the need to maintain this hierarchy with the current registration methodology in order to support the current Internet architecture. Their argument can be countered with the rationale based on the technical nature of the domain server itself. It can be argued more plausibly that the location of the root server or top level domain that contains the domain registration in the distributed domain hierarchy should be given more weight precisely because the root is the top and technically most important server in the hierarchy. And since the root server is geographically located within the forum of the registrar, in this case often the U.S. *situs*, the U.S. can have at least a *de facto* jurisdiction[381].

Yet, despite such a rationale, the *de facto in rem* assertion in turn faces some resistance since for one it could be held unconstitutional due to the fact that the foreign registrant, e.g. a foreign cyber-squatter, may not have sufficient contact with the U.S. forum[382].

The second contention is that the U.S. approach to unilaterally prescribe the *in rem* jurisdiction via the ACPA could entice other regulators to create or introduce '*alternative root servers*'[383]. This could entail an unwanted outcome where the domain name system becomes segregated and the original purpose of technically more feasible and efficient centralized management of domains gets eroded. So far; however, this tendency has not materialized yet.

In any event, with respect to relevance to offshoring, first

---

[381] Id. at 3.

[382] Id. at 2.

[383] Id. at 3

there is the potential that an offshoring service FDI could maintain an e-commerce website with the implication that the digital investor also owns one or more domain names. Secondly, it is highly likely that this FDI interacts with its clients globally in an e-commerce capacity, where legal disputes can be expected. Further there is a potential that such disputes will involve questions of both personal and *in rem* jurisdictions.

The issue of jurisdiction (whether *in rem* or *in personam*) could very well become a central point of contention due to multiplicity of foreign parties and circumstances with which such disputes are entangled. Although jurisdictional questions may be resolved with an appropriate choice of law clause[384] that can be included in the e-commerce website, there is no guarantee that such clauses can prevent the digital investor from being subject to litigation somewhere. Under circumstances, there is a potential for the FDI to be subject to *in rem* or at a minimum to personal jurisdiction everywhere in the world.

d) Personal Jurisdiction in Cyberspace under U.S. Laws

The next logical question from the preceding discussion is how issues of personal jurisdiction in particular are addressed under the current jurisprudence. We will take the U.S. point of view as an example to see how personal jurisdiction in light of cyberspace is handled by U.S. courts. Obviously the treatment of personal jurisdiction becomes complicated with the involvement of cyberspace, specifically the Internet technology, which defies geographical limitations.

---

[384] This is said to be the best solution at least from the e-commerce operator stand point to limit this potential; see GERALD R. FERRERA ET AL., CYBER LAW: TEXT AND CASES 32 (2000).

Viewing jurisdiction in cyberspace from the perspective of the U.S. legal system, one can easily observe a legal plurality both in judiciary and scholarly contributions. There is a variety of theoretical and judicial viewpoints developed and adopted over the years to questions of personal jurisdiction in general which more likely give rise to similarly varied solutions in cyberspace cases as well. For this reason, resolving issues with personal jurisdiction will depend on such prevalent views. Specifically courts will look at parties' loci, particularly defendant's location in the first place, and secondly whatever compelling theory or judicial precedent a given tribunal finds better suited to address the issue at hand.

Courts' jurisdiction over a person could be fairly easy or straightforward depending on the loci of the parties to a dispute. For example, if parties in a digital investment dispute are physically located in the U.S., a U.S. court's *in personam* jurisdiction over the investor or a U.S. resident won't be too much of an issue to determine. And the same may be true wherever parties have specifically agreed upon valid terms with regard to choice of law and jurisdiction. However, it becomes less straightforward if the defendant (e.g. a third party) resides in another forum, a foreign state, while maintaining a business dealing with the foreign investor in the U.S. This means absent a valid jurisdictional clause between the parties, any dispute between them related to their business relationship will more likely result in jurisdictional questions. That is where a variety of interpretations and jurisdictional doctrines both from civil and case law systems' points of view come into play.

Personal jurisdiction often becomes a point of controversy in cyberspace, more so than *in rem* jurisdiction, and there is no a simple way of solving the problem. There are quite a few proposals out there to approach jurisdiction on cyberspace.

To put this into perspective, with respect to the treatment of an *in personam* cyberspace related jurisdiction in the U.S., for example, there are a few theoretical and case law instances that can be analyzed here. American jurisprudence for personal jurisdiction is generally based on long-arm statutes[385], yet strongly influenced by case law. Personal jurisdiction has also been hugely influenced by the constitutionally mandated due process clause of the Fifth and Fourteenth amendments. Both amendments come into play in terms of defining judicial jurisdiction over a foreign defendant and limiting this jurisdiction.[386] The due process clause requires two-pronged analysis: minimum contacts and traditional notions of fair play and substantial justice.

Historically, both theory and practice in the U.S. jurisdictional jurisprudence have evolved over the years from territorial to minimum contact to specific jurisdiction within the due process analysis[387]. The old strictly territorial doctrine that could be equated with what is sometimes known as subjective territoriality principle[388] is primarily based on *Pennoyer v. Neff* [389].

---

[385] For example, the revised version of the Federal Rule of Civil Procedure 4 and several states have similar statutes; see GARY B. BORN; INTERNATIONAL CIVIL LITIGATION IN U.S. COURTS: COMMENTARY AND MATERIALS, 69 (4th Ed. 2006)..

[386] Due process clause limits also authorizations provided by the federal and states' long-arm statutes; see BORN, supra note 385, at 70; for details on two-pronged analysis, see GERALD R. FERRERA ET AL., CYBER LAW: TEXT AND CASES 20 (2000).

[387] Jared H. Beck, A "Category-Specific" Legislative Approach to the Internet Personal Jurisdiction Problem in U.S. Law, at 8 (2004).

[388] Contrary to the more controversial objective territoriality principle that expands jurisdiction to the location of the victim without regard to national boundaries, the subjective territoriality is the most basic principle associated with state's rights to exert jurisdiction within its territory and recognized in the international law; see also Henrik Stakemann Spang-Hanssen, A Just World

This strict approach has generally declined over time and certainly would not be a good fit for cyberspace. Pennoyer approach was later replaced by the constitutional due process standard in *International Shoe Co. v. Washington*[390], both doctrines adopted, developed, and adjusted by the U.S. Supreme Court. Even the due process approach has slightly changed in the course of its application. The contemporary due process analyses generally distinguish between general[391] and specific jurisdictions[392] when dealing with personal jurisdiction.

Other legal systems, in contrast, are neither bound by a constitutional mandate similar to the due process analysis nor adopt methodologies like those developed under the auspices of rulings by the U.S. Supreme Court in determining personal jurisdiction. For example, the use of territoriality principles in some EU countries somewhat diverges from that of the case law jurisprudence, especially the U.S. for mainly two reasons.

First, in the EU the territoriality principle appears to also apply in cyberspace, e.g. the location of the affected computer system regardless of the origin becomes a decisive element in this regard. For instance, the forum where a computer system is a

---

Under Public International Law in Cyberspace: Jurisdiction. Annual Survey of International and Comparative Law, Vol. 13, at 12 (Spring 2007).

[389] Id. at 7.

[390] Id.

[391] Permits a court to adjudicate any claim against a defendant based on nationality, domicile, or incorporation criteria; see BORN, supra note 385, at 77. But for ubiquitous websites and cyberspace cases, defendant of which is originating from abroad, general jurisdiction may not be suitable.

[392] GARY B. BORN; INTERNATIONAL CIVIL LITIGATION IN U.S. COURTS: COMMENTARY AND MATERIALS, 77 (4th Ed. 2006).

target for cybercrime can assert territorial jurisdiction over a foreign hacker who resides outside the territory[393]. This is true even if the crime does not originate from this territory since the affected computer becomes the main reasons for the territorial jurisdiction determination. Territoriality becomes an important element even when the same case can be prosecuted under the effects theory, where the perpetrator can be subjected to the location of the crime; in this case that of the affected computer. This is justified through the rationale that the victim's state can go after transnational criminals as the state is obliged to safeguard its citizens. Secondly, personal jurisdiction in EU is not supported by constitutional standards. Hence, the EU countries, mostly those of civil law tradition in particular are not affected by such due process limits[394].

When the due process test is applied to cyberspace; however, it is no longer accepted that a mere online presence is taken as sufficient for minimum contact. This is evidenced in the fact that the judiciary, notwithstanding its previous position in this regard had later adopted what is now called 'sliding scale' for websites as evidenced in *Zippo Manufacturing Co. v. Zippo Dot Com, Inc* [395]. The sliding scale approach, obviously based on

---

[393] European Convention on Cybercrime has recognized this expanded territoriality principle in its Art 22, where this principle is also expected to apply against offences based on the location of the victim or impacted computer system, so called "objective territoriality doctrine", see Robert Uerpmann-Wittzack, Principles of International Internet Law, in the German Law Journal, Vol. 11, No. 11, at 1254 (2010), p.1254, whereas the U.S. equivalent would be the effects doctrine as territoriality is still strictly interpreted here with respect to the location of the offence.

[394] Denis T. Rice, Jurisdiction and e-Commerce Disputes in the U.S. and EU, Presentation at the Annual Meeting of the California Bar, at 1 (2002).

[395] Id. at 2.

specific personal jurisdiction, categorizes websites into three to determine the minimum contact needed to satisfy the due process requirement: interactive (e.g. e-commerce), partially interactive, and non-interactive, but tends to exercise personal jurisdiction on websites that are interactive. Yet, even with respect to interactive sites, since website providers cannot always foresee an active interaction of a user with their sites in every forum, this test too leads to an unfair conclusion especially with respect to predictability. And predictability being "the *sine qua non* of the due process," [396] due process analysis based on the minimum contact test will not always be easier to determine jurisdiction given the simultaneous presence of websites across cyberspace. Turns out Web based service providers/businesses are particularly vulnerable to assertion of personal jurisdiction everywhere around the globe due to the web's inherent ubiquitousness (regardless of their being interactive), which can only be made fair through limits provided by the minimum contacts test. But due to the ubiquitous nature of websites, the minimum contact test too needed to be limited or adjusted for cyberspace with foreseeability described above. That is, commercial activity and interactivity of the website alone would not suffice to pass the minimum contact test and assert personal jurisdiction, i.e. more in terms of level of interaction is needed of the website. Hence, the unpredictability of the sliding scale test itself has recently led courts to a slight shift in position away from this approach.

Courts have sought other options, albeit inconsistently, partly in favor of more polished approaches in the due process

---

[396]Minimum contact will ensure defendants' liberty afforded under the constitutional Due process clause based on the Fifth and Fourteenth Amendments; see Jared H. Beck, A "Category-Specific" Legislative Approach to the Internet Personal Jurisdiction Problem in U.S. Law, at 3 (2004).

consideration. Many courts have used Zippo's sliding scale in somewhat modified manner, where they not only tested the nature of websites in terms of commercial activity and interaction, but also checked reasonability when jurisdiction is exercised in relation to non resident aliens. One such approach proposed was the question as to whether it is entirely appropriate to subject a non-resident website operator to U.S. personal jurisdiction merely because the website was accessed by U.S. users regardless of the websites interactivity. The appropriateness consideration in using the sliding scale has become apparent when courts realized that exercise of jurisdiction over non-resident aliens based on just web based contact could be unreasonable. Such a basic contact, although sufficient for and consistent with public international law requirements[397], could lead to an influx of cases. That is, non-resident website operators from anywhere in the world could be called into the U.S. court rooms without sufficient evidence of foreseeability on their part, which is what the principle of fair play and substantial justice demands to protect. Therefore, let alone a mere website access by users in the U.S. but even more than just interacting with the site is needed in favor of the predictability for the site operator to force the same demand the same to appear before U.S. courts. This modified approach appeared to be fair for web publishers who otherwise would be subject to the U.S. court system indiscriminately.

However, as the following cases show, courts needed more ways of refining the minimum contacts test to better meet the

---

[397]Mere contact per se, on the other hand, seems to suffice to meet one of the two basic requirements: link or contact and reasonableness needed to justify jurisdiction; see Henrik Stakemann Spang-Hanssen, A Just World Under Public International Law in Cyberspace: Jurisdiction. Annual Survey of International and Comparative Law, Vol. 13, at 6 (Spring 2007).

due process requirement. Notice that, while courts continued to adjust the minimum contacts test from the two-pronged due process clause analysis formulated for *International Shoe Co v. Washington* that partially culminated in the specific jurisdiction to the foreseeability test, the notion of the due process itself continues to be alive and well. The refining process does not end as can be seen in the recent rationale provided by the Supreme Court in *Burger King Corp. v. Rudzewicz*[398]. The Burger King case sought for a continued relationship (which by the way does not seem to be problematic *in re* websites) instead of a single contact where the defendants must have purposefully availed themselves of the U.S. forum state to establish the required minimum contact.

Turns out neither the modified minimum contact tests nor the sliding scale have provided plausible solutions for web based presence in a given forum. Hence in an attempt to also affirm the protection provided by the due process clause, courts have further introduced the 'effects' test. This constitutes their shift in focus from the nature of the website to the analysis on the actual effects of the minimum contact due to web-presence. The effects doctrine, generally accepted in criminal law as well by even most restrictive, territorially based criminal law systems[399], allows courts to reasonably subject a foreign defendant website operator

---

[398] Burger King Corp. v. Rudzewicz, 471 U.S. 462 (1985); see Jared H. Beck, A "Category-Specific" Legislative Approach to the Internet Personal Jurisdiction Problem in U.S. Law, at 8 (2004).

[399] Courts of many countries have recognized jurisdiction based on effects of offenses without regard to nationality or domicile of the offender; see GARY B. BORN; INTERNATIONAL CIVIL LITIGATION IN U.S. COURTS: COMMENTARY AND MATERIALS, 497-499 (4th Ed. 2006); also see Robert Uerpmann-Wittzack, Principles of International Internet Law, in the German Law Journal, Vol. 11, No. 11, at 1254 (2010).

to personal jurisdiction. This is based on the premise that a website operator must have known or had intention based on specific actions that its website would have effects in any forum to be subject to personal jurisdiction there, and thus to pass the effects test[400]. So, for instance, an e-commerce operator must have intended to do business in a forum by specifically allowing users to interact with the e-commerce site through filling out submitting forms, making payments, or digitally signing contracts. This could include for example specifically allowing users from certain countries to buy and sell products and services by using their local currencies. In doing so, the operator must have expected the effects including legal consequences of these transactions. Having a reasonable expectation of these effects defeats any foreseeability defense on the operator's part.

Generally; however, it must be noted that courts in both EU and U.S. are either divided or inconsistent in applying more established approaches even with regard to cyber jurisdiction whereby many cases lead to unacceptable outcomes[401]. For example, even though the due process analysis has become more persuasive for cyber cases as well, U.S. courts either disregard it or are not consistent with its consideration. Courts in civil law forums, on the contrary, are not bound by the due process limits, but tend to give effect to the effects test.

Unfortunately, this is not an issue just for EU and U.S. The question of jurisdiction varies as much as applicable substantive

---

[400] Rice, supra note 372, at 1.

[401] For instance the mere fact that a website can be seen alone could form a basis for asserting personal jurisdiction, an approach that pretty much subjects the website operator to lawsuits in every forum in the world. See Rice, supra note 372, at 2.

laws or other applicable laws multiplied by the overall legal systems or number of countries. Given the fact that there are variations in culture, value, customs, and yes legal systems, web operators will have to deal with various legal systems not only differently but sometimes with unfavorable outcomes. Diversity in this regard means that anything displayed on a website may or may not be welcomed or received in good terms everywhere in the world. The ones (in many cases sovereign states) that do not like it or consider it against their policy, law, customs, or value could base their jurisdiction on these grounds alone and very well attempt to go against an alien as well. That is a daunting fact from an offshoring investor point of view and scary in terms of the possibility and risks the global marketplace entails for the digital investor. These risks are not limited to business environment alone but those associated with facing multiple legal systems in potential lawsuits[402].

There is no doubt that these risks have negative consequences on business decisions for global digital investor. It can be argued that the uncertainty with forum jurisdiction more likely discourages web-based businesses. Seen from a different angle, an offshore investor that relies on an e-commerce website to sell service products both in an FDI forum and outside may fear the consequences of its being subjected to many jurisdictions

---

[402] The famous French court order initially against Yahoo! enforcing the French penal code that prohibits display of Nazi memorabilia exemplifies this; see Joel R. Reidenberg, The Yahoo Case and the International Democratization of the Internet, Fordham Law & Economics Research Paper No. 11, at 5 (April 2001). This case helped pronounce the division between Internet 'separatists' who took the pro free speech position that later helped Yahoo win the case (see The Center for Democracy and Technology (CDT), available at: http://www.cdt.org/grandchild/jurisdiction#2, (last visited July 6, 2011), for the chronology of the case) and those who denounce the Nazi acts also argued that the state has every right based on its sovereignty to legislate and enforce laws.

based on web-based transactions. This may ultimately act as a disincentive for such a business engagement not just from the host forum perspective per se but overall.

Finally the last question above is concerned with possible impact of jurisdictional problems on an offshore engagement. The answer depends on a particular legal system where jurisdiction of the local court is disputed. In the case where an investor maintains e-commerce, the investor risks the possibility of being subjected to long-arm jurisdiction. In the long-arm approaches the exercise of personal jurisdiction is not limited to the investment forum alone. Indeed, the fact that a website operator can come into contact with numerous users and forums globally, makes it susceptible to multiple legal proceedings. Depending on the nature of an offshore investment, a legal system that tends to expand assertion of personal jurisdiction over an investor as a defendant will help multiply the number of forums the defendant will have to respond to in a dispute. Clearly the fact that the investor sees the possibility to be subjected to lawsuits everywhere in the world or at least in multiple jurisdictions is not without consequences. It has a negative impact on either a decision to do business in an offshore setting or to maintain an e-commerce website as part of the offshoring service engagement. In the end, since potential legal conflicts abound due to the fact that an e-commerce FDI is subject to various jurisdictions, this alone suffices to discourage this type of an FDI engagement.

e) Prescriptive Jurisdiction over the Internet

The question as to who should control cyberspace involves the debate about whether nation-states should regulate cyberspace, the Internet in particular, or combine global efforts to create international regulatory norms. While this debate continues, whether or not states should control and regulate cyberspace including the Internet really depends on whether or not they can and want to exercise sovereignty over cyberspace[403]. The question of control over the Internet by one or a group of nations is nearly impossible as every other nation will claim the same power. In other words, there is no merit in suggesting that one or more nations should control the Internet portion of cyberspace. But at least with regard to the portions of cyberspace that may fall under the purview of nations, it makes some sense to propose control by nations. So in this regard, the question of sovereignty becomes something that needs further analysis. Assuming it is not disputable that states can own, operate, and control their portion of cyberspace behind main gateways, the next question becomes can states successfully exercise their sovereignty on their portion of cyberspace? There are several challenges which point to the fact that complete control over those cyber portions may not be achievable after all for many nations. This leads to another situation where it becomes unclear whether sovereignty over cyberspace that is not necessarily controlled is possible.

As described above, it is no longer a disputed fact states should not only be able to control their borders where their ICTs connect to international gateways, but they should also be able to manage the cyber traffic that rides on their ICTs with appropriate regulations. But this responsibility comes with additional

---

[403] Control over state's territory and cross-border in terms of cyberspace traffic is decisive to exert sovereignty but convincing states to own and exercise this right appears to be among the challenges of control over cyberspace; see Patrick W. Franzese, Sovereignty in Cyberspace, in The Law Review, 64 A.F. L. REV. (66), at 31 (2009).

challenges. Is it always easy and possible for these states to technically achieve the daunting task of identification and tracking sources of incidents within their territories, let those originating beyond their borders. Needless to say, this is not achievable for those that do not have adequate technical means at their disposal. This is generally true with respect to especially developing nations for lack of resources. Yet, everybody else still has the technical problem of attribution, identification, and successfully segregating cyberspace. Nevertheless, despite technical limitations, some states may still attempt to exert their sovereignty powers over cyberspace individually through policy, as well as regulatory means.

Theoretically, such a sovereignty exercise may be possible through applying the traditional principle of territoriality. The realm of cyberspace may have; however, made it nearly impossible for nation-states to extend their sovereignty based territoriality concept to the Internet. Indeed, the realm of cyberspace is said to have totally eroded the traditional notion of territoriality in the context of cyberspace by transcending physical or geographical boundaries. This reality has resulted in heated debates by scholars, who propose a variety of solutions[404]. Their arguments can generally be grouped into two extremes: those who still support sovereignty and rely on the territoriality principle, and those who call for self regulation.

The sovereignty model will extend the territoriality principle from real-space to cyberspace arguing that if no state sovereignty power is exerted in an expanded manner, cyberspace is bound to

---

[404] Some insist that the state should maintain sovereignty also on cyberspace since cyberspace is not immune from state sovereignty for many reasons including infrastructural/physical and legal support that should be provided locally, for detail, id. at 12.

become an uncontrolled/unregulated sphere that can be a source of anarchy and breeding ground for all cybercrimes with no enforceable norm, as well as force against it. This argument has some merit when it comes to cyberspace abound with all the security issues today. Neither currently known complex incidents nor future potentially more sophisticated issues seem to be fully controlled without formal, enforceable regulations that are currently only possible at national levels. These regulations are apt to be in place more quickly by national regulators at least in some jurisdictions[405].

However, the fact that cyberspace is both national and global at the same time might make it more difficult to limit the scope of any regulatory norm applicable to it. That is legal provisions applicable to cyberspace may have effects beyond national limits by potentially being applicable at both national and global levels as well thereby causing legal plurality and jurisdictional conflicts. State's power to regulate cyberspace, thus, will only be justified or free from problems of conflict of laws when the regulatory norms address cyber conducts, if possible, within the national ICT portion of the global ICT in cyberspace. The extraterritorial reach of nations through such regulations should be limited. To reduce legal conflicts, it makes a lot of sense to reserve normative sources with multinational effects on

---

[405] Practice shows that international law-making process takes much more time and even if norms become in effect, it takes time for nation-states to adhere to, ratify, and incorporate the norms to national laws, let alone any efficacy for timely enforcing such norms. In regards cyber security, due to diversity in terms of values, customs, standards, and legal, as well as social systems, it is much harder to come up with internationally acceptable and enforceable cyberspace laws without going through lots of vetting and negotiations that may last for years. Hence, as it stands currently, especially universally applicable international cyberspace conventions or statutes will not seem to come to light to rescue the mostly unregulated space of the internetworking anytime soon.

cyberspace for cooperative efforts which use instruments like treaty regimes; such as, cybercrime convention[406].

To those who advocate self regulation, it is clear that any attempt to regulate the Internet by individual nation-states will create conflicting global jurisdiction. If national jurisdiction is given effect on cyberspace, each state eventually feels entitled to and ends up exercising regardless of effects beyond its territorial limits[407]. Self regulation model will support the idea that cyberspace should be treated as an independent sphere while this sphere should be able to regulate itself just like some other business/industry sectors do, e.g. credit card industry[408]. Regulating cyberspace, the Internet in particular, nationally will lead to an unwarranted control by nation-states and will undermine technological innovations. As this position further contends innovation tends to be possible only under free enterprise as it has also been the case so far with the Internet itself.

The self regulation model further justifies its position with the argument to the extent that in addition to jurisdictional conflicts, national regulation for cyberspace can affect some

---

[406] Signed by some OECD member countries to combat attribution issues, entered into force for the U.S. in 2007, see a Department of Justice document, International Aspects of Computer Crime, available at: http://www.cybercrime.gov/intl.html#Vb, (last visited June 4, 2011).

[407] It must be noted that global jurisdiction is different from universal in that universal is available to all nations whereas global is attempted to be exercised by one or more nations; also see Henrik Stakemann Spang-Hanssen, A Just World Under Public International Law in Cyberspace: Jurisdiction, Annual Survey of International and Comparative Law, Vol. 13, at 3 (Spring 2007).

[408] See Jane K. Winn, Electronic Commerce Law: Direct Regulation, Co-Regulation and Self-Regulation, CRID 30th Anniversary Conference Forthcoming, Cahiers du CRID, 4 (September 2010).

aspects of fundamental human rights; such as, freedom of speech, rights to privacy, and it results in unnecessary censorship limiting thereby a free flow of information[409]. It is more persuasive and plausible that some form of more liberal regulation other than a strict national regulation of cyberspace or the Internet itself could lead to thriving technology and innovation. Less regulation could mean limited number of requirements that can affect free enterprise. Free enterprise could help galvanize innovation thereby contributing to advance in technology, part of the attributes which may become more controlled and, thus, negatively impacted by more regulation. Some content that not any level of regulation by states, but self regulation empowers those who tend to be more adept at a given specific type of technology with decision making ability[410].

Yet the self regulation approach too is lacking because it has not answered the central question as to how to effectively combat cybercrime resulting from the unregulated cyberspace and help control the impending anarchy in cyberspace.

Moreover, the self regulation argument is weak with respect to the question of enforcement and certainly cannot provide for effective deterrence mechanisms since it cannot impose criminal sanctions, among other things, on perpetrators. Little or no enforcement and policing are provided by self

---

[409] Such control via regulation has clearly evidenced in countries like China and a few Middle East Countries; See Kanuck, supra note 348, at 1591; Chinese Internet companies filter content published within the nation: See http://www.rsf.org/article.php3?id_article=23924; http://en.rsf.org/internet-enemie-china,39741.html, (last visited June 14, 2011); see also Roberts et al., supra note 231, at 3.

[410] See Richard M. Marsh, Jr., Legislation for Effective Self-Regulation: A New Approach to Protecting Personal Privacy on the Internet, 15 Mich. Telecomm. Tech. L. Rev. 543, at 553 (2009).

regulation options in both civil and criminal cases[411]. Only the state can enforce criminal law norms using its criminal procedures and power available through enforcement jurisdiction. Hence, free enterprise and more innovation come at the cost of anarchy and security. There should be some mechanism to balance both extremes, whereby it is possible to ensure continuously thriving innovation and free enterprise with regulatory intervention to account for illicit events.

Perhaps the best option could be some combination of both extremes, a middle ground contrary to the two extremes. I would propose an option where certain aspects from both self regulatory and national regulation models can be implemented at national levels, which must be augmented by globally applicable norms.

In regards globally applicable norms, those already in existence or yet to be formulated, it must be noted that the challenge clearly is enforceability. Developing globally enforceable norms beyond "soft laws", which can be adhered to by the international community to effectively compensate national laws, has always been a challenge. Soft laws, meanwhile, won't address issues with cyberspace as much as what is possible through national jurisdictions.

So under this third option, states could regulate and control cyberspace as it relates to their national ICT, i.e. Internet infrastructure that falls within their national geographical boundary. This would allow them to exercise all three types of jurisdiction (prescriptive, adjudicative, and enforcement) in civil as well as criminal matters involving and emanating from cyberspace within their territorial ICT. To exercise adjudicative and enforcement jurisdiction over cross-border criminal cases;

---

[411] Id. at 555.

however, national courts would have to rely on international cooperation. Jurisdiction outside national limits can be exercised by global tribunals, which could apply international, as well as regional cyberspace laws.

With respect to enforcing cybercrime with cross-border effects, a second option would be enforcing transcending cyber offences under international or more standard national provisions utilizing some form of universal jurisdiction by a national or global tribunal. Applying universal jurisdiction in cases with international connection is nothing new. This jurisdiction has already been practiced with international crimes like war crimes while resorting to national or international legal norms. Use of universal jurisdiction is; however, limited to elevated crimes called *delicti jure gentium*. Elevating jurisdiction on cyberspace to global level or affording a cybercrime universal jurisdiction as some suggest[412] will need some justification since it means that cybercrime is being qualified as crime comparable to a crime against humanity just like war crimes.

For war crimes, the actor may theoretically be subject to all jurisdictions in the world, hence universal jurisdiction. Such expansion for a cybercrime is questionable as the cybercrime may not equate with the war crime, again because cyberspace based criminal activities are not equally considered or treated by international community as a criminal offence that needs severe consequences everywhere in the world. And the rationale could be that due to difference in values, customs, legal norms, and

---

[412] Cyberterrorism is recommended as suited for universal jurisdiction as it is as heinous an act as traditional terrorist acts observed, for instance, in 2001, and in fact more so justified because of its being hard to detect or prosecute; see Gable, supra note 17, at 43. Others propose use of the Internet for human trafficking, a form of "modern slavery", as another aspect for such jurisdiction; see Spang-Hanssen, The Future of International Law: CyberCrime, 11 (2008).

other considerations with respect to cyberspace not every society views every cybercrime as egregious as war crime[413].

On the other hand, it is also possible to compare terrorist acts with crimes against humanity, war crimes, and genocide, and answer the applicability of universal jurisdiction to all these in the positive due to the degree of heinousness they are all capable of inflicting into society[414].

By the same token, equally convincing is the argument that if heinous crimes like traditional terrorist acts similar to what the world has observed particularly since 2001 can be equated with war crimes, not every cybercrime, but at least cyberterrorism or cybercrime with severe consequence for life and liberty should be treated the same way[415]. An act of cyberterrorism or any capable organized group including state-sponsors is not only capable of inflicting similar damages to society or humanity, but also the fact that it is hard to trace, detect, prosecute, or attribute most cybercrimes, makes this elevated cybercrime conspicuously worrisome. This characteristic, in particular, makes it a good candidate for the fact that this crime too should be accounted for with the most extreme tool of jurisdiction, universal jurisdiction.

Therefore, nation-states should assert jurisdiction over cases involving cybercrimes with severe consequences based on universal jurisdiction in addition to other national jurisdictional

---

[413] When it comes to cybercrime, countries think differently and have hugely diverging norms, thus, what is a crime in Singapore may or may not a be a crime in Germany thereby raising further question for example in terms of extradition; see Susan W. Brenner & Bert-Jaap Koops, Approaches to Cybercrime Jurisdiction, 4 J. High Tech. L. 1, at 3 (2004).

[414] Universal jurisdiction can be based on customary international law or convention and since acts of terrorism are recognized by various treaties, it is a good candidate for universal jurisdiction; see Gable, supra note 17, at 45.

[415] See Gable, supra note 17, at 44.

rights they may possess. This again is based on the same premise as that of similarly egregious crimes. Given the heinousness of the effects of such a crime, states should have the tools to not only prosecute terrorists and other criminals but to use the deterring effects of this extended jurisdiction against organized crimes.

f) Jurisdiction Based on Destination or Origin of Cyber Incidents

Exertion of a jurisdictional power on a perpetrator for cybercrime, in particular can be based on location of the effects or origin of the act. That being said, however, the effects approach has not been consistently applied. There is a tendency to renounce the destination principle and resort instead to the country of origin principle in cross-border e-commerce, as advocated by the Commission for European Union[416]. But this will have to be limited to civil disputes. Any attempt to expand this approach beyond civil cases, otherwise either doesn't make a lot of sense when it comes to transient effects on criminal acts on cyberspace or may not always work for cybercrime. The rationale is that if this principle were to be extended to cybercrime, it would sort of change the course of jurisdictional practice in cybercrime in that states would have exclusive jurisdiction over crimes committed in their territory regardless of the crimes' effects. This would seem to suggest that countries which control the ICT where an issue might originate from should also be able to

---

[416] This approach appears to rely on an analogy of the Law of the Sea "which states that the Flag State has exclusive jurisdiction on its ships on the High Seas", see Henrik Stakemann Spang-Hanssen, A Just World Under Public International Law in Cyberspace: Jurisdiction. Annual Survey of International and Comparative Law, Vol. 13, at 8 (Spring 2007).

assert an exclusive jurisdiction not just in civil and commercial matters at a minimum, but in cybercrime.

The problem with that is not every incident might be of interest for every forum to allocate resources and pursue the incident deserving some level of criminal sanction. For example, if a cyber criminal conduct originates in forum A, but has negative economic or criminal effects in forum B. At least economically, it does not make a lot of sense for A to allocate resources and exercise its jurisdiction to prosecute the actor and account for the incident even when it has an exclusive jurisdiction as a country of origin.

Therefore, also contrary to the strictly territoriality based outcomes, as exemplified in the U.S. Supreme Court's emphasis on the origin of conduct as evidenced in one of its older decisions[417] , it makes more sense in the information age to allow B to assert jurisdiction following at least the effects principle. The effects consideration from IT standpoint has more weight. No wonder that more scholars seem to agree with this position[418]. This is more practical for B absent any other competing jurisdiction. Even when there is competing jurisdiction, countries generally have the right to prosecute a criminal for the same act since the level of impact and interest to bring the perpetrator to justice for the

---

[417] The court in the old case of American Banana Company v. United Fruit Company, 213 U.S. 347, 356 (1909), held that the lawfulness of an act must be determined by the law of the location of the act; also see Susan W. Brenner & Bert-Jaap Koops, Approaches to Cybercrime Jurisdiction, 4 J. High Tech. L. 1, at 6 (2004).

[418] This is based on the well established international principle allowing states to regulate any offence that adversely affects domestic interests; see Scott J. Shackelford, From Nuclear War to Net War: Analogizing Cyber Attacks in International Law, Berkeley Journal of International Law Vol. 27:1, at 210 (2008); see also Restatement (Third) of Foreign Relations § 402(1)(C) (1987) for the treatment of this theory in the United States.

same crime might be different in various fora. So in the example above, if the incident was a virus created in forum A, its damages/consequences may vary in different forums (B, C, D, etc) depending on protection mechanisms in place, types of systems, and criticality of information housed in the systems affected, etc.

Therefore, it is not reasonable to expect C and D not to pursue criminal proceedings against the perpetrator in A if B or A has already filed suits. From this, it follows that in the case of cybercrime, regardless of whether A makes use of its jurisdictional power; B, C, or D should be able to apply its power without regard to the exclusivity.

To conclude the discussion surrounding the question of jurisdiction on cyberspace, it must be conceded that jurisdiction as it relates to cyberspace should also be assessed and asserted based on various factors. Jurisdiction on cyber matters can be determined the same way as it can be determined for other non-cyberspace matters involving cross-border transactions. The only caveat is that cyberspace has made jurisdiction more complex and its exercise a lot more frequent, i.e. many cyber cases can involve multiple parties and states simultaneously. Though the unique characteristics of virtual space embodied in cyberspace can complicate and multiply the question of jurisdiction, it should not by itself lead to a conclusion that nation-states should be limited or even entirely excluded from entertaining their jurisdictional rights and applying their laws on cyberspace.

Regardless of whether it is personal, subject matter, or *in rem* jurisdiction, nation-states can rely on prescriptive measures to assert jurisdiction, or to apply effects test on criminal and civil matters. States can also enforce their criminal jurisdiction on cyber matters, among others, with the help of international cooperative measures.

Clearly, jurisdiction for enforcement presents the most challenge again as a result of national differences in cultural and socio-political settings, as well as legal standards, e.g. conflicting laws, lack of treaties, or absent double criminality - with respect to extradition. While these challenges remain to be part of major hurdles in international jurisprudence, there is a possibility that even problems with enforcement in international cybercrimes can be resolved for the most part. The solution for enforcement issues could include appropriate agreements (bilateral or multilateral) fostering cooperation within the international law enforcement.

Chapter 4 Part Two Summary

This chapter discussed in detail the fundamental characteristics of service FDI also termed as offshoring as it relates to digital investment, the technical details of information security associated with offshore investment, and essential legal and policy frameworks available or missing to protect cyber security related to offshoring business model. Part of the discussion involved cyber security issues affecting IT enabled offshore investment, whereas the focus was not on counter measures from technical point of view as much as it was on describing threats posed by the global cyberspace.

The emphasis in terms of counter measures that should help protect cyberspace was on the analyses of effectiveness and adequacy of existing legal, as well as policy measures geared to counteract those threats. In particular, the challenges of cyber security and attempts to address cyber security issues with existing or new, cyberspace specific regulations were analyzed.

The central problem of cyberspace and the Internet: their being transnational/global and territorial simultaneously, which have resulted in legal and technical challenges of securing cyberspace was discussed.

Based on these analyses and evidence presented, one must conclude the following. Cross-border transactions involving offshoring service FDI often utilize global cyberspace as part of the business process. The use of cyberspace by an offshoring service FDI may be in the form of forum based e-commerce or direct use of cyberspace, the Internet in particular, to transmit information assets back and forth between the FDI forum facility and other locations around the world. These transactions are vulnerable to all the discussed cyberspace threats.

Any legal disputes involving civil and criminal laws with regard to cyber incidents emanating from compromised investor digital assets will result in litigation costs for the investor, jurisdictional conflicts, and legal as well as technical issues with attribution and identification of illicit actors. Legal, policy, ideological, and cultural, etc. diversity within the global community result in various legal, policy, and ethical standards. And this variation is the road block in the attempt to standardize cyber security, develop standard cyberspace regulations globally, or enforce cybercrime elsewhere.

Cyberspace is not well defined in law, but legal conflicts arising from cyberspace may implicate several aspects of law: contract, criminal, intellectual property, and jurisdiction. Yet legal conflicts cannot always be solved with existing legal norms in ways which satisfy all parties involved. In terms of jurisdiction, in particular the disparity in legal standards causes legal uncertainty as to which principle or approach to apply to resolve cyberspace related jurisdictional disputes.

Certain countries have attempted to protect cyberspace

with regulations that have extraterritorial reaches thereby creating potential legal conflicts with other jurisdictions, which may neither recognize such prescriptive jurisdictional rights nor enforce these laws.

Attempts to regulate cyberspace by both home and host countries may interfere with efforts to promote offshore digital investment as some regulations are either too restrictive/protective (pro consumer) or too lax, and thus discouraging for potential digital investors.

National security can be affected by cyberspace and vice versa. So some legal regimes are wary of this circumstance and thus attempt to protect their national security by resorting to restrictive measures mostly at the cost of technological innovation, privacy, and Internet freedom. In the name of national security, some of these nation-states even have implanted far-reaching measures on cyberspace within their national limits, where they filter, analyze, and censor the Internet traffic. Such far-reaching national security measures both from home and host countries can have a negative impact on offshoring FDI.

On the contrary, some legal regimes do not adequately address cyber security issues in their regulatory and policy instruments which will also negatively affect the potential to attract digital investment in the form offshoring FDI.

All things considered, both home and host countries must do due diligence to promote and protect digital assets of investors doing business across national borders by taking into consideration all relevant factors and necessary steps when dealing with cyberspace. Regulatory measures need to address security aspects of offshore investment while at the same time promoting investment in digital economy. In other words, governments should ensure that these measures support cyber security and do not adversely impact innovation, and the ability to attract foreign direct investment in IT and IT-enabled services in particular, in their economies.

Part III

Conclusions

This interdisciplinary discourse has touched upon the vast array of important issues associated with offshore undertakings dealing with digital assets, cyber security for such digital assets, and the ability/inability to provide regulatory protection to these assets.

This book extends studies and inquiries surrounding one of the most controversial issues in global Cybersecurity – the questions of whether or not it is possible to effectively regulate and secure cyberspace, and deter cybercrime. It offers a new perspective on service oriented FDI activities with a focus on IT and IT enabled services involving offshoring business models. The topic invokes interdisciplinary approaches to investigate underlying problems, discuss opposing arguments, and present alternatives.

Most current and hotly debated issues that have won relevance in information security, international law, and economics literature have been analyzed and looked at from various angles. However, it cannot be claimed to the extent that this work exhaustively raised, presented, and discussed all relevant issues brought up in the course of this investigation due to limitations that must have been imposed on the scope. Yet an attempt has been made to identify and discuss the most important items that should also call for and inspire further research, readings, and discussions.

Problems with national cyber security measures have been compounded by the multitude of elements involved in the global market place along with the ubiquitous presence of cyberspace globally. In light of the threats cyberspace poses to digital investors in the global market place, the central question of whether such investors can be legally protected became an essential part of the research.

Therefore, the emphasis has been on the existence, effectiveness, and adequacy of law, as well as policy measures aimed at counteracting those threats, rather than technical solutions. As digital assets utilize cyberspace, their security is as good as the security of cyberspace itself. Thus, the discussion of protecting these primarily intangible assets with possible legal and policy measures centers around the security of cyberspace.

While the use of global cyberspace poses security challenges, these challenges are specially pronounced in the lack of technical capabilities for attribution and identification of illicit actors. Legal, policy, and cultural diversity within the global community essentially creates variations in value, legal, and ethical standards. Consequently, it becomes difficult to standardize cyber security, to develop all-inclusive legal regimes globally, or enforce national cyberspace laws elsewhere. Various research sources have shown that national regulations have failed for the most part to account for illicit cyber events across the globe due to attribution and enforcement challenges and there is no viable solution from international sources in sight.

In my observation, cyberspace is not fully covered by law, but legal conflicts arising from cyberspace abound, which implicate several aspects of law: contract, criminal law, intellectual property, and jurisdiction. Oftentimes some of these conflicts cannot be resolved with existing legal norms in ways which satisfy all parties involved.

I also find that regulations; such as, those aimed at national security, cyber security, or privacy by both home and host countries interfere with efforts to promote offshoring service FDI at host locations as some regulations, especially those geared to protect national security are too restrictive and thus discouraging for potential investors. Overall it is worth noting that, while it seems difficult to strike a balance between incentives for digital investment and strict national security measures that may backfire, regulatory and policy measures should help safeguard the national ICT infrastructure. These measure need to address security aspects of investment in digital economy while at the same time ensuring that those measures do not adversely impact innovation or efforts to attract offshoring.

As much as there are nations that have cyber security regulations, albeit with some loopholes, there are those which do not have any. This is the case in particular in the developing world, the best example being a few countries in the Sub-Saharan region.

The Sub-Saharan region also houses perhaps the least technologically enabled countries in the world to support cyberspace. These countries have the lowest penetration rates in ICT and Internet usage. I find that these countries have neither the resources to implement well functioning and secure ICT networks nor the need to regulate cyberspace since wherever there is no ICT capabilities, there is little or no incentive to regulate it.

In sum, clearly lack of ICT capabilities has been the primary deterrent factor for digital investment in form IT offshoring in SSA. This region on the one hand has more acute FDI impediments to account for in order to attract offshoring, and on the other hand, there is a yawning capital resource gap to account for the majority of these problems.

All in all, it is my sincere hope that this contribution has pointed out important problems and identified ponderable, as well as critically assessed observations. Yet the findings also point to an unfinished research agenda.

First, there is an immediate need to do more research to help nations cope with securing their portions of cyberspace with appropriate legal and policy measures thereby being more attractive for digital investors.

Secondly, there is a research need to address the yawning digital divide that continues to grow and set the developing world apart from the rest thereby limiting developing countries' ability to access global market place using global cyberspace. It seems prudent to do more research to help find solutions for these countries in their quest for connection to the rest of the world.

At least there is an ethical obligation for technologists, government officials, and scholars to consider the digital gap as a serious issue, something that need immediate attention from the rich and poor. Otherwise, countries with poor information technology infrastructure continue to lag behind and never be able to catch up just like those in poverty's vicious circle that some countries never seem to be able to exit. The only way to help countries which are left behind in the digital age seems to be a proactive support through inclusiveness, rather than isolation. One needs to look into all possible alternatives to help them build new ICT infrastructure if none is available or to improve existing infrastructure and foster connectivity. Eliminating such a digital gap and ensuring active participation of developing nations in the digital economy will allow them to reap all the benefits of the information age including their ability to take advantage of international electronic trade and digital investment, among other things.

BIBLIOGRAPHY

Alok Aggarwal, William Aspray, Orna Berry, Stefanie Ann Lenway, Valerie Taylor; The Big Picture; In the Globalization and Offshoring of Software; A Report of the Association for Computing Machinery (ACM) Job Migration Task Force, 2006 ACM 0001-0782/06/0200

Álvaro Calderón, Michael Mortimore, Carlos Razo and Márcia Tavares; Foreign Investment in Latin America and the Caribbean, 2008; Unit on Investment and Corporate Strategies of the ECLAC Division of Production, Productivity and Management

Andrew D. Mitchell, Electronic Commerce, Legal Studies Research Paper No. 353, 2006

Antonio R. Parra, Provisions on the Settlement of Investment Disputes in Modern Investment Laws, BITs and Multilateral Instruments on Investment, 12 FDI Journal, 1997, p.287

Arjun Kalyanpur, Firoz Latif, Sanjay Saini, Surendra Sarnikar; Inter-organizational E-Commerce in Healthcare Services - The Case of Global Teleradiology, 2006

Arvind Panagariya, E-Commerce, WTO and Developing Countries; Policy Issues in International Trade and Commodities Study Series No. 2, UNCTAD, 2000

Assafa Endeshaw, Intellectual Property and the Digital Divide; Journal of Information, Law & Technology (JILT), 2008 (1)

Audrey Guinchard, Criminal Law in the 21st century: The Demise of Territoriality? Notes for the Critical Legal Conference on Walls (2007)

Beata K. Smarzynska, Composition of Foreign Direct Investment and Protection of Intellectual Property Rights in Transition Economies, University of Oxford - Department of Economics; World Bank - Development Research Group (DECRG); Centre for Economic Policy Research (CEPR), June 1999

Beata k. Smarzynska, Composition of Foreign Direct Investment and Protection of Intellectual Property Rights: Evidence from Transition Economies; The World Bank Development Research Group Trade, February 2002

Beth Bacheldor, What Google vs. China Says About Security and Offshore Outsourcing, also see: http://advice.cio.com/beth_bacheldor/what_google_vs_china_says_about_security_and_offshore_outsourcing, Accessed 5-3-2011

Bezzawork Shemelash, The Formation, Content and Effects of an Arbitral Submission under Ethiopian Law, in the Journal of Ethiopian Law, Vol. XVII, December, 1994

Bierce & Kenerson, P.C, Cyber Security Threat Management in Outsourcing: The Coming National Security Regulation of ITO, BPO and KPO, Posted January 29, 2010; see http://www.outsourcing-law.com/2010/01/cyber-security-threat-management-in-outsourcing-the-coming-national-security-regulation-of-ito-bpo-and-kpo/, last accessed 4/18/11.

Bierce & Kenerson, P.C., Privacy, Data Protection and Outsourcing in the United States http://www.outsourcing-law.com/jurisdictions/countries/united-states-of-america/privacy-data-protection-and-outsourcing-in-the-united-states/, Accessed 4/27/11

Bit Law Legal Resources: http://www.bitlaw.com/copyright/fair_use.html; accessed 4-7-2011.

Catherine L. Mann, International Trade in the Digital Age: Data Analysis and Policy Issues; Testimony Subcommittee on International Trade, Customs, and Global Competitiveness of the Senate Committee on Finance, November 2010

Catherine L. Mann, Offshore Outsourcing and the Globalization of U.S. Services: Why Now, How Important, and What Policy Implications? The United States and World Economy

Catherine L. Mann, Technology, Trade in Services, and Economic Growth; OECD Trade Committee Conference: Trade, Innovation, and Growth "Global Forum on Trade" 15-16 October 2007

Catherine Struve, Polak Wagner; Realspace Sovereigns in Cyberspace - Problems with the Anticybersquatting Consumer Protection Act (ACPA), 2002

Catherine T. Struve, R. Pole Wagner; Realspace Sovereigns in Cyberspace: Problems with the Anticybersquatting Consumer Protection Act (ACPA). Berkeley Technology Law Journal, Vol. 17, No. 1, Sept. 2002

Charles Pfleeger P., Security in Computing, 3rd Edition, 2003

Charlie Kaufman, Radia Perlman, Mike Speciner: Network Security; Private Communication in a Public World, 2002.

Choudhury Barnali, Recapturing Public Power: Is Investment Arbitration's Engagement of the Public Interest Contributing to the

Democratic Deficit? Vanderbilt Journal of Transnational Law, 2008

Chris Dent, Copyright as (Decentred) Regulation: Digital Piracy as a Case Study; the Monash University Law Review, Volume 35, Number 2, 2009

Christian N. Okeke, "Science, Technology and the Law" (1992). Lectures & Speeches. Paper 2. Also available at: http://digitalcommons.law.ggu.edu/lectures/2; Accessed 10/18/2011

Christine Bruinsma, Peter Wemmenhove; Tone at the Top is Vita! A Delphy Study; in the ISACA Journal, Volume 3, 2009

Christoph Engel, The Role of Law in the Governance of the Internet Preprints aus der Max-Planck-Projektgruppe: Recht der Gemeinschaftsgüter, Bonn 2002

Christoph Schreuer, Full Protection and Security; Journal of International Dispute Settlement, (2010), pp. 1–17

Christoph Schreuer, The Relevance of Public International Law, in International Commercial Arbitration

Christopher Joyner, Catherine Lotrionate, Information Warfare as International Coercion: Elements of Legal Framework, 2001

Christopher Kuner, An International Legal Framework for Data Protection: Issues and Prospects, 2009.

Committee on National Security Systems; National Information Assurance (IA) Glossary; CNSS Instruction No. 4009, April 26, 2010.

Common Criteria for Information Technology Security Evaluation, Part 2: Security functional components, July 2009

Computerworld; Heartland data breach sparks security concerns in payment industry; Available at: http://www.computerworld.com/s/article/9126608/Heartland_data_breach_sparks_security_concerns_in_payment_industry

Couzyn Hertzog, Electronic Contracts in South Africa - A Comparative Analysis, in the Journal of Information, Law & Technology; Lex Informatica Conference, 21st -23rd May 2008 Pretoria, South Africa.

Dan Ciuriak, Claudius Preville; Ethiopia's Trade and Investment: Policy Priorities for the New Government, September 2010

Daniel B. Garrie, Bill Spernow; Legally Correct But Technologically Off the Mark; North Western Journal of Technology and IP, Vol. 9, No. 1

Daniel J. Gilman and James C. Cooper, There Is a Time to Keep Silent and a Time to Speak, the Hard Part Is Knowing Which Is Which: Striking the Balance Between Privacy Protection and the Flow of Health Care Information, 16 Mich. Telecomm. Tech. L. Rev. 279 (2010)

Daniel J. Solove "I've Got Nothing to Hide" and Other Misunderstandings of Privacy, 2007

Danielle Langton, U.S. Trade and Investment Relationship with Sub-Saharan Africa: The African Growth and Opportunity Act and Beyond; Congressional Research Service Report to Congress; Updated October 28, 2008

David A. Gantz, Investor-State Arbitration Under ICSID, the ICSID Additional Facility and the UNCTAD Arbitral Rules (2004)

David A. Wheeler, Techniques for Cyber Attack Attribution; Institute for Defense Analyses, 2007

David Collins, Applying the Full Protection and Security Standard of Protection to Digital Investments; The City Law School, City University, London 2010.

David D. Elliott, Tonya L. Putnam; International Responses to Cyber Crime, 2001

David L. Willson, Keeping Cyberspace Professionals Informed: When does electronic espionage or a cyber attack become an 'act of war'?, NSCI CyberPro May 2010

David Navetta, The Legal Defensibility Era; the (ISSA) Journal May 2010.

Dax Eric Lopez, Not Twice for the Same: How the Dual Sovereignty Doctrine is Used to Circumvent *Non Bis In Ide,* in the Vanderbilt Journal Transnational La, Volume 33, Number 5: October 2000

Dejo Olowu, Cyber-Crimes and the Boundaries of Domestic Legal Responses: Case for an Inclusionary Framework for Africa, in the Journal of Information, Law & Technology, 2009

Denis T. Rice, Jurisdiction and e-Commerce Disputes in the US and EU, Presentation at the Annual Meeting of the California Bar, 2002.

Duncan B. Hollis, An e-SOS for Cyberspace, 2010

Economic Commission for Latin America and the Caribbean (ECLAC); Foreign Direct Investment in Latin America and the Caribbean, 2008

Elizabeth Asiedu, Foreign Direct Investment in Africa: The Role of Natural Resources, Market Size, Government Policy, Institutions and Political Instability; UN University 2006

Elizabeth Asiedu, Foreign Direct Investment to Africa: The Role of Government Policy, Governance and Political Instability (2003)

Elizabeth Asiedu, Policy Reform and Foreign Direct Investment in Africa; Absolute Progress but Relative Decline; Development Policy

Review, 2004, 22(1): 41-48

Eric Neumayer and Laura Spess, Do Bilateral Investment Treaties Increase Foreign Direct Investment to Developing Countries? (May 1, 2005). World Development, Vol. 3, No. 1, pp. 31-49, 2005, Available at SSRN: http://ssrn.com/abstract=616242 or doi:10.2139/ssrn.616242

Erran Carmel, Rafael Prikladnicki; Does Time Zone Proximity Matter for Brazil? A Study of the Brazilian IT Industry, Industry Report of July 20, 2010

Erwin van der Zwan, Security of Industrial Control Systems; in the ISACA Journal, Volume 4, 2010

Fawzia Cassim, Formulating Specialised Legislation to address the Growing Spectre of Cybercrime: A Comparative Study, PER 2009 VOLUME 12 No 4

Federal Information Processing Standard 199 (FIPS 199), Standards for Security Categorization of Federal Information and Information Systems, Publication 199, Feb 2004

Fred H. Cate and Robert Litan, *Constitutional Issues in Information Privacy*, 9 Mich. Telecomm. Tech. L. Rev. 35 (2002), p.40; *Available at* http://www.mttlr.org/volnine/cate.pdf

Gary B. Born; International Civil Litigation in US courts: Commentary and Materials, 4th Edition 2006.

George M. Marakas; Decision Support Systems in the Twenty-first Century, 1999

Georgios Zekos, *Foreign Direct Investment in a Digital Economy*, European Business Review, Vol. 17 No. 1, pp. 52-68 (2005)

Gerald R. Ferrera, Stephen D. Lichtenstein, Margo E. K. Reder, Ray August, William T. Schiano, Cyber Law: Text and Cases, 2000.

Getachew/ Abebe/ Mengistu, Ethiopian Supreme Court Journal of Law, vol. 2, No. 1, (Amharic version)

Global Economic Prospects, Electronic Commerce and Developing Countries; World Bank, 2000

Graeme W. Austin, *Importing Kazaa - Exporting Grokster,* Arizona Legal Studies Discussion Paper No. 06-08, (April 2006)

Graham H. Todd, Armed Attack In Cyberspace: Deterring Asymmetric Warfare with an Asymmetric Definition; in The Air Force Law Review, 64 A.F. L. REV. (66) (2009).

Gralf-Peter Calliess, Transnational Consumer Law: Co-Regulation of B2C-E-Commerce; Comparative Research in Law and Political Economy (CLPE) Research Paper 3/2007; Vol. 03 No. 03 (2007)

Grant Eskelsen, Adam Marcus W. Kenneth Ferree; The Digital Economy Fact Book 10th Edition, 2008-2009; The Progress & Freedom Foundation Washington, D.C., 2009.

Guido S. Tawil, UNCTAD, Dispute Settlement: ICSID Disputes - Applicable Law, in The Course on Dispute Settlement in International Trade, Investment and Intellectual Property, United Nations, 2003

Hailegabriel G. Feyissa, The Role of Ethiopian Courts in Commercial Arbitration, Mizan Law Review Vol. 4 No.2, Autumn 2010, pp. 298ff

Hailu Abatena, Globalization and Development Problems in Sub-Saharan Africa; Presented at the 18th Annual Conference of the *Global Awareness Society International* - May 2009

Hal Roberts, Ethan Zuckerman, and John Palfrey, 2007 Circumvention Landscape Report: Methods, Uses, and Tools; The Berkman Center for Internet & Society at Harvard University, March 2009

Hari Hara Das, Principles of International Law and Organization, New Delhi, 1995.

Henrick W Kaspersen, Cybercrime and Internet Jurisdiction, March 2009.

Henrik Stakemann Spang-Hanssen, A Just World Under Public International Law in Cyberspace: Jurisdiction. Annual Survey of International and Comparative Law, Vol. 13, Spring 2007. Available at SSRN: http://ssrn.com/abstract=1092389

Henrik Stakemann Spang-Hanssen, Cyberspace or Sovereign States? (March 22, 2010). Twelfth United Nation Crime Prevention and Criminal Justice Congress, Brazil, April 12-19, 2010 . Available at SSRN: http://ssrn.com/abstract=1582645

Henrik Stakemann Spang-Hanssen, The Future of International Law: CyberCrime (2008); Available at SSRN: http://ssrn.com/abstract=1090876

Hollis Ashbaugh-Skaife, Daniel W. Collins, William R. Kinney, Jr., Ryan LaFond; The Effect of SOX Internal Control Deficiencies on Firm Risk and Cost of Equity, June 10, 2008

Ibrahim F.I. Shihata, Towards a Greater De-politicization of Investment Disputes: The Roles of ICSID and MIGA

Ignaz Seidl-Hohenveldern, Collected Essays on International Investments & on International Organizations, 1998, pp. 204f.

International Telecommunication Union – Telecommunication Standardization Sector (ITU-T), Recommendation ITU-T X.1205, 4/2008.

ITU Global Cybersecurity Agenda, High-level Experts Group, Global Strategic Report, 2008

ITU Toolkit for Cybercrime Legislation; Developed through the American Bar Association's Privacy & Computer Crime Committee Section of Science & Technology Law With Global Participation, Draft February 2010

Ivohasina Razafimahefa, Shigeyuki Hamori; An Empirical Analysis of FDI Competitiveness in Sub–Saharan Africa and Developing Countries, 2005; in *Economics Bulletin,* Vol. 6, No. 20 pp. 1–8

James Gannon, The Middle Lane on the Information Superhighway: A Review of Jack Goldsmith's and Tim Wu's Who Controls the Internet? Illusions of a Borderless World (2006)

James R. Langevin, Michael T. McCaul, Scott Charney, Lt. General Harry Raduege, James A. Lewis: Securing Cyberspace for the 44th Presidency: A Report of the CSIS Commission on Cyber-security for the 44th Presidency. Center for Strategic and International Studies, Washington, DC, December 2008

Jane K. Winn, Electronic Commerce Law: Direct Regulation, Co-Regulation and Self-Regulation, CRID 30th Anniversary Conference, *Cahiers du CRID* September 2010

Jared H. Beck, A "Category-Specific" Legislative Approach to the Internet Personal Jurisdiction Problem in U.S. Law

Jason Cox, Regulation of Foreign Direct Investment After the Dubai Ports Controversy: Has the U.S. Government Finally Figured Out How to Balance Foreign Threats to National Security Without Alienating Foreign Companies? The Journal of Corporation Law, 34:1 (2008)

Jason Webb Yackee, Do Bilateral Investment Treaties Promote Foreign Direct Investment? Some Hints from alternative evidence, the Virginia Journal of International Law Association, Volume 51 — Number 2 — Page 397, 2010

Jean Camp, Seymour Goodman, Charles H. House, William B. Jack, Rob Ramer, Marie Stella; Offshoring: Risks And Exposures; In the Globalization and Offshoring of Software; A Report of the Association for Computing Machinery (ACM) Job Migration Task Force, 2006 ACM 0001-0782/06/0200

Jennifer A. Chandler, Security in Cyberspace: Combating Distributed Denial of Service (DDoS) Attacks, University of Ottawa, 2004.

Joanna Kulesza, Internet Governance and the Jurisdiction of States Justification of the Need for an International Regulation of Cyberspace, 2003

Joanna Kulesza, Internet Governance and the Jurisdiction of States; Justification of the Need for an International Regulation of Cyberspace, 2003

Joel R. Reidenberg, States and Internet Enforcement; University of Ottawa law & technology journal; (2003–2004) 1 UOLTJ 213

Joel R. Reidenberg, The Rule of Intellectual Property Law in the Internet Economy. Houston Law Review, Vol. 44, No. 4, pp. 1074-1095, 2007; Fordham Law Legal Studies Research Paper No. 1012504. Available at SSRN: http://ssrn.com/abstract=1012604

Joel R. Reidenberg, The Yahoo Case and the International Democratization of the Internet (April 2001). Fordham Law & Economics Research Paper No. 11. Available at SSRN: http://ssrn.com/abstract=267148 or doi:10.2139/ssrn.267148

John Palfrey, Urs Gasser, Miriam Simun, Rosalie Fay Barnes; Youth, Creativity, and Copyright in the Digital Age; Research Publication No. 2009-05; June 2009

Jonathan Zittrain, Benjamin Edelman; Documentation of Internet Filtering in Saudi Arabia; Berkman Center for Internet & Society Harvard Law School: http://cyber.law.harvard.edu/filtering/saudiarabia/; Accessed 5-13-11

Joseph D. Piotroski, Suraj Srinivasan; Regulation and Bonding: The Sarbanes-Oxley Act and the Flow of International Listings, January 2008

Joseph P.H. Fana, Randall Morckb, Lixin Colin Xuc, and Bernard Yeungd; Does 'Good Government' Draw Foreign Capital? Explaining China's Exceptional FDI Inflow, Draft paper (2006)

Jota Ishikawa, Hodaka Morita, FDI in Services and Market Access: A Paradox of Trade Liberalization, 2006

Judge Stein Schjolberg, Amanda Hubbard; International Telecommunication Union, Harmonizing National Legal Approaches on Cybercrime WSIS Thematic Meeting on Cybersecurity, Geneva, 28 June – 1 July 2005.

Jurgen Kurtz, A General Investment Agreement in the WTO? Lessons from Chapter 11 of NAFTA and the OECD; Multilateral Agreements on Investment; in the Journal of International Economic Law, 23:4, 2003

Justin Hughes, The Internet and the Persistence of Law, Boston College Law Review, Vol. 44, Pages 289-290 (2003), available at: http://www.bc.edu/content/dam/files/schools/law/lawreviews/journals/bclawr/44_2/04_FMS.htm

Karl P Sauvant, World Investment Prospects to 2010: A backlash

Against Foreign Direct Investment? 2006.

Kelly A. Gable, *Cyber Apocalpyse Now: Securing the Internet Against Cyber Terrorism and Using Universal Jurisdiction as a Deterrent* (August 14, 2009), also available at: SSRN: http://ssrn.com/abstract=1452803 (last visited Dec. 25, 2011)

Kendra Simmons, Ron Keys, Charles Winstead: Cyberspace Security and Attribution, in National Security Cyberspace Institute (NSCI); July, 2010

Kenneth J. Vandevelde, The Political Economy of a Bilateral Investment Treaty, AJIL, October 1998, pp. 9-13.

Larry K. McKee, Jr., International Cyberspace Strategies Kathryn Stephens, NSCI; June, 2010.

Lawrence B. Solum, Minn Chung; The Layers Principle: Internet Architecture and the Law; University of San Diego School of Law Public Law and Legal Theory Research Paper 55 June 2003.

Leon E. Trakman, Foreign Direct Investment: Hazard or Opportunity? The George Washington Int'l L. Rev. [Vol. 41] 2009

Leon Trakman, Foreign Direct Investment- An Australian Perspective (January 23, 2010). UNSW Law Research Paper No. 2010-4, available at: SSRN: http://ssrn.com/abstract=1540289

Lieutenant Colonel Patrick W. Franzese; Sovereignty in Cyberspace: Can it Exist? The Air Force Law Review, 64 A.F. L. REV., (2009)

Lilach Nachum, Srilata Zaheer; MNES in The Digital Economy? ESRC Centre for Business Research, University of Cambridge Working Paper No. 236, June 2002.

Linda Schmid, Africa Harnessing a Broadband Boom; Ways Journal of E-Government Policy and Regulation 32 (2009) 219–227

Lukas Feiler, The Legality of the Data Retention Directive in Light of the Fundamental Rights to Privacy and Data Protection; in the European Journal of Law and Technology, Vol 1, Issue 3, 2010

Madhu T. Rao, Key Issues for Global IT Sourcing: Country and Individual Factors; in Information Systems Management Journal, Summer 2004

Maeve Dion, Keeping Cyberspace Professionals Informed, in NSCI CyberPro December 2009

Malcolm Shaw, International Law, 4th Edition, 1997

Marc Proksch, Selected Issues on Promotion and Attraction of Foreign Direct Investment in Least Developed Countries and Economies in Transition

Marco Gercke, International Telecommunication Union – Understanding Cybercrime: A Guide for Developing Countries, Draft 2009

Michael W Nicholson, Intellectual Property Rights, Internalization and Technology Transfer; Federal Trade Commission, 2001

Mohamed S. Abdel, Identity Theft in Cyberspace: Issues and Solutions, spring 2006

Nathalie Bernasconi, Background Paper on Vattenfall v. Germany Arbitration, International Institute for Sustainable Development (IISD), 2009

Nathalie Bernasconi-Osterwalder, Lise Johnson; International Investment Law and Sustainable Development - Key cases from 2000–2010

Nathan Associates Inc., Foreign Direct Investment, Putting it to Work in Developing Countries, U.S. Agency for International Development (USAID), June (2005)

NIST Special Publication 800-144, Guideline on Security and Privacy in Cloud Computing (Draft), January 2011

NIST Special Publication 800-145, The NIST Definition of Cloud Computing (Draft), January 2011

NIST Special Publication 800-60 Volumes I & II Revision 1, Guide for Mapping Types of Information and Information Systems to Security Categories, August 2008

Norbert Lebale, Patrick Osakwe, Janvier Nkurunziza, Martin Halle, Michael Bratt, Adriano Timossi; The Economic Development in Africa Report; South-South Cooperation: Africa and The New Forms of Development Partnership; UNCTAD, NY 2010.

OECD Conference on Empowering E-consumers Strengthening Consumer Protection in the Internet Economy: Background Report, Washington D.C., 8-10 December 2009.

OECD Foreign Government-Controlled Investors and Recipient Country Investment Policies: A Scoping Paper *January 2009*

OECD Guidelines for Recipient Country Investment Policies Relating to National Security; Recommendation Adopted by the OECD Council on 25 May 2009.

OECD, International Investment Perspectives: Freedom of Investment in a Changing World 2007

OECD, Security-Related Terms in International Investment Law and in National Security Strategies; May 2009

Organization for Economic Co-Operation and Development (OECD), Guidelines for Consumer Protection in the Context of Electronic Commerce, 2000

Osita C. Eze, The Legal Status of Foreign Investments in the East African Common Market, 1975.

Patrick W. Franzese, Sovereignty in Cyberspace; in The Air Force Law Review, 64 A.F. L. REV. (66) (2009)

Paul E. Paray, Cost Effective Risk Management of Health Information; the (ISSA) Journal February 2011.

Paul Rosenzweig, National Security Threats in Cyberspace, September 2009; Report from a Workshop Conducted by: American Bar Association Standing Committee on Law and National Security and National Strategy Forum part of the McCormick Foundation Conference Series.

Pauline C. Reich, Stuart Weinstein, Charles Wild & Allan S. Cabanlong, Cyber Warfare: A Review of Theories, Law, Policies, Actual Incidents - and the Dilemma of Anonymity in European Journal of Law and Technology, Vol. 1, Issue 2, 2010

Peter Iliev, The Effect of SOX Section 404: Costs, Earnings Quality and Stock Prices, 2008

Peter Mutharika, Creating an Attractive Investment Climate in the Common Market for Eastern and Southern Africa (COMESA) Region, ICSID Review FDI Journal 12/97, p.238

Polk R. Wagner and Catherine T. Struve, Realspace Sovereigns in Cyberspace: Problems with the Anticybersquatting Consumer Protection Act (ACPA). Berkeley Technology Law Journal, Vol. 17, No. 1, Sept. 2002. Available at SSRN: http://ssrn.com/abstract=321901 or doi:10.2139/ssrn.321901

Ramanan R. Ramanathan; E-business: Trust Inhibitors, in the ISACA JournalOnline, 2008

Rashmi Banga, Foreign Direct Investment in Services: Implications for Developing Countries, Asia-Pacific Trade and Investment Review Vol. 1, No. 2, November 2005

Rashmi Banga, Foreign Direct Investment in Services: Implications for Developing Countries; Asia-Pacific Trade and Investment Review Vol. 1, No. 2, November 2005

Report of the Group of Governmental Experts on Developments in the Field of Information and Telecommunications in the Context of International Security to the UN General assembly 65th Session, July

2010

Richard A. Mann, Smith and Roberson's Business Law, 11th Edition, 2000

Richard D. Smith, Foreign Direct Investment and Trade in Health Services: A review of the literature; in Social Science & Medicine 59 (2004) 2313–2323

Richard Johnston, Ken Slade; Jurisdiction, Choice of Law, and Dispute Resolution in International E-Commerce; Boston Bar Association: International Arbitration Committee, January 2000

Richard M. Marsh, Jr., Legislation for Effective Self-Regulation: A New Approach to Protecting Personal Privacy on the Internet, 15 Mich. Telecomm. Tech. L. Rev. Vol. 543 (2009)

Rob van den Hoven, Trading Privacy for Security; Amsterdam Law Forum, 2009

Robert A. Hillman, Jeffrey J. Rachlinski; Standard-Form Contracting in the Electronic Age, 2000, page 3

Robert Uerpmann-Wittzack, Principles of International Internet Law, in the German Law Journal, Vol. 11, No. 11, 2010

Robert Z. Lawrence, Jennifer Blanke, Margareta Drzeniek Hanouz, John Moavenzadeh, The Global Enabling Trade Report; World Economic Forum, 2008

Ron Keys, Jim Ed Crouch, International Cyberspace Considerations, NSCI CyberPro May 2010

Ronald L. Mendell, Dealing with the "Insider Threat"; the Information Systems Security Association (ISSA) Journal May 2006

Rory Macmillan, Connectivity, Openness, and Vulnerability: Challenges Facing Regulators, Trends in Telecommunication Reform (2009)

Rudy Hirschheim, Beena George, Siew Fan Wong; Information Technology Outsourcing: The Move Towards Offshoring, 2004

S. Ibi Ajayi, Foreign Direct Investment in Sub-Saharan Africa: Origins, Targets, Impact and Potential; African Economic Research Consortium, 2006

Sacha Wunsch-Vincent, IP's Online Market: The Economic Forces at Play, World Intellectual Property Organization (WIPO) Magazine #6, Geneva, December 2010

SafeNet, Inc; Understanding Man-in-the-Browser Attacks and Addressing the Problem, 2010

Saundarjya Borbora, ICT Growth and Diffusion: Concepts, Impacts and Policy Issues in the Indian Experience with Reference to the International Digital Divide; in Digital Economy: Impacts, Influences and Challenges, page 236, 2005

Scott J. Shackelford State Responsibility for Cyber Attacks: Competing Standards for a Growing Problem, 2009

Scott J. Shackelford, From Nuclear War to Net War: Analogizing Cyber Attacks in International Law; Berkeley Journal of International Law Vol. 27:1 2008.

Scott N. Carlson, International Investment Laws and Foreign Direct Investment in Developing Countries: Albania's Experiment, International Lawyer, Vol. 29 No. 3, 1995.

Sean Kanuck, Sovereign Discourse on Cyber Conflict Under International Law, Texas Law Review, Vol. 88:1571, 2010

Sokchea Kim, Bilateral Investment Treaties, Political Risk and Foreign Direct Investment, in MPRA paper #21324 March 2010

Solveig Singleton, Privacy and Human Rights: Comparing the United States to Europe; Cato White Papers and Miscellaneous Reports, December 1, 1999

Sonia Verma and Upvan M. Prakash, Jurisdictional Disputes and Intermediary Liability in Cyberspace (April 1, 2011). Available at SSRN: http://ssrn.com/abstract=1800837

Stein Schjolberg, Solange Ghernaouti-Helie; A Global Treaty on Cybersecurity and Cybercrime, 2nd edition 2011, also available at: http://www.cybercrimelaw.net/documents/A_Global_Treaty_on_Cyber security_and_Cybercrime,_Second_edition_2011.pdf, (last visited December 10, 2012)

Stephan Manning, Silvia Massini, Arie Y. Lewin; A Dynamic Perspective on Next-Generation Offshoring: The Global Sourcing of Science and Engineering Talent, in the Academy of Management Perspectives, 2008

Steve Luebke, The Evolving Legal Duty to Securely Maintain Data; the (ISSA) Journal January 2011.

Steve Luebke, Trade Secrets: An Information Security Priority; the (ISSA) Journal December 2006.

Steven Swanson R. , Google Sets Sail: Ocean-Based Server Farms and International Law (February 1, 2011). Connecticut Law Review, Vol. 43, p. 709, 2011. Available at SSRN: http://ssrn.com/abstract=1783159

Subramanian Rangan, Metin Sengul; Information technology and transnational integration: Theory and evidence on the evolution of the modern multinational enterprise; Journal of International Business Studies (2009) 40, 1496–1514

Sudin Apte, Shattering the Offshore Captive Center Myth, 2007

Susan W. Brenner, Bert-Jaap Koops; Approaches to Cybercrime Jurisdiction; 4 J. High Tech. L. 1 (2004)

Sushil K. Sharma, Socio-Economic Impacts and Influences of E-Commerce in a Digital Economy; in the Digital Economy: Impacts, Influences, and Challenges; Hershey 2005

Tabrez Ahmad, Copyright Infringement in Cyberspace and Network Security: A Threat to E-Commerce, Bhubaneswar, India 2009.

Tang Lan, Zhang Xin, Harry D. Raduege, Jr., Dmitry I. Grigoriev, Pavan Duggal, and Stein Schjølberg; Global Cyber Deterrence: Views from China, the U.S., Russia, India, and Norway, April 2010

The United States Attorney's Office, Office of Public Affairs: Department of Justice takes Action to disable International BotNet, April 13, 2011

The US Department of State, Bureau of Economic and Business Affairs; Openness to Foreign Investment, 2006/2007 Highlights: httpwww.state.goveeebifd2008100861.htm; Accessed 7/27/11

The White House, National Strategy for Trusted Identities in Cyberspace: Creating Options for Enhanced Online Security and Privacy, 2010

The World Bank Group, Cyber Security: A New Model for Protecting the Network in International Policy Framework for Protecting Critical Information Infrastructure: A Discussion Paper Outlining Key Policy Issue July 2006

Thomas Anderson, MNC Investment in Developing Countries, 1991

Thomas C. Folsom, Defining Cyberspace (Finding Real Virtue in the Place of Virtual Reality), Tulane Journal of Technology & Intellectual Property, Vol. 9, p. 75, 2007, Available at SSRN: http://ssrn.com/abstract=1350999

Thomas J. Smedinghoff, The Legal Challenges of Implementing Electronic Transactions; UNIFORM Commercial Code Law Journal [Vol. 41 #1], 2008

Thomas M. Kerr, Standardizing Environmental Assessment of Foreign Investment Projects in Developing Countries, Int'l Lawyer Vol. 29 No 1, 1995, p. 153.

Thomas R. Lee, In Rem Jurisdiction in Cyberspace Washington Law Review Association:

http://cyber.law.harvard.edu/property00/jurisdiction/lee.html

Timothy B. Lee, The Durable Internet Preserving Network Neutrality without Regulation, Policy Analysis No 626, (November 2008) available at: http://www.cato.org/pubs/pas/pa-626.pdf

Torfinn Harding & Beata Smarzynska Javorcikr, *Developing Economies and International Investors: Do Investment Promotion Agencies Bring Them Together?* The World Bank, Policy Research Working Paper #4339 (2007)

UNCITRAL, Promoting Confidence in Electronic Commerce: Legal Issues on International Use of Electronic Authentication and Signature Methods; UNCITRAL 1996 Model Law on Electronic Commerce; UN, 2009.

UNCTAD, Economic Development in Africa: Rethinking the Role of Foreign Direct Investment, 2005

UNCTAD, Information Economy Report 2007-2008; Science and Technology for Development: the new paradigm of ICT

UNCTAD, Information Economy Report 2010: ICTs, Enterprises and Poverty Alleviation

UNCTAD, Investment and Enterprise Responsibility Review: Analysis of Investor and Enterprise Policies on Corporate Social Responsibility; UN, New York and Geneva, 2010.

UNCTAD, Investor-State Disputes: Prevention and Alternatives to Arbitration II, NY 2011

UNCTAD, World Investment Report - The Shift Towards Services; United Nations New York and Geneva, 2004.

UNCTAD, World Investment Report 2010: Investing in a Low-Carbon Economy

UNCTAD, World Investment Report 2011: Non-Equity Modes of International Production and Development

UNCTAD, World Investment Report; FDI from Developing and Transition Economies: Implications for Development, 2006

United States Government Accountability Office (GAO), Offshoring of Services: An Overview of the Issues; Report to Congressional Committees, November 2005

Varinder P. Singh, Harbhajan Kehal; Digital Economy: Impacts, Influences, and Challenges; Hershey 2005.

Vishnu Konoorayar, Regulating Cyberspace: The Emerging Problems and Challenges; Cochin University Law Review, 2003

Vivian C. Jones, U.S. Trade and Investment Relationship with Sub-Saharan Africa: The African Growth and Opportunity Act; Congressional Research Service (CRS) Report to Congress, February 2010

Wulf A. Kaal and Richard W. Painter; Extraterritorial Application of US Securities Law – Will the US become the Default Jurisdiction for European Securities Litigation? (August 24, 2010); available at SSRN: http://ssrn.com/abstract=1664809, (last visited January 12, 2012)

Index

www.ingramcontent.com/pod-product-compliance
Lightning Source LLC
Chambersburg PA
CBHW071407050326
40689CB00010B/1781